NEGOTIAUCTIONS

NEGOTIAUCTIONS

NEW DEALMAKING STRATEGIES FOR
A COMPETITIVE MARKETPLACE

GUHAN SUBRAMANIAN

W. W. NORTON & COMPANY
New York   London

For information about permission to reproduce selections from this book,
write to Permissions, W. W. Norton & Company, Inc.,
500 Fifth Avenue, New York, NY 10110

For information about special discounts for bulk purchases, please contact
W. W. Norton Special Sales at specialsales@wwnorton.com or 800-233-4830

Manufacturing by Courier Westford
Book design by Helena Berinsky
Production manager: Anna Oler

Library of Congress Cataloging-in-Publication Data

Subramanian, Guhan.
Negotiauctions : new dealmaking strategies for a competitive
marketplace / Guhan Subramanian.
p. cm.
Includes bibliographical references and index.
ISBN 978-0-393-06946-4 (hardcover)
1. Negotiation in business. 2. Auctions. I. Title.
HD58.6.S83 2010
658.4'052—dc22

2009038974

W. W. Norton & Company, Inc.
500 Fifth Avenue, New York, N.Y. 10110
www.wwnorton.com

W. W. Norton & Company Ltd.
Castle House, 75/76 Wells Street, London W1T 3QT

1 2 3 4 5 6 7 8 9 0

To Helen

CONTENTS

INTRODUCTION

On Wednesday, January 21, 2004, at approximately 8:30 a.m., representatives from seven bidding groups convened at the offices of a well-known investment bank in midtown Manhattan for the auction of Cable & Wireless America (CWA), the bankrupt American division of British-based Cable & Wireless PLC. After a brief introduction, the bidders were sequestered into separate conference rooms, and for the next twenty-one hours, CWA's bankers and lawyers went from room to room negotiating privately with each of them. A month earlier, the stalking-horse bid process had implicitly valued CWA at $125 million. But by 6:00 a.m. on January 22, the best bid was in only the mid–$60 million range.

CWA's bankers and lawyers assembled in a conference room overlooking Park Avenue. With more than a century of dealmaking experience among them, they asked themselves a simple question: What do we do now?[1]

This book tries to answer the question "What do we do now?" for both buyers and sellers in situations like the sale of Cable & Wireless America. It will come as no surprise that the CWA bankers and lawyers did not run to their bookshelf for guidance. The reason is that existing negotiation theory is inadequate in these complex dealmaking situations. In many fields, the gap between what practitioners want and what academics can provide simply reflects the limits of the existing knowledge base. It would be nice, for example, if financial economists could provide practitioners with a single, definitive, and completely precise way to value assets. But existing finance theory cannot do this.

In negotiations, the gap between what sophisticated dealmaking practitioners want and what academics can offer is not for lack of knowledge. Rather, it is the failure of negotiations as a field to incorporate elements of auction theory that are highly relevant to how deals are actually made. Aside from fixed-price processes (such as buying lettuce at the grocery store), auctions and negotiations are the only two ways in which assets are transferred in any market economy. It is therefore surprising that the academic thinking on these two mechanisms has developed in separate silos.

The broad-brush history goes like this: Auction theory has its roots in game theory and microeconomics. It generally assumes that the structure of the situation is well specified and that all parties are rational, and then develops optimal strategies for sellers and buyers. Negotiation theory starts with basic microeconomics, but it has developed in a direction that includes experimental economics, social psychology, behavioral economics, and the legal profession, among other fields. Despite the same underlying subject matter (the transfer of assets), the two fields have grown further apart over time, as auction scholars have become more technical and negotiation scholars have become more applied. This trajectory is the opposite of what their inherent interconnectedness would seem to require.

Rather than trying to solve problems from inside these two academic silos, I try in this book to guide practitioners in solving problems as they present themselves in the world. Specifically, this book brings together the two parallel streams of research in auctions and negotiations to provide guidance to practitioners who are involved in what I call "negotiauction" situations. Professor Jeffrey Teich of New Mexico State University trademarked the term in 2001, in conjunction with his computer algorithm and Internet software that combines auction and negotiation processes.[2] Independently, I introduced the term in a 2004 article with Professor Richard Zeckhauser from Harvard University, to capture the murky middle ground that falls between pure one-on-one negotiations and pure Sotheby's-style auctions. In my definition, a *negotiauction* is the commonplace situation in which negotiators are fighting on two fronts—across the table for sure, but also on the same side of the table, with known, unknown, or possible competitors.

Visually, a negotiauction can be represented as in Figure 1. The competitive pressure in a negotiation comes mainly from the across-the-table dynamics. In contrast, in an auction the competitive pressure comes primarily from same-side-of-the-table dynamics. Once the seller has established the process in an auction, he becomes a passive participant. Competition among the bidders does most of the work in pushing up the price.

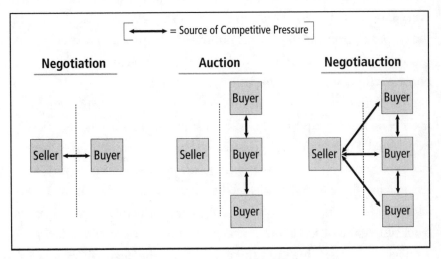

Figure 1. Negotiations, Auctions, and Negotiauctions Compared

The key point in the diagram is that most real-world situations include aspects of both same-side-of-the-table competition *and* across-the-table competition—what I call a negotiauction. I have spent the last decade studying negotiauctions, through Harvard Business School case studies, consulting work, expert witness testimony, and empirical studies. In this research I initially thought about negotiauctions as a subset of all negotiations, a special kind of negotiation that had auction elements. But in my executive education teaching and in conversations with businesspeople, I discovered that the term resonates with what they experience every day in an increasingly competitive marketplace. As a result, I stopped asking, "What kinds of negotiations are negotiauctions?" and began asking, "What kinds of negotiations *aren't* negotiauctions?" There are answers to this question, of course, but they are fewer than I imagined.

There is of course the proverbial risk that when you have a hammer, everything becomes a nail. The litmus test for me came when I began teaching about negotiauctions to executive education groups at the business school, the law school, and the Kennedy School of Government at Harvard. Across these diverse audiences, the negotiauction concept resonated strongly with what these practitioners experienced every day in their negotiating lives. From salespeople trying to get in the door, to government officials putting public procurement contracts out to bid, to general counsels trying to secure outside legal services, negotiauctions were everywhere.

I came to realize that the negotiauction concept resonates with dealmakers because it captures the way most high-stakes assets are actually transferred. Furthermore, in my research I have found that (1) even experienced dealmakers make costly mistakes in negotiauction situations; (2) recognizing these mistakes, dealmakers crave guidance on how to play in a more sophisticated way; and (3) general principles can be derived from systematic observation of negotiauction successes and failures.

The CWA case illustrates these points. As the negotiauction began on January 21, 2004, the main banker for the sellers told the assembled bidders, "The rules that we're setting as ground rules may change. If we change them, we will advise all of you, but we reserve the right to change the rules throughout the process."[3] In an interview afterward, the banker explained to me that "a lot of this [running an auction] is being nimble in the moment." Another CWA participant put it to me more starkly: "It's a free-for-all in these situations; the only rule is that there are no rules."

Although "being nimble in the moment" sounds desirable in principle, in the CWA situation it deterred bidders from putting their best bid on the table because the seller never credibly committed to a process that would "show bidders the finish line." Instead, the seemingly never-ending process led to a bidding strategy to simply "stay in the building"—that is, not get kicked out of the auction. And because CWA threatened to kick bidders out but failed to do so, staying in the building did not require the bidders to bid very much. So it is not surprising that the bidding stalled in the mid–$60 million range. Clear process rules, including a firm commitment to kicking low bidders out, would have changed the calculation among the bidders and pushed the price up more quickly.

In addition, the stalled bidding process reinforced itself, because bidders were learning from the moves of other bidders. Each bidding group had entered the auction with a valuation in mind, and with the benefit of hindsight (see the outcome of the deal described next) we know that many of those valuations were significantly higher than the mid–$60 millions. But when bidders saw the sluggish bidding, they thought either that they could get the company for less than their valuation suggested, or that their valuation was too high. In either case, the slow pace of bidding reinforced their instincts to bid low.

Transcripts of the sale process reveal that the sellers were dangerously close to accepting a price in the mid–$60 million range. At one point early in the morning on January 22, the main banker for CWA told the assembled bidders, "If we don't hear any [further] bids, we will wrap up the bidding and be done."[4] The high bid at that point was $64.7 million. A few hours later, at 7:15 a.m., the banker told the bidders that he was basically finished with all of them. The high bid at that point was $66.2 million.

Fortunately for CWA, its bankers hit upon the idea of holding "Survivor Rounds" (named after the popular TV show in which one contestant is voted off the island each week), in which the lowest one or two bidders would be "excused" from the process after each round. This firm process commitment had the effect of significantly pushing up the bidding: $70 million . . . $80 million . . . $100 million . . . $120 million. The lead banker recounted,

> The numbers started to go up, and it started to excite a lot of bidders. We stopped at one point because probably all the bidders were above the number they thought they would have to bid to win . . . I think it's when we went across $143 million that the entire room gasped . . . When we hit that number, a number of bidders said, gee, that's a very big number. But our two bidders kept going.[5]

Savvis Communications, a leader in virtual private network (VPN) software, and Gores Technology, a private-equity firm, were the last bidders standing. CWA's bankers switched to an open-outcry auction in the main conference room between these two. In the end, Savvis won. Its winning bid was $168.3 million.

CWA reached a number that was well beyond its expectations, yet Savvis's stock rose 33 percent on the announcement of the deal, suggesting that it could have paid even more. (In Chapter 3, I provide some explanations for why the market responded so positively.) Moreover, Savvis promptly sold five CWA data centers to Dupont Fabros, a competing bidder in the auction, for $52 million, and leased them back for fifteen years.[6] CWA's bankers and lawyers could have brokered this sale-and-leaseback deal, had it identified Savvis's cash flow needs. So these are some lessons for the *process setters*, the parties who establish the rules by which a negotiauction proceeds.

There are lessons for the buy-side *process takers* too. In hindsight, we know that at least two bidders had something around $160 million "in their pockets," but the seller's initial process rules had failed to extract this value. Instead of playing passively, one of the bidders could have changed the game by putting a preemptive bid on the table coupled with a threat: "$80 million; accept it in the next five minutes or we are out of here." It seems possible that such a preemptive move would have been successful, given where the bidding stood and the seller's fear of losing the highest bidder. Instead, six bidders invested thirty-three hours each but came away with nothing. The winning bidder got the prize but might have been able to pay significantly less by making a preemptive move earlier in the process.

Two weeks later, as Savvis was taking ownership of the CWA assets, the *Washington Post* conveyed a similar exasperation among participants in the deal:

> In 40 hours of negotiations, a Wednesday morning dragged into Thursday evening—with no showers, beds, and a steady diet of takeout. Tempers frayed; voices were raised; procedure was disputed . . . Seventy-five people camped out in those rooms for the two days: executives of the seven companies bidding, their lawyers, the auction managers, and a stenographer. As the auction drew to a close, Sprayregen [a Kirkland & Ellis lawyer involved in the deal] realized . . . he had consumed 30 Diet Cokes.[7]

The question is whether there is a better way to play in these sorts of situations, on both the buy-side and the sell-side. In this book I suggest that there is, and the lessons presented here extend well beyond the world of corporate acquisitions. They apply to the sales representative trying to land a new account. They apply to the procurement officer trying to reduce input costs for a company while preserving quality and reliability. They apply to important personal transactions, such as buying a car or selling a house. In fact, the lessons from this book apply to every dealmaking situation in which there is competition from across the table and from the same side of the table. In my research and other experience, this characterization would seem to capture just about every deal that is done in our increasingly complex and competitive marketplace.

The book proceeds in two parts. Part I begins with the conceptual framework for negotiations as it has developed in the academic and practitioner literature. There are hundreds of articles and dozens of excellent books on negotiations, and this part does not try to provide a complete survey of this literature. Instead, I put forward the basic model for negotiation analysis that has developed in the past thirty years. Part I then provides a similar review of the auctions literature. It starts with a basic question—when to auction and when to negotiate?—and then dives in to examine the specific kinds of auctions, and when to use each type. Part I closes with an explanation of why the frameworks that have developed for negotiations and auctions are inadequate, prescriptively and descriptively, for most complex deals today.

Part II focuses on negotiauctions—the murky middle ground that falls between pure negotiations and pure auctions. I begin by defining the negotiauction concept and providing examples of negotiauction situations. I then examine how to play effectively in this complex arena, where the rules are ambiguous and often in flux. In my research I find that the most effective dealmakers in negotiauctions are simultaneously negotiating deal process along with substance. Specifically, as process setters, dealmakers are continually assessing whether and when to use auction-like mechanisms (to exert same-side-of-the-table pressure) or negotiation-like mechanisms (to exert across-the-table pressure). As process takers, dealmakers are continually assessing the viability of three kinds of moves:

1. *Setup moves* establish terms of entry into a negotiauction situation.

2. *Rearranging moves* reconfigure the assets, the parties, or both, in a way that creates additional value in the deal.

3. *Shut-down moves* prematurely cut off same-side-of-the-table competition.

In negotiauctions, these three kinds of moves are mutually exclusive and collectively exhaustive. Part II provides examples of these three kinds of moves, describes when they should be considered, and specifies the conditions under which they can be successful.

Part II ends with an examination of the legal "shadow" of nego-tiauctions. To what extent is it permissible to bluff about competing bidders? Is hiding your identity in a negotiauction allowed? Is it legal to collude with a competitor to stifle competition? The book closes with descriptions of the kinds of dilemmas that often confront dealmakers when lawyers are not present and that are therefore important for deal-makers to know about firsthand.

Before jumping in, let me say a few words about my intended audi-ence and objectives. This book is not meant to be a comprehensive guide on how to negotiate everything—in part because I believe there is no one-size-fits-all approach to negotiations. The tools that are most effective for negotiating with your spouse are not the same as the tools that are effective in negotiating with your colleague at work, which are not the same as the tools that are effective in negotiating with a sup-plier or customer.

Rather than offering a universal approach, this book focuses on complex business deals. In my experience, when sophisticated deal-makers hear negotiation prescriptions such as "Understand your walk-away alternative" and "Identify the bargaining zone," they say, in effect, "Tell me something I don't know." When sophisticated deal-makers hear about auction theory, they say, in effect, "Huh?" The rea-sons for this disconnect between theory and practice are described in Chapter 6. This is not to say that existing theory is useless—just that it does not fully meet the needs of dealmaking practitioners today. This book tries to fill that gap, offering advice that will allow even sophisti-cated dealmakers to "take their game to the next level."

As you will see, several of the examples in this book come from the mergers and acquisitions (M&A) industry. Most of my technical and academic writing over the past decade has examined different kinds of deals and deal structures in this arena. I have come to realize that the tools and techniques developed on Wall Street have broader appli-cation, yet they have not migrated very far. This book is, in part, an effort to learn from the experimentation that has taken place in M&A, and to deploy it outside of this narrow world. I believe that such dissemination can create significant value for dealmakers and the marketplace generally. Investment bankers are paid a lot of money to be dealmaking entrepreneurs, so they have to stay on the cutting edge. Their experience is one helpful data point for triangulating professional best practices.

This is not to say that Wall Street bankers are infallible, or generally introspective about what they do. To the contrary, I find investment bankers to be far less interested in thinking about the theory of corporate dealmaking than, say, corporate lawyers are. But this book tries to capture the latent insight in their decades of experience. My goal is to bring relevant tools and techniques from the cutting edge into everyday dealmaking practice.

Although the focus is squarely on real-world problems, this book gets somewhat technical in places. When it does, I hope you will not lose sight of the big picture. As the global marketplace grows more competitive, negotiauctions are becoming the standard way in which assets are bought and sold in our economy. This book shows you how to play in this increasingly commonplace and important arena.

PART I

Negotiations and Auctions

CHAPTER 1

PREPARING TO NEGOTIATE

If you are a TV sitcom fan like me, you probably remember the hit television show *Frasier*, which amassed a huge viewership and twenty-nine Emmys (second only to *The Mary Tyler Moore Show*) in the 1990s and 2000s. You probably remember that *Frasier* featured the pompous yet perpetually insecure psychiatrist Dr. Frasier Crane, who got divorced from his wife, moved from Boston back to his hometown of Seattle, and attempted to begin life anew as the host of a radio advice show. What you probably don't know is that in February 2001—after eight years of critical acclaim and more than a billion dollars in profits— Paramount Studios (the producer of the show) and NBC (the network that aired the show) were at odds over whether *Frasier* would continue on NBC. The main point of contention was the price per episode that Paramount should receive. In this chapter we review the critical steps in preparing to negotiate, using the *Frasier* case to illustrate various elements along the way.[1]

This chapter focuses on the four essential elements of preparation: understanding (1) the parties, (2) their interests, (3) alternatives to agreement on all sides, and (4) incentives of the people at the table. It is a bare-bones set of concepts, intended to make sure you don't miss anything important, while still leaving room for the kind of creative think-ing that is described in Part II of this book. I use the *Frasier* example to illustrate various elements along the way.

UNDERSTANDING PARTIES AND INTERESTS

The first step in preparing for any negotiation is to think carefully about the parties to the negotiation and their interests. In the case of *Frasier*, Paramount and NBC were the parties at the table. Two other major television networks—CBS and ABC—were also relevant par-ties, in two ways: they would be likely suitors for the show if Para-mount's negotiations with NBC broke down, and NBC would likely have to steal an existing show from one of them if it walked away from *Frasier*.

CBS, in particular, hinted none too subtly that it was interested in buying the show. Just as the *Frasier* negotiations were getting under way, CBS President Les Moonves told the press, "If a great show became available, we'd always listen. It might be an offer we couldn't refuse."[2] Fueling this fire, the press spotted Kelsey Grammer, the star of the show, having dinner with Moonves and his entertainment chief, Nancy Tellem. Although the meeting was reportedly about putting new shows from Grammer's production company on CBS, several stories suggested that plans to subvert NBC were also discussed. CBS and Paramount were both owned by Viacom—a fact that helped grease the wheels toward a CBS-Paramount deal.

In addition to CBS, ABC, and Viacom, Kelsey Grammer was an important party in the Paramount-NBC negotiation. Without Gram-mer, there was no *Frasier*. Grammer clearly wanted a high price per episode from NBC, which would create a higher price umbrella in his negotiation with Paramount, but he had two other interests that were more important than money. First, he wanted the show to stay on NBC because market research showed that TV shows lose significant audi-ence share when they move to a different network. Second, regardless of what network the show was on, Grammer wanted an ironclad commitment to air the show for three more seasons.

Why three seasons? TV buffs will remember that Dr. Frasier Crane had spent nine seasons sitting on a barstool in *Cheers*, the TV series about the Boston bar "where everybody knows your name." Three more seasons of *Frasier* on top of the eight prior seasons would give Frasier Crane twenty seasons total—tying Matt Dillon, who was played by James Arness for twenty seasons on *Gunsmoke*—for the record of longest-running primetime character in TV history. After the negotiations were finished, Kelsey Grammer told the press, "I spent the last month biting my nails, being lost in a controlled frenzy."[3] For Grammer, the NBC-Paramount deal was not really about the money; it was about his claim to TV history.

Then there were the chief negotiators on each side of the table. The leader of the NBC team was Marc Graboff, a lawyer by training. Graboff had spent fifteen years practicing entertainment law at a major Los Angeles firm before joining CBS in 1998. In 1999, Graboff had gained public attention and credit in the industry for his instrumental work in bringing the hugely popular *Survivor* series to CBS. Described by the *New York Post* as the "*Survivor* Swami," Graboff had developed the business model for CBS that enabled the network to create original programming during the otherwise slow summer months.

Graboff's performance caught the attention of Scott Sassa at NBC, who offered him the job of executive vice president, NBC West Coast. Graboff joined NBC in October 2000, just in time to be the point person for the *Frasier* negotiating team. In January 2001, TV wunderkind Jeff Zucker joined NBC as president of NBC Entertainment, providing further support for the Graboff-Sassa negotiating team. The trio sometimes involved Bob Wright, CEO of NBC, who maintained a keen interest from the outset in how the negotiations were progressing.

Across the table was Kerry McCluggage, a seasoned veteran at Paramount Studios. After graduating from Harvard Business School in 1978, McCluggage joined Universal Television Studios, where he helped create and produce a string of popular shows that included

Magnum, P.I.; *The A-Team*; *Miami Vice*; *Murder, She Wrote*; and *Law & Order*. In 1991, McCluggage left Universal to become president of Paramount's television group. In that role McCluggage led high-stakes deals such as the *Frasier* negotiation, though he was frequently joined at the table by Gary Hart, president of Paramount Network TV.

THREE CORE CONCEPTS: BATNA, RESERVATION VALUE, AND ZOPA

Many parties in the *Frasier* negotiation have not been mentioned—the press, the viewing public, advertisers, and the other stars of the show, to name just a few. The omission is not to say that these parties were not important; arguably, David Hyde Pierce and John Mahoney—who played Frasier's brother and father, respectively—were almost as important to *Frasier* as Kelsey Grammer was. For now, though, we will keep it simple and move on to the next step in effective preparation: figuring out the "BATNA" for each party.

The term *BATNA* was coined in the seminal negotiations book *Getting to Yes*, by Roger Fisher, Bill Ury, and Bruce Patton. It stands for "*b*est *a*lternative *t*o a *n*egotiated *a*greement." It's the "What do you do?" if you don't reach a deal.

In the *Frasier* negotiation, NBC's BATNA was to buy a show from another network or "pilot" a new show. (In theory, NBC could run color bars for thirty minutes in place of *Frasier*, but this probably was not its *best* alternative.) Ideally, the replacement would be another comedy that could provide a comparably sized audience. Graboff and Sassa eyed ABC's *Dharma & Greg* as a possible replacement if NBC walked away from *Frasier*. The pair then came to an important insight in their BATNA analysis: What would ABC do if it lost *Dharma & Greg*? ABC, of course, wouldn't run color bars for thirty minutes; it would steal a similar show from another network, maybe even from NBC.

With a scarcity of high-rated comedies at the time, Graboff and

Sassa feared that walking away from *Frasier* could trigger a bidding war in which all three of the major networks vied for each other's top programs. In a worst-case scenario, Graboff and Sassa speculated that there could be a drastic increase in programming costs for all three networks. CBS might indirectly benefit from this increase in programming costs, through its sister studio, Paramount; and ABC might indirectly benefit through its parent company, Walt Disney; but NBC, which didn't have an affiliated production company, would definitely lose. NBC's BATNA, in short, was lousy.

The general lesson is to think through what will *really* happen if there is no deal—not just one step ahead (buy another show) but two or three steps ahead (potential bidding contest). Best-practice BATNA analysis requires constantly asking yourself, "And then what happens?" until you are satisfied that all parties involved have reached stable ground and won't react to your moves any further.

Of course, you need to assess both your own BATNA and the other side's BATNA in order to fully understand the implications of your negotiation strategy. In the *Frasier* negotiation, Graboff was a seasoned veteran in the TV business and felt confident that Paramount's BATNA was to sell the show to CBS: "ABC wasn't a player at the prices that we were already talking about, because it wouldn't have made sense for them, though Paramount kept promising us that ABC was very interested in it." In 2001, if you were NBC and ABC wasn't a player, that left CBS as Paramount's BATNA.

Kerry McCluggage confirmed Graboff's assessment of the Paramount BATNA. In an interview several years after the deal was completed, he told me,

> Clearly, CBS was our best alternative to a negotiated agreement. But that wasn't a great alternative. It's a big step down from concluding a deal with your home network [NBC] . . . I wanted to do what I considered to be our fiduciary responsibility to the show, which was to make the best possible deal that we could. And in this context the best deal was far and away to have the show at NBC.

So there were clear indications that we could sell the show to CBS. But they knew our point of view about that, which was that we really didn't want to do that . . . Clearly CBS would have earned less money on the show than NBC could.[4]

The BATNA analysis for both sides leads naturally to another important concept in negotiation analysis: *reservation value*. Your reservation value is your walk-away number—the lowest amount you would be willing to accept as a seller or the highest amount you would be willing to offer as a buyer. Your reservation value should reflect your BATNA—in NBC's case, for example, its bad BATNA (potential bidding war) meant a higher reservation value. The reservation value has nothing to do with what you hope to pay, what you "should" pay, or what is a "fair" price in the negotiation. It simply reflects the point at which you are creating value *in* the deal versus *away* from the table in your best alternative to a deal. It's an important number to keep in mind as you enter the room.

In the *Frasier* negotiation, the reservation value for both sides started with the break-even license fee. Graboff estimated that NBC would break even on the show if it paid approximately $5 million per episode. And what about CBS? As you will recall, Graboff had joined NBC in October 2000, after two years as the main person buying TV shows—for CBS. The consequence was, as Graboff put it, "I knew better what CBS's economics were at that time than I knew what NBC's were." With this inside perspective, Graboff estimated that CBS's break-even license fee would be about $3 million per episode. As McCluggage had noted, it was a "big step down" from NBC's willingness to pay.

Then there were other sources of value that had to be added on both sides. On NBC's side, for example, there was the value of avoiding a potential bidding contest. For both NBC and CBS, there was significant value from the so-called *tent pole effect* (the ability to promote and develop other shows in the time blocks adjacent to *Frasier*) and the benefit of keeping the show off a rival network.

It's hard to pin down for sure what these intangibles were worth, but some additional insights from the Paramount side of the table can help us triangulate a value. McCluggage estimated that his own walk-away price was between $5.25 million and $5.5 million per episode, because that is what CBS would have been willing to pay. "We knew that if we didn't end up with that price from NBC, then CBS would pay that price."[5] McCluggage's assessment implied that these "softer" sources of value would enable CBS to pay $2+ million more than its break-even license fee of $3.0 million per episode.

Shifting to the NBC side of the table, it seems reasonable to assume that NBC's increment over its break-even license fee would be at least as much: NBC's tent pole (*Frasier*) and its interest in keeping it away from a rival were as large as CBS's, and NBC had an additional source of value—its strong interest in avoiding a bidding contest. On the basis of these additional sources of value, NBC's reservation value (the amount it was willing to pay) was somewhere in the neighborhood of $7.25 million to $7.5 million per episode. We will see in a moment that other factors pushed this reservation value downward. But this relatively simple analysis makes clear that NBC was willing to pay significantly more than its break-even license fee, if it had to, in order to keep the show. Graboff confirmed this conclusion:

> Sometimes you're prepared to break even. Sometimes you won't do a deal unless you're going to make money. We steeled ourselves to the idea of paying a license fee that was more than our break-even, and more than what we were then paying [$5.0 million per episode]. We said, "Okay, we're prepared to lose more money than normal on this show; now let's try to limit that loss."

Putting these points together brings us to the final basic concept in negotiation analysis: *ZOPA*, which stands for "*zone of possible agreement*." Given your assessment of your own BATNA and your own reservation value, and (equally importantly) the other side's BATNA and reservation value, you can determine, at least as a first pass, whether a

ZOPA exists. The ZOPA analysis tells you whether there is value to be created in the negotiation. In some cases, one or both parties have very attractive BATNAs, and there is simply no ZOPA (sometimes referred to, mostly in jest, as a "NOPA" situation). In many other cases, the question of whether a ZOPA exists is unclear, and the initial challenge in the negotiation process is to figure out whether it does and, if so, where it is.

In the *Frasier* negotiation, there was a big ZOPA, and everyone knew it. The year 2001 was the high point of the "Must-See TV" era on NBC, when *Frasier* was part of an array of blockbuster shows that included *ER* and *Friends*. Significantly fewer "eyeballs" would be on *Frasier* if it left the NBC roster.

The numbers confirmed this conclusion. McCluggage believed that CBS would pay somewhere around $5.25 million for the show, and bootstrapping this estimate to the NBC side indicated that NBC would be willing to pay approximately $7.25 million. So the ZOPA was somewhere in the neighborhood of $5.25 million to $7.25 million per episode. If you multiply the $2.0 million size of the ZOPA by 24 episodes per season and the 3 seasons that Grammer was insisting on, you get $144 million of value "on the table" for NBC and Paramount to either capture or destroy.

To put this number in perspective, NBC's net profit was $1.6 billion and Paramount's net profit was $263 million in 2001.[6] So the value on the table in this single deal amounted to almost 10 percent of NBC's net profit and more than half of Paramount's net profit for the year.

Just before the parties sat down to negotiate the *Frasier* deal, the *New York Times* observed,

> Like a mighty fortress on a bluff, impervious to attack and threat-ening to all that dare to invade its territory, NBC's Thursday night lineup has towered over the rest of the television industry through an entire generation of viewers . . . Now NBC's total command of Thursday—and the massive advertising revenue that pours in

because of it—is being challenged, and the stakes are enormous . . .
The challenge, by CBS, sets up the most important battle in recent
prime-time history.[7]

Clearly, this was a negotiation that both sides wanted to get right.

UNDERSTANDING INCENTIVES

This leads us to a final aspect of preparation: thinking through the
incentives of the individuals who will be negotiating. Research shows
that people are highly aware of differences within their own group,
but these same people tend to treat other groups as monolithic.[8] This
is a mistake. Even people who are trying to do the right thing for their
organization can have subtle and powerful incentives that diverge from
their organization's interests.

Most financially significant negotiations occur between organizations, not individuals—yet individuals, not organizations, negotiate
deals. It's therefore crucial to consider the incentives of the individual
across the table: How is she compensated? How long has she worked
for the company? What are her long-term aspirations? These questions
are essential as part of effective preparation.

In the *Frasier* negotiation, consider Marc Graboff's incentives.
Graboff had a powerful advantage because he knew CBS—maybe even
better than CBS knew CBS at the time. Therefore, he knew Paramount's
BATNA with reasonable confidence.

Graboff also faced certain challenges because he was new at NBC
and wanted to start off on the right foot. After *Frasier*, exclusive negotiating periods for *The West Wing* and *Just Shoot Me* were just around
the corner. A *Frasier* deal, Graboff reasoned, could prove useful in
future rounds with other producers. One stake in the ground, from
Graboff's perspective, was *Friends*, a similar but even more successful
NBC comedy at the time. Any deal for *Frasier* that was more expensive

than *Friends* would be perceived as a bad deal for NBC. Although public accounts varied, the *New York Times* reported that NBC was paying approximately $6 million per episode for *Friends*.[9]

Paramount understood this general point but questioned where the ceiling actually was. According to McCluggage, "Our information was that the *Friends* license fee was higher than that . . . So yes, *Friends* was a ceiling, but unless we got it wrong, [NBC's] license fee [for *Friends*] was closer to $6.5 million, at least as we analyzed it."[10]

Regardless of whether the license fee for *Friends* was $6.0 million or $6.5 million per episode, Graboff's incentives to set a strong precedent severely constrained the ZOPA. Even if NBC's reservation value for *Frasier* on a stand-alone basis was as high as $7.0 or $7.5 million per episode, Graboff wasn't going to pay more than something in the neighborhood of $6 million. Analytically, Graboff gained reputational value by taking a hard line in the *Frasier* negotiation that would yield future benefits. This reputational value was particularly large for Graboff because he was new at NBC, and all eyes were on him to see what he would do in his first deal. Understanding Graboff's incentives leads to the conclusion that the ZOPA was severely constrained— something like $5.25 million on the low end to $6.0 million per episode on the high end.

In this chapter we have discussed the four essential steps of preparation: understanding (1) the parties, (2) their interests, (3) BATNAs on all sides, and (4) the incentives of the people at the table. It is a barebones set of concepts, intended to make sure you don't miss anything, but still leaving room for creative thinking about context-specific factors. In the next chapter we continue the story with an examination of at-the-table tactics in the *Frasier* deal.

CHAPTER 2

AT THE TABLE

In early 2001, Marc Graboff and Kerry McCluggage were gearing up for a thirty-day exclusive negotiating period that would begin on February 1. Rumors floated in the press that Paramount wanted $8.0 million per episode for *Frasier*—an enormous increase over the existing price per episode of $5.0 million. Graboff speculated that interested outside observers, not Paramount, had floated the $8 million number: "A couple of the agents, who represent some of the producers and the talent on the show, had a strong interest to get the price as high as possible. So that's how the $8 million got leaked."[1] McCluggage had a different assessment of where the number came from:

> It read to us like NBC planted that [$8 million] number, knowing that they were having a tough time getting to the numbers they wanted . . . It felt to me like they were positioning the studio as having been unreasonable and asking for more money than the show deserved, which would have made losing the show more justifiable. I don't know that that's actually how it happened, because the press is easily capable of getting it wrong on its own

. . . But we did look at that as a tactic on their part and it didn't play well with us.

As the exclusive negotiating period began, Paramount's first serious offer was $6.0 million per episode, a 20 percent increase over the existing price. McCluggage admitted, "We didn't expect it to end up at $6.0." NBC countered with $4.75 million per episode, a 5 percent reduction from the existing level. It was an enormous gap. Graboff recalls, "Usually when you're negotiating licenses, you're tens of thousands of dollars apart, not millions of dollars apart."

As the clock ticked toward the March 1 deadline, Paramount came down to $5.5 million and then dug in its heels. NBC came up to $5.0 million and then also refused to make further concessions. The parties were stuck with a $500,000 gap in their "best and final" offers. Multiplying by 24 episodes per season and by the 3-year term that Paramount was insisting on, NBC and Paramount were fighting over $36 million. Figure 2 brings together the ZOPA analysis from Chapter 1 with the dance of concessions thus far in the deal.

The parties were at a standoff, with NBC willing to pay a maximum of $5.0 million per episode but Paramount demanding a minimum of $5.5 million per episode. As Graboff recalls,

They wouldn't budge, and they were telling us that other networks were interested, and that it [*Frasier*] was going to go to another network if we didn't come up with this price. It all became a question of, do we want to call their bluff? Do we want to allow this to go the marketplace and see whether they're telling the truth or not? That was really what we were faced with . . . There were several meetings where we looked at each other across the table and we were at a standoff. We walked away from the table a couple of times when they brought up a couple of points that they claimed were on the table that had never been on the table. We just got really angry and we walked away. We threatened them a bunch of times, and they threatened us as well. For a while, it got really ugly.

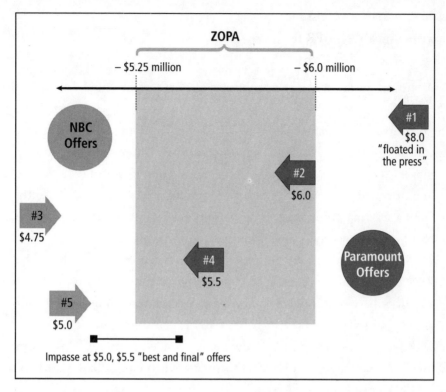

Figure 2. The Dance of Concessions in the *Frasier* Negotiation

McCluggage offers a similar account:

> It was very tense at the end, particularly when we felt we were offering a reasonable deal at $5.5 million, and they were still spending a lot of time talking about numbers below $5 million, which were just non-starters.

The NBC-Paramount deal illustrates some of the key aspects of the basic negotiation model. We work through these elements in the remainder of this chapter.

ANCHORING AND FIRST OFFERS

A natural question in any negotiation is whether you should make the first offer. Some people believe you should *never* make a first offer. Of course, if both sides take this view, then they both sit, sphinx-like, waiting for the other side to suggest a number. Others understand that making a first offer can "anchor" the negotiation in your favor. A long line of research shows that negotiators tend not to adjust sufficiently from a starting point once a number has been thrown out. This failure to adjust adequately is a well-known cognitive bias.

Anchoring works by influencing your perceptions of where the ZOPA lies. Imagine that, on the basis of prior research, you think the ZOPA is between about $30 and your reservation value of $60. But when your seller makes a first offer of $75, you shift your expectations without even realizing it. Suddenly, you wonder if the seller's bottom line isn't really $50, and you feel fortunate when you get a deal at $55. You have just been anchored.

Should you always make a first offer in order to make use of the anchoring phenomenon? Not quite. There are two distinct risks in making a first offer. One risk is that you anchor too aggressively, well outside the ZOPA. When this happens, you have a choice of either making big concessions to get into the ZOPA or walking away from the deal even though a ZOPA exists. Both alternatives are problematic. The other risk is that your first offer is too conservative, so you unknowingly give away a substantial piece of the ZOPA in your very first move.

In addition, an important caveat about the anchoring effect is that it works only when the other side is uncertain about where the ZOPA is. To take an extreme case, if the other side knows the bargaining range with 100 percent confidence, then your first offer is unlikely to influence the other party's perception of it. The more the other side knows about the ZOPA, the less effective anchoring becomes.

To balance these competing factors, I offer a few guidelines to help you determine whether to make a first offer that go beyond the conventional wisdom of "always" or "never":

- When you have a pretty good sense of where the ZOPA is, you should consider making a first offer in order to anchor the negotiation in your favor. The "sweet spot" is when you know where the ZOPA is but the other side does not. In this scenario, consider a "hard" first offer that puts a stake in the ground: "$30 is really the best we can do here." Then move just a bit from that starting point to seal the deal.

- When you don't know where the bargaining range is, hang back, listen, learn more, and maybe even let the other party make a first offer. To the extent you want to make a first offer in this scenario, you might consider setting a "soft" anchor: "We're thinking about something in the ballpark of $30" or "My people tell me that $30 is a fair price." You haven't actually made an offer, but you have floated a number that may stick if it is in the ZOPA or close to it.[2]

- When you don't know where the bargaining range is but the other side does, you're at a big disadvantage. If the other party is smart, they will make a first offer in this scenario. Your most important defense is awareness of the phenomenon. Rather than letting the cognitive bias take hold, resist the tendency to change your perception of the ZOPA unless the other side's first offer contains real information (for example, a breakdown of their costs).

Figure 3 summarizes my approach to thinking about the important question of whether to make a first offer.

If you go through this analysis and decide that you should make a first offer, how high (or low) should you aim? Recent research by Professors Richard Larrick and George Wu provides helpful guidance on this question. Larrick and Wu find that negotiators systematically underestimate the size of the ZOPA; that is, people think the other side can give less than is actually possible. Larrick and Wu call this the *small-pie bias*. If you think the pie is smaller than it actually is, then you will naturally overestimate how much of the pie you have claimed (what Larrick and Wu call the *large-slice bias*).

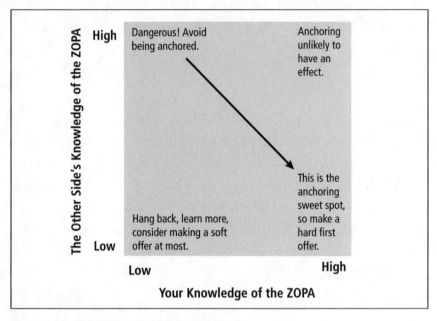

Figure 3. When Should You Make a First Offer?

Consider a simplified example. You are the seller and the bargaining range is between $0 and $100, but you think the other side won't pay any more than $80 (small-pie bias). When you end up with $50, you feel pretty good, because you think you claimed 63 percent of the pie ($50/$80), even though you actually claimed only 50 percent of the pie. In one experiment, students in a lab (more on laboratory investigations in Chapter 6) estimated that they had claimed 65 percent of the pie, on average, in a fixed-pie negotiation.[3] This is impossible: in a fixed-pie negotiation, each negotiator claims exactly half the pie on average.

These findings imply that you should make a first offer that is more aggressive than your instincts might lead you to make. I like the approach offered by Professors Max Bazerman and Deepak Malhotra. They recommend asking yourself, "What is the highest number I can justify?"[4] The question invites you to stretch beyond where your instincts might take you. It suggests not an outlandish number, but one that you can "tell a story" around.

The *Frasier* negotiation provides a nice illustration of these points. Recall that Paramount's first offer was $6.0 million, at the very high end of the ZOPA. Paramount was able to tell the story of why $6.0 million made sense, but it was certainly an aggressive offer that may have anchored the negotiation toward the high end of the deal space.

But didn't Marc Graboff at NBC have a strong sense about the ZOPA too? As I described in Chapter 1, Graboff had just left CBS, the likely competitor for the show, so the theory would tell us that Graboff shouldn't be influenced by Paramount's anchor. That may be true, but the value of the "soft stuff" in the deal on the CBS side added a wild card to the negotiation. As Graboff explained, Paramount's reservation value was likely to have been much better than the pure economics would suggest:

> I knew that the only way it goes to CBS is if [CBS CEO] Les Moonves convinces [Viacom COO] Mel Karmazin that putting *Frasier* on CBS is a triple whammy. It gets it off NBC. It gets it on CBS, where it becomes a tent pole. And third, I knew that there was a power struggle going on between certain levels of CBS and Paramount, and that getting *Frasier* on CBS would help CBS's political cause. That was purely political, but it was a factor nonetheless.

This uncertainty, and the major risk it created for NBC, may have allowed Paramount's anchor to have a greater effect than it otherwise would have had.

COUNTEROFFERS, AND MANAGING YOUR
PATTERNS OF CONCESSION

Once a first offer is made, the usual negotiation dance requires a counteroffer from the other side. If you are on the receiving end of a first
offer, the *midpoint rule* is the most important principle to consider as
you shape your counteroffer. Even my five-year-old son knows how it
works:

> "I'll throw you five more pitches, and then it's time for dinner."
> "Come on Dad . . . [pause for thought] ten more."
> "Seven."
> "Nine."
> "Eight."
> "OK, deal."

After the eight pitches are thrown and we're sitting at the dinner table,
my five-year-old looks at me with a sly grin: "Hey Dad, guess what—I
only *wanted* eight pitches!"

I've never felt prouder.

Even if you haven't heard of it, you probably know the midpoint
rule intuitively: by far the best predictor of the final deal price is the
midpoint of the first semireasonable offer and counteroffer. The rule
is not a law of physics, so the correlation between the midpoint of
the first offer and counteroffer and the final deal price is not a perfect one. Nevertheless, the midpoint is the most powerful explana-
tory variable for where the final deal price ends up. Use the midpoint
to your advantage in a negotiation. Think about where you want to
end up, and start with a counteroffer that gets you to that number as
a midpoint.

A few years ago, my wife and I were buying the house that we currently live in. Our inspection turned up $80,000 worth of things that
were problematic with the house, ranging from gutters that needed to

be replaced to large trees that needed to be pruned. I asked our broker what we should do.

He responded that there were three alternatives. The first alternative, he said, would be to let it go—the house is an 1880s Victorian, so some problems, even significant problems, shouldn't be terribly surprising.

I wasn't thrilled with this alternative, so I asked him what else we could do. The second alternative, he said, would be to split the difference. "You didn't know about these problems, and the seller presumably didn't know about these problems, so a $40,000 reduction from the purchase price seems like a reasonable resolution." This idea I liked a lot more.

The third alternative, our broker continued, would be to ask for an $80,000 reduction in the purchase price. "You made an offer not knowing about these problems," he explained. "And so the house will be worth your offer price only after these problems are fixed."

After some discussion, my wife and I decided that splitting the difference seemed like the fair resolution. But remembering the midpoint rule, I instructed our broker to present our list of problems to the seller and to ask for an $80,000 reduction in the purchase price.

One day later, the seller came back with a counteroffer of $10,000. After a few iterations, we agreed to a $37,500 reduction in the purchase price. Would we have gotten to this number if we had started with a split-the-difference offer from the outset? We'll never know, but it seems far less likely. Thinking about where we wanted to end up, we started with a number that got us there as a midpoint.

The first offer and counteroffer are followed by the usual dance of concessions between the parties to see if they can bridge the gap. The norm here is reciprocity: you make a concession, then I make a concession, then you make a concession again, and we go back and forth until we reach either a deal or an impasse. In managing this dance of concessions, it is important to "signal the end of the road." Make smaller and smaller concessions as you go to indicate that you are reaching your limit. As with the midpoint rule, plan in advance to converge your concessions to a desirable outcome.

SEARCHING FOR VALUE-CREATING MOVES

So far in this chapter, I have tried to summarize best-practice negotiation strategies for carving up a fixed pie, using the *Frasier* negotiation to illustrate various points. First offers, counteroffers, and patterns of concession are all important parts of this game. Negotiation theory, however, tells us that this is often the wrong game to be playing. The "fixed pie" assumption is usually incorrect. It's not necessarily true that more for me must mean less for you.

One of the core challenges in negotiations is to identify *value-creating moves*: things that are cheap for me to give and valuable for you to receive, and vice versa. To be clear, "making the pie bigger" isn't necessarily good in itself. In the end what you care about is how big your slice is, but it is obviously a lot easier to get a big slice if the overall pie is bigger.

Let's return to the *Frasier* example. For most of the exclusive negotiation period, NBC and Paramount were playing the traditional, zero-sum game. According to Graboff, these early negotiations were focused "purely on price," or, at best, "price, and some ancillary things which really were, if you boil it down, price-related." When you are playing solely a price game, a dollar more for you must mean a dollar less for the other side.

As the possibility of an impasse between NBC and Paramount began to loom—recall that the parties were $500,000 apart—they began to explore value-creating opportunities. For example, NBC offered money in the form of "development commitments" for Paramount, for Kelsey Grammer's production company (Grammnet Productions), and for *Frasier*'s executive producer's production company (Grub Street Productions). These development commitments are the equivalent of "take or pay" contracts in other industries, in that if a network decides not to air a producer's pilot or at least six episodes of the series, the development commitment mandates that the network still pay the producer a predetermined amount. "Development commitments boil down to money," explained Graboff, "but it came out of a different pool of money for us, so in some ways it was easier to give." A classic value-creation move: cheap(er) for NBC to give, and valuable for Paramount to receive.

A more important win-win move in the *Frasier* negotiation was the introduction of ratings-based increases and decreases in the purchase price. Making use of the different expectations that Paramount and NBC had about the show created value for both parties. Paramount was optimistic that the ratings would be strong, and therefore liked ratings-based increases that would reward them for a good show. NBC was more pessimistic about what the next three seasons would look like in terms of ratings. As Graboff explained, "Our big concern was that the show was starting to show signs of age." NBC liked ratings-based decreases because it meant a lower purchase price if they were correct.

In general, differences in expectations about the future often create value in negotiations. These kinds of bets, known as "contingent contracts" in the negotiation lingo, have three major benefits:[5]

1. They align the incentives of the parties. In the *Frasier* negotiation, once a ratings-based incentive is built into the contract, Paramount has a strong financial incentive to produce shows that keep the ratings up, which is exactly what NBC wants too.

2. They allow the parties to diagnose the honesty of the other side. If Paramount insists that the ratings will be high, NBC should respond by offering a ratings-based increase. If Paramount refuses this offer, NBC has just learned something: Paramount isn't willing to put its money where its mouth is with regard to the future ratings of the show.

3. They enable the parties to share the risk. If the show does great, NBC makes a lot of money, and therefore doesn't mind paying Paramount a higher fee because of a ratings-based increase. And if the show does poorly, NBC pays less to Paramount—a benefit

that NBC particularly values because it would have less cash in the door from advertisers.

THE NEGOTIATOR'S DILEMMA

Value-creation opportunities such as ratings-based increases and decreases can seem quite obvious once "all cards are on the table" (or, more colorfully, in an "open kimono" negotiation). The problem is that in real negotiations we don't put all our cards on the table. If we are fully forthcoming about our interests, the other side can use this information to extract all of the value that is created. Imagine if NBC had said, "We are deeply concerned about the ratings for the show, so we would very much value a ratings-based decrease in the purchase price." Paramount would have said in response, "Well, since you want a ratings-based decrease so much we'll give it to you, but it's going to cost you a lot in terms of the price per episode."

The core of the problem is this: in order to identify value-creation opportunities in a negotiation we need to disclose information; but disclosing information can expose us to value-claiming tactics by the other side. In a pathbreaking book from the mid-1980s, David Lax and Jim Sebenius coined the term *Negotiator's Dilemma* to capture this inherent tension.[6] To formalize the intuition, Lax and Sebenius construct a hypothetical scenario involving two individuals, Ward and Stone, negotiating over several issues. Ward and Stone have a choice: they can each *Create* in the negotiation, which means adopting an open, forthcoming approach; or they can *Claim*, which means a closed, more fixed-pie mindset.

Lax and Sebenius construct the matrix in Figure 4 to indicate the various choices and the outcomes that would result. As the matrix shows, if Ward and Stone both Create, they will each get a Good outcome. The open and forthcoming approach enables them to identify the value-creation opportunities, which they will then split evenly.

If instead Ward and Stone both Claim, they will both get a Mediocre outcome. The guarded approach makes it far less likely that the value-creation opportunities will be identified. Ward and Stone will fight over a smaller pie, which they will divide approximately evenly.

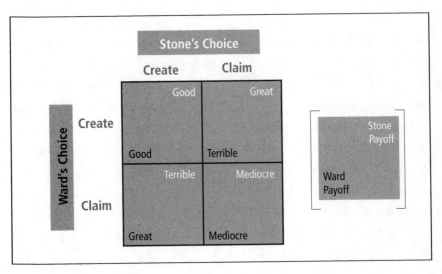

Figure 4. The Negotiator's Dilemma

The third possibility, reflected on the other diagonal in the matrix, is that one of them will Claim and the other will Create. For example, if Ward Claims and Stone Creates, Ward will get a Great outcome and Stone will get a Terrible outcome. Stone will be very forthcoming with his interests; Ward knows his own interests, so he will be able to identify the value-creation opportunities and capture all of that value. The pie will be big, as in the Create/Create scenario, but Ward will have claimed most of it.

Should Ward choose Create or Claim in this negotiation? The answer requires an assessment of what Stone might do. If Stone chooses Create, then Ward's best response is to Claim: Stone is open and forthcoming, and Ward can use the information to identify and capture for himself all of the value-creation opportunities (rather than playing Create and having to share the value with Stone). Great is better than Good, so if Stone plays Create, Ward should play Claim.

What if Stone chooses Claim? Here again, Ward's best response is to play Claim, to avoid being taken to the cleaners by Stone. Mediocre is better than Terrible, so if Stone plays Claim, Ward should play Claim too.

The punch line is this: no matter what Stone does, Ward's "best response" is to Claim. The payoff diagram in the Negotiator's Dilemma is symmetric, making Stone's assessment the same: Regardless of what Ward does, Stone's best response is to Claim. Lax and Sebenius demonstrate that Claim/Claim is a "dominant strategy" in the negotiation, meaning that both Stone and Ward do better by playing Claim, regardless of what the other party does. The result is a Mediocre outcome for both Stone and Ward, which is troubling because there was a better outcome that *both* of them could have achieved by playing Create/Create. The Negotiator's Dilemma leads rational negotiators to leave value on the table. (Students of game theory will recognize that the structure of this problem, and its analytical result, is the same as the well-known Prisoner's Dilemma.)

Dozens of books provide strategies for how to overcome the Negotiator's Dilemma. In general, these books advocate asking lots of questions, probing for underlying interests, revealing information reciprocally, and offering "packages" rather than negotiating issue by issue, to maximize the likelihood of identifying and capturing value-creation opportunities. For our purposes, the important point is that the Negotiator's Dilemma provides a structural reason to believe that many value-creation opportunities are missed in negotiations. This point provides the theoretical foundation for much of the empirical research and writing in negotiation over the past two decades. I revisit this point in more detail in Chapter 6.

THE *FRASIER* AFTERMATH

So, what happened with *Frasier*? When we left off, NBC and Paramount were stuck at "best and final" offers of $5.0 million and $5.5 million, respectively. As the March 1 deadline approached, the parties began to explore value-creating opportunities to break the impasse—things like development commitments and ratings-based increases and decreases in the purchase price. However, one of the biggest sources of value creation was explicitly taken off the table. As described by Marc Graboff,

> Our big concern was that the show was starting to show signs of age. We felt that it had one good year, maybe two, left in it after the eighth season, but that the third year could potentially be disastrous. We didn't want to have to commit to the third year. If we were going to lose money in years one and two, we were going to get clobbered in year three under our projection. We made several proposals that had a three-year pick-up but a cutback right that said if the ratings fell below a certain number in our 18 to 49 demographic in the second year—which was kind of a disaster-scenario number—we didn't have to pick up the show in the third year. Our argument was, by that time, everybody's embarrassed.

NBC feared that the show didn't have "legs," so a cutback right was extremely valuable to it. Paramount should have been willing to give the cutback right in exchange for a higher price per episode. If Paramount really believed that the show would have solid ratings in the third year, NBC wouldn't exercise the cutback right anyway. Textbook value creation: NBC gets something that it perceives to be very valuable; Paramount gives something that it thinks is cheap and gets a higher price per episode for accepting the risk of no third season.

The roadblock was Kelsey Grammer, the star of the show. Graboff explained:

> Their attitude [on the cutback right] was, "That's a non-starter. Kelsey will be insulted. You don't want to do this." So Scott [Sassa] went and talked to Kelsey, and asked him squarely, "Is three years really that important to you?" And Kelsey basically said, "Look, at the end of the day, you're not going to be embarrassed here, because we're not going to do it just to do it." So that gave us the comfort we needed to say okay, this issue was off the table.

Notice the flaw in the logic. If Grammer really wasn't going to "do it just to do it," then he couldn't possibly have minded a cutback right— he was going to stop doing the show anyway if the show tanked. Grammer's intransigence on the cutback right revealed that he wasn't as confident about the show's "legs" as he claimed to be.

In the end, the parties reached a deal at approximately $5.4 million per episode, with some other development commitments and modest ratings-based increases and decreases. (Notice that this outcome is very close to what the midpoint rule would predict, in view of the first offers of $6.0 million and $4.75 million.) Graboff describes the endgame:

> Jeff, Scott, and I had to leave that night to go to a cocktail party. It was around 8:30 pm, and the Paramount guys wanted to stay at the table all night figuring this out. I said that we had to leave, and Jeff and Scott ran out the door. I was putting my jacket on, and the Paramount guys pulled me aside and caved on the last point. I told them, "Well, I've got to talk with Jeff and Scott before we can close this deal because we want to look each other in the eye now that we're at the closing point." So Kerry [McCluggage] and Gary [Hart] went home . . . I went to the party, grabbed Jeff and Scott, and we all left and sat in Jeff's car for five minutes talking about the deal. Then Jeff picked up the cell phone in his car, called Kerry McCluggage at home, and closed the deal.

Frasier stayed on NBC for three more seasons. Just as Graboff had feared, the show declined significantly in the ratings. What had previously been a perennial top-ten contender dropped into the forties and fifties for most of the last three seasons. Despite his insistence that he wouldn't "do it just to do it," Grammer persisted for all three seasons, thereby tying the record for longest-running character in TV history. In May 2004, the show went out with a whimper, not a bang.

There is one last piece to the story. After reaching its deal with NBC, Paramount had to sit down with the stars: Kelsey Grammer and David Hyde Pierce. As described by Graboff:

> One of the things that we had made a condition to the deal was the services for all three years of Kelsey Grammer and David Hyde Pierce, who plays Niles, because without them, there is no show. You would think that, as a studio, Paramount, before they made this deal with us, would have locked in the services for Kelsey and David for those three years, because once we made that deal and it became public (which these things invariably do) that gave Kelsey and David a bit of negotiating power with the studio. And unfortunately Paramount did not have deals in place with either of those guys.

So Kelsey Grammer became a toll collector on a very narrow bridge. McCluggage explained this important sequencing issue from Paramount's perspective:

> We would have preferred to have locked them down [Kelsey Grammer and David Hyde Pierce], but it wasn't really possible . . . Their agents didn't want to close the deal without knowing exactly what the size of the pie was [from NBC]. Of course, it's more difficult when you do it that way, because you are putting a gun in their hands and saying, "Shoot me" . . . But we actually ended up pretty close to where we wanted to be.

In June 2001, three months after Paramount and NBC had come to an agreement, Grammer reached a deal with Paramount to work on

Frasier for three more seasons. The terms: $1.6 million per episode, making him the highest-paid actor in sitcom history. Paramount got a rich price from NBC but then delivered a lot of that money to its star Kelsey Grammer. As Graboff recounts, "At the end of the day, they weren't happy and we weren't happy, which are the hallmarks of a good deal."

In these first two chapters I used the *Frasier* case to illustrate core ideas from the standard negotiation model: concepts such as BATNA, reservation value, ZOPA, and the Negotiator's Dilemma. In Chapter 7, I return to the *Frasier* negotiation to assess NBC's and Paramount's moves using a negotiauction lens.

CHAPTER 3

WHEN TO AUCTION, WHEN TO NEGOTIATE?

On October 3, 2008, President George W. Bush signed into law the Emergency Economic Stabilization Act (EESA) of 2008, beginning the most significant US government intervention into the economy since the Great Depression. The centerpiece of the EESA was the Troubled Asset Relief Program (TARP), which gave Treasury Secretary Henry Paulson the right to spend $700 billion (in two tranches) to buy up so-called toxic assets. In the deluge of commentary on the EESA, relatively little attention focused on how, exactly, Secretary Paulson would go about buying up the toxic assets. Would he negotiate individual deals with the troubled financial institutions? Or would he hold a reverse auction to set the price? Sections 113(b) and (c) of the Act provide the only legislative guidance on the question of whether to auction or negotiate:

(b) USE OF MARKET MECHANISMS. In making purchases under this Act, the Secretary shall—

Make such purchases at the lowest price that the Secretary determines to be consistent with the purposes of this Act; and

Maximize the efficiency of the use of taxpayer resources by using

31

market mechanisms, including auctions or reverse auctions, where appropriate.

(c) DIRECT PURCHASES. If the Secretary determines that use of a market mechanism under subsection (b) is not feasible or appropriate, and the purposes of the Act are best met through direct purchases from an individual financial institution, the Secretary shall pursue additional measures to ensure that prices paid for assets are reasonable and reflect the underlying value of the asset.

Under the reverse auctions that were envisioned by Section 113, the Treasury Department would specify a class of security, and then troubled banks would compete in the auction to sell their securities that fit the specification back to the government. The price would be bid down and the lowest price would win, thereby providing the biggest bang for the buck for the American taxpayer.

The instinct to hold a reverse auction might have been due in part to the positive experience that the US government has had using auctions to sell securities. Every week the government sells US Treasurys into the marketplace, and the competitive bidding process is generally thought to yield fair market prices. Even after the financial crisis was well under way, the US government was easily able to sell billions of dollars of US Treasurys in this way. In one auction conducted in November 2008, for example, the *Wall Street Journal* reported that the offering was more than three times oversubscribed.[1] And in February 2009, in the midst of unprecedented spending plans from the Obama administration that would balloon the federal deficit, the *Wall Street Journal* headlined with "The World Still Lines Up for Treasurys."[2]

An auction mechanism makes a lot of sense for the US government to use in selling Treasurys. Among other reasons, the asset is homogeneous, and there are many potential buyers. The same is not true with a reverse auction for toxic assets; these assets, unlike US Treasurys, are heterogeneous. At least 100,000 different mortgage-related securities are outstanding, with different vintages, maturities, interest rates, geographic locations, payment histories, and FICO scores, to name a few characteristics.[3] The government could hold different auctions for different types of securities, but it would be impossible to perfectly control for all the variation across these toxic assets. Even if the government controlled for the most important features, there would be a tension between specifying the asset precisely and getting a reasonable number of bidders to show up. The more the government specified the asset it wanted to buy, the more auctions it would have to run, and the fewer sellers who would show up for each auction.[4]

Thus, the US government was caught between a rock and a hard place in designing its reverse auction. On the one hand, the government could have specified the asset so precisely that only a few sellers (or maybe only one) would own assets that would qualify for sale in the auction. Too few sellers would be bad, for obvious reasons. On the other hand, the government could have broadened the asset specification so that more sellers competed, but doing so would have made the asset heterogeneous in both observable and unobservable ways. The winner in this broader auction would be the seller with assets that were the most toxic, because that seller would be motivated to cut its bid the most. So the government would be getting less than it was expecting for the money it paid.

Some might say it's okay to overpay a little bit for the toxic assets, because an implicit goal of the TARP is to give the financial institutions a government handout. Even if you subscribe to this view, mark-to-market rules created an even bigger problem for the securities that were *not* sold into the reverse auction process. In November 2007, the Federal Accounting Standards Board (FASB) promulgated Rule 157 ("FAS 157"), which requires financial institutions to mark trading and "available for sale" securities to market values. Once the Treasury Department began running reverse auctions for toxic assets, the banks would get pressure from their outside auditors to mark their own toxic assets to the prices that were set in these auctions. As one commentary put it, "If auctions for troubled assets appear successful, it would seem difficult, absent a suspension of FAS 157 by the SEC, to ignore the auction price, not only for the specific class of securities auctioned, but also for other substantially identical securities."[5]

Recall that the auction prices would be set by the value of the worst toxic assets within the class of security. The best toxic assets (if that's not an oxymoron) would be left unpurchased in the reverse auction process, and then (under FAS 157) would have to be marked to the "market price" set in the reverse auction. Banks would be writing their toxic assets down to values that were below their actual, hold-to-maturity values. In effect, banks would be punished even more severely than the economic fundamentals of their balance sheets would dictate. This would seem to be precisely the opposite of what the TARP was intended to do. All of this supports the conclusion that buying back the toxic assets through a reverse auction was a lousy idea.

On November 12, 2008, a little more than a month after the TARP was established, the Treasury Department ditched the plan. Secretary Paulson announced that instead of buying toxic assets directly, the TARP would be used to inject equity into financial institutions in order to spur lending. According to the *Wall Street Journal*, "Mr. Paulson's move signals a new, albeit awkward second phase for Treasury's rescue plan just weeks before a new administration is seated."[6] But on January 16, 2009, after $350 billion in TARP funds funneled to banks had not, in fact, spurred lending, the Treasury returned to its original plan of buying toxic assets. According to the *Journal*, "the idea of buying up bad bank assets echoes the original idea of Treasury Secretary Henry Paulson . . . Mr. Paulson abandoned that idea in favor of investing directly in banks after he concluded that the program would be too slow, costly, and difficult to implement."[7]

It is clear that Treasury's back-and-forth in deploying TARP funds damaged its reputation. In fact, commentators attribute some of the meltdown in the stock market during this period to the concern that the Treasury Department didn't know what it was doing. The instinctive preference for auctions, as codified in Sections 113(b) and (c) of the EESA, illustrates the conventional wisdom that an auction is the best method for getting a good price. Just hold an auction, interested parties will show up, and the price will be bid up or down (depending on whether you are buyer or seller) to your advantage. As another example of this conventional wisdom, one well-known mergers and acquisitions handbook states:

> Auctions are still generally believed to be the best way of ensuring that the highest possible price is obtained. The same sentiment probably drives the seller to use auction methods for sales of divisions or subsidiaries of companies. Also, who can fault a corporate executive for the price he or she agrees to if it was the result of a competitive bid procedure?[8]

This conventional wisdom manifests itself in real deals all the time. For example, Noel Dunn, a senior investment banker at JPMorgan Chase in New York City and a sounding board for several of the ideas contained in this book, e-mailed me to say:

> I am in the middle of one auction where we represent the most likely buyer vis-à-vis a motivated seller who wants "value" (purchase price + timing + certainty of execution). However, the seller is following a strict auction process almost like a car manual even though we and they know that the universe of qualified buyers is strictly limited. I am waiting for the appropriate moment to instigate a "shut down" move.[9]

Two prominent auction theorists, Professors Jeremy Bulow and Paul Klemperer, have developed a theoretical model of auctions and negotiations validating the conventional wisdom that an auction always maximizes value. Bulow and Klemperer conclude from their analysis that "with independent signals, and risk-neutral bidders, therefore, an auction with N+1 bidders dominates any negotiation with N bidders . . . The result suggests that the value of negotiating skill is small relative to the value of additional competition."[10]

The conventional wisdom, even when bolstered by Bulow and Klemperer's theoretical model, is wrong. There are serious drawbacks and risks with auctions that the theoretical models and the conventional wisdom do not capture. As an illustration, consider the ongoing debate in the procurement industry about the wisdom of e-auctions. Over the past decade e-auctions have brought dramatic and highly visible price reductions to companies' input costs. Software vendors such as Ariba make it very easy for a procurement officer to set up an online auction, have suppliers bid in real time over the Internet, and walk away with dramatic cost savings just thirty minutes later. In the late 1990s, e-auctions hit the procurement industry like a tidal wave. According to one top procurement executive, "when auctions first came on the scene, they were very much in vogue and were tried for pretty much anything, with varying degrees of success."[11]

Over the ensuing decade, companies learned, often the hard way, that auctions were not the best way to buy everything. One problem that companies encountered was the difficulty in capturing non-price items in the e-auction process. E-auctions are excellent at creating competition on price, but not good at providing meaningful competition on non-price terms like quality. As a result, procurement officers began to recognize an important distinction between commodities, which were appropriate for e-auction, and more complicated goods and services, which were not.

Over time, an increasing number of suppliers refused to participate in e-auctions. Part of this trend was, of course, fueled by the perception that it was difficult to earn reasonable profits from participating in e-auctions. A more subtle problem was that e-auctions created a win-lose situation between supplier and customer, the opposite of supplier-customer "partnerships," which are thought to be best practice today. In 2001, a survey of 230 suppliers conducted by Oxford University's Said Business School revealed that more than 60 percent did not use e-auctions and had no plans to do so within the next two years.[12] A November 2007 survey by *Supply Management* magazine, which caters to procurement professionals, confirmed this conclusion under the headline "Most Buyers Shun E-Auctions."[13]

The evidence from the procurement industry, then, doesn't square with the theoretical prediction that you should always hold an auction.

My research in the M&A arena also supports this assessment. Experienced investment bankers consistently tell me that pure auctions are usually not the best way to sell an asset. It's not that practitioners have not yet caught up with cutting-edge academic thinking on the question; rather, in the real world important complexities need to be considered in determining whether to auction or negotiate. In the remainder of this chapter I offer a framework for thinking through this important question.

Before jumping in to the analysis, some definitions. An *auction* is a mechanism in which the seller is a passive participant after the process has been set, and the primary source of competitive pressure arises from competition among the buyers. A *negotiation* is a mechanism in which the primary source of competitive pressure arises in across-the-table dynamics between buyer and seller. For now, I treat auctions and negotiations as pure cases. In Part II, I will explore more complex mechanisms that combine both auction and negotiation features.

Finally, throughout the analysis that follows I assume that the process is being set by the seller of the asset; that is, the seller is the process setter. When the buyer determines the process, the situation is known as a *reverse auction*. The analysis remains the same, but the labels "seller" and "buyer" are just flipped in this situation.

When deciding whether to hold an auction or negotiate privately with potential buyers, you should consider four factors: (1) the profile of potential bidders; (2) asset characteristics; (3) your own profile, as the seller; and (4) contextual factors. In the remainder of this chapter I describe each of these elements in more detail.

1. Profile of Potential Bidders

NUMBER OF BIDDERS. The starting point for most process setters in determining a deal process is the number of potential bidders. Unfortunately, this is often the ending point as well: If there are lots of bidders, sellers hold an auction; if not, sellers negotiate privately. The number of potential bidders is certainly an important aspect of the bidder profile, and I provide more details on how to think about this factor in the discussion that follows. I also introduce three other aspects of the bidder profile that are often missed: (1) the degree of certainty as to who the potential bidders are; (2) the bidders' incentives to participate; and (3) the likely difference in valuations among these bidders.

The starting point is what you already know: You should be more likely to auction as the number of serious potential buyers increases. When there are many buyers, there is lots of same-side-of-the-table competition to take advantage of. Hold an auction, and let buyers do the work of driving up the price.

To be a little more precise, imagine the following stylized situation. You are using an auction to sell an asset that you value at zero. As potential buyers enter the room, they draw their valuations from a barrel containing a hundred balls labeled from $1 to $100. Once the auction begins, each participant will bid up to the value indicated on his or her ball (the amount is known only to the participant), and then drop out.

If the first bidder draws $99 and the second bidder draws $100, they're off to the races and you win big, even though there are only two bidders. But you can't expect to be so lucky. In general, you can expect to receive slightly more than the second-highest bidder's valuation, which is the point at which the second-highest bidder drops out of the auction and there is only one bidder left standing. That value, in turn, depends on the number of potential buyers who show up to draw balls out of the barrel. With a little math, we can determine that the expected outcome is $33 with two potential buyers, $67 with five potential buyers, and $82 with ten potential buyers.[14] As we all know, increased competition drives up the selling price. Figure 5 shows the expected revenue to the seller from this stylized auction as a function of how many bidders draw balls from the barrel.

It's no surprise that the expected revenue goes up as the number of bidders increases. But notice also that the value of each incremental bidder goes down as the total number of bidders goes up; that is, the curve flattens out quickly. At about ten bidders, you are getting 85 percent of the expected revenue that you would get from fifty bidders. In the absence of any particular advantage, each additional bidder who shows up has a smaller and smaller chance of being the highest bidder (who wins) or the second-highest bidder (who sets the price). And these are the only two bidders you care about in the end.

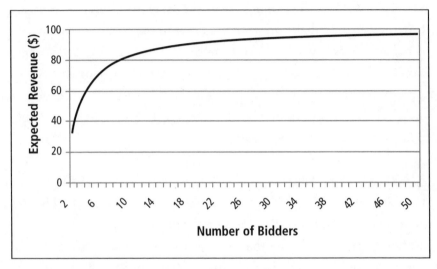

Figure 5. Expected Revenue to Seller from Stylized Auction

You might say that as long as the expected revenue keeps going up, you want as many bidders as possible to show up at the auction. The problem is that there are costs to having a completely wide-open process. On your side is the complexity of managing so many potential bidders; on their side is the risk that some bidders (even high-value bidders) will not play if the field is so wide open. The latter risk is particularly likely if bidders must incur costs—real or intangible—to make a bid.

In the end, you definitely want more than one participant in an auction, but twenty is not necessarily better than ten. The "magic number" will depend on things like the complexity costs on your side and bid costs on their side—as complexity costs and/or bid costs increase, you will want to decrease the number of bidders.

In many contexts, practitioners consider the magic number to be somewhere between five and eight bidders. When UK private-equity powerhouse Apax Partners sold Xerium Technologies in April 2002, it immediately winnowed down forty indications of interest to seven bidders on the basis of the bidders' reputations, credibility, and the likelihood that they would close the deal. Xerium CEO Tom Gutierrez explained, "You can't really handle more than seven serious bidders. It's incredibly time-consuming."[15] In the Cable & Wireless America (CWA) case study that I presented in the Introduction, the lead investment banker acknowledged afterward that "it was almost burdensome, frankly, to try to get all seven contracts in the same spot so that we could have the auction."[16] So when the number of potential buyers is large, use an auction to maximize value, but beware that it's possible to have too much of a good thing.

CERTAINTY ABOUT WHO THE BIDDERS ARE. Another important aspect of the bidder profile is your degree of certainty as to who the bidders are. If you are the US government seeking to build a next-generation aircraft carrier, you know that only a few private companies in the world are qualified to deliver on this kind of multibillion-dollar contract. In this case there would be no point in holding an auction; you would just go talk to the three companies that have the capability to build the ship. Although this point may seem intuitive, recall Noel Dunn's comment at the beginning of this chapter: "The seller is following a strict auction process almost like a car manual even though we and they know that the universe of qualified buyers is strictly limited."

In other situations, you don't know who the high-value buyer is, and it would take a lot of time and effort to find out. In this scenario, "search costs" are high, so you should hold an auction, announce it to the world, and let the high-value buyers find you. Consider the following account from the lead banker for CWA, describing the market canvass that was conducted:

> We went broadly. We talked to strategic buyers, we talked to financial buyers, we talked to international buyers. We had a very high turn-down rate. But that's what you do. You go out way beyond

what you would expect. Also, bidders called us . . . We were very satisfied that we did not miss somebody . . . We were confident that anybody that had an interest in this asset and could pay more than $50 million [the stalking-horse bid] had been contacted or had heard of it and had decided to pass.[17]

As you will recall from the Introduction, Savvis Communications won the auction with a bid of $168.3 million. After the fact, the selling banker admitted he was surprised that Savvis had won the auction:

None of us thought Savvis would be the winning bidder . . . I have to tell you we did not put them in the best, most central conference room, but they kept saying to us "we're going to win." A good friend of mine was their lawyer and he said these people are seriously going to win. So I think that the surprise, probably of the day, was that the winning bidder was Savvis.[18]

If the seller had conducted a more closed process, it seems likely that Savvis would have been missed and the seller would have received less.

BIDDERS' INCENTIVES TO PARTICIPATE. Bidders are generally wary about participating in auctions. In some situations you will have to use a more closed, negotiation-like process to bring bidders to the table. For example, in Chapter 10 I describe an auction for a new car that I tried to conduct using an online service offered by Edmunds.com. None of the four Boston-area dealers were willing to bid in my auction, presumably because their experience told them that participating just wasn't worth the effort. I infer that these dealers were too busy selling to showroom customers to bother with my Internet auction. In effect, I had guessed incorrectly about the dealers' BATNAs (best alternatives to a negotiated agreement), and the result was a busted auction. For the rest of the story, skip ahead to Chapter 10. For now, the point is that when bidders' BATNAs are good, you may need to negotiate privately to get them to come to the table.

Alternatively, some bidders might not participate in auctions because other bidders can get a free ride off their expertise. In Chapter 5 I illustrate how bidders can learn from other bidders' moves in open-outcry auctions. If bidders understand this point (and research examining eBay auctions suggests that they do),[19] then experts might simply decline to participate in open-outcry auctions. If you want to deal with them, you will have to negotiate privately, or at least hold a sealed-bid auction.

Some assets are easy to value, so expertise isn't worth very much. For example, laptop PCs are bought and sold every day by non-experts because prices are highly visible and readily accessible on the Internet. For these kinds of assets, you don't need to worry about inducing participation by experts, so you can comfortably hold an auction. Some assets, however, are difficult to value without expertise. An antique sword, for example, could be worth $100 or $100,000, and only an expert would know the difference. If it's a must-have for a serious collector, then you can happily hold an auction and let the non-experts learn from the experts' bids. If the item is not a must-have, the experts can walk away from your auction, resulting in a price that is set by non-experts (risky), or a busted auction that brings you back to private negotiations with the experts. In this scenario you should negotiate privately from the start.

DISTRIBUTION OF VALUATIONS. A fourth aspect of the bidder profile is the distribution of valuations among the bidders. Even if there are lots of bidders, you may want to negotiate privately if the top two valuations are far apart. Recall that the predicted outcome in an auction is the second-highest valuation, plus a little bit. If the top two valuations are close to each other, then getting the second-highest valuation plus a little bit is a pretty good deal for the seller because it pushes the high bidder close to his or her bidding limit. But if the top two valuations aren't close, then the seller is leaving a lot of value on the table by holding an auction.

In fact, we saw this point already in the Introduction. Savvis Communications was the winning bidder for Cable & Wireless America, with a bid of $168.3 million. This number was well beyond the seller's expectation, to be sure, but it was likely well under Savvis's reservation value for the asset. The Savvis CFO testified after the fact that operational synergies with CWA "may be as high as $60 million a year and maybe higher," implying that synergies alone would pay for the deal in three years.[20] In addition, and perhaps even more important, before acquiring CWA Savvis was in a precarious position because it relied on two customers—Reuters and Moneyline Telerate—for 55 percent of its revenues. (Eventually, Reuters bought Telerate, which would have made Savvis's reliance even more precarious.) Such reliance makes financing difficult—and in the investment-heavy telecommunications business, access to financing is essential for survival. Buying the CWA assets suddenly gave Savvis hundreds of new customers, and Reuters/Telerate shrank to just 15 percent of total revenues. The deal reduced Savvis's business risk in a way that was unique among the seven bidders who were present at the January 2004 auction.[21]

In contrast, Gores Technology, the second-highest bidder in the auction, was a well-known private-equity firm. Although Gores had other portfolio companies in the same industry as CWA, buying CWA would have been primarily a "financial play," meaning that Gores would have tried to improve operations and capital structure, and hope for "multiple expansion," in order to sell CWA for a profit down the road. Unlike Savvis, Gores had no synergies with existing operations, no fixed costs that it could leverage across a larger customer base, and no benefits from customer diversification.

Robert McCormick, the Savvis CEO, was in the room to confirm his $168.3 million winning bid at 6:12 p.m. on January 22, thirty-four hours into the auction. Savvis's stock jumped 33 percent on the announcement of the deal. This increase amounted to an additional $85 million in market capitalization for Savvis after adjusting for market movements, implying that Savvis's full valuation for CWA was in the ballpark of $250 million. If this sounds like a high number, it is supported by the fact that Savvis was absolutely certain it was going to win the auction. Recall the account from the seller's lead banker: "They

[Savvis] kept saying to us, 'we're going to win.' A good friend of mine was their lawyer, and he said these people are seriously going to win." Not a difficult prediction to make when you have a quarter billion dollars in your pocket.

After the fact, McCormick was effusive about the deal he got, calling it a "transforming transaction" and a "quantum leap forward" for Savvis.[22] Three years later, the subsequent Savvis CEO, Phil Koen, confirmed that recreating the CWA assets would have cost "multi-billion dollars."[23] Taken as a whole, this evidence suggests that Savvis paid less than its full valuation for the target. It was able to do this because it had to beat the Gores bid by only a little bit.

Nothing in the US Bankruptcy Code or the local rules of the bankruptcy court required CWA's bankers to auction the company, yet most bankers and lawyers tend toward auction processes in order to satisfy the bankruptcy judge that they achieved a fair price.[24] In fact, when the distribution of valuations is large, a seller will be leaving considerable value on the table by holding an auction.

2. Asset Characteristics

After examining various characteristics of the bidders, the next factor to consider in determining whether to auction or negotiate are features of the asset itself. In considering asset characteristics, three related points are important: (1) if you can specify the asset you're trying to buy or sell, an auction is probably the better option; (2) if the potential for value creation is high, negotiation is probably better; and (3) if relationship and service are important aspects of what you are buying or selling, you will probably want to negotiate instead of holding an auction.

These three aspects of asset characteristics are often correlated. For example, being able to specify the asset you're trying to buy often means that the value-creation potential is low and relationship and service are not terribly important. Nevertheless, I treat the three aspects independently in the discussion that follows because they are not perfectly correlated.

ABILITY TO SPECIFY THE ASSET. An important consideration in determining whether to auction or negotiate is your ability to specify what the asset is. In my view, this is the main reason that the TARP auctions for toxic assets were a bad idea—the Treasury would have had a difficult time specifying exactly what it was seeking to buy in each auction.

The procurement context provides another illustration of this point. All else equal, the more you are able to specify what you want, the more likely it is that an auction will be a better option than a negotiation. The ability to specify the asset is sometimes, though not always, determined by whether the asset is a commodity. If you are trying to buy paper clips in bulk, by all means hold an e-auction and let same-side-of-the-table competition drive down the price. Even some services can be so well specified that an e-auction is justified. But this is not very often the case.

A recent academic article, focusing on e-auctions in the procurement context, rejects this "myth" that e-auctions are suitable only for commodities. Using interviews with thirty procurement officers, the researchers acknowledge that "the more commodity-like the product and/or service, the easier the online auction process," but they argue that even services can be auctioned if the process setter spends sufficient time doing the preparatory work, so that "everything is laid out very clearly in the RFQ [request for quote]."[25]

The problem with this advice is that it eliminates the possibility for capturing win-win opportunities, which can be important if the product is not a commodity. Consider the following excerpt from a recent request for proposal (RFP) for business services that tries to "lay everything out clearly":

SUPPLIER must use the prescribed format to submit its proposal. Any deviation from the format or requirements stated in the RFP and associated documents may render SUPPLIER's proposal invalid. SUPPLIER must accept, without exception, all of CLIENT's standard terms and conditions of contract set forth in this RFP and to price its proposal accordingly. Failure to do so (for risk, liability or any other reason) may result in removal of SUPPLIER from the RFP process. Any element of the SUPPLIER's proposal that is subject to or alludes to being contingent upon further discussion or clarification with CLIENT, or review, consent or further approval from any person, group, committee, board or other authority of the SUPPLIER, may be rejected.[26]

This is not exactly a process that is conducive to value creation. The general point is that beyond baseline must-have requirements, product specifications cannot be determined in isolation from price. Doing so makes it quite likely that participants will miss value-creating opportunities.

A better approach for non-commodities is to hold a multi-attribute auction. The process setter establishes a scoring system that establishes weights for each issue and points for each option within each issue. Bids are then scored against this point system. Recent theoretical work demonstrates that the process setter should openly disclose this scoring system to the bidders, so that they can optimally structure their bids across the various issues.[27]

A scoring system works well if the process setter can specify all the issues and the value associated with each option within each issue. But if the issues are themselves up for negotiation, and/or the options within each issue are not well-defined choices, a scoring system can break down. Even when a scoring system is feasible, most software programs require "additive preferences," meaning that your preferences for the various options on one issue are independent of your preferences on other issues. This assumption can be unrealistic in many negotiauction situations—instead, what you get on one issue will influence whether and how much you want another issue.

To sum up, if you are buying or selling a commodity, by all means use an auction. Or if your asset is not a commodity but you can construct a scoring system that accurately captures your preferences, a multi-attribute auction can work well. But if neither of these conditions is met, you should be more inclined to negotiate privately with one or more potential counterparties.

POTENTIAL FOR VALUE CREATION. A second, and often related, factor in deciding whether to auction is the potential for value creation. Auctions do a great job of boiling everything down to price, but boiling everything down to price is exactly the opposite of what you want to do in order to identify value-creating opportunities.[28] If there is some possibility of win-win moves, it is better to negotiate with one or more potential counterparties than to hold an auction. As described in Chapter 2, negotiations give you the opportunity to learn each others' preferences, make trade-offs across different issues, and craft a deal that yields a larger pie overall.

Recent research supports this point. Professor Patrick Bajari and two coauthors examined private-sector commercial building contracts awarded in northern California between 1995 and 2000.[29] Out of approximately four thousand contracts in their data set, about half (43 percent) were negotiated deals, while the remainder were awarded through auction mechanisms. The authors found that the most powerful explanation for the decision to auction or negotiate was the complexity of the project: as complexity increased, the buyer was more likely to negotiate privately with one or more potential builders. Buyers in this marketplace were intuitively aware that complex projects, with multiple issues in play and not necessarily conflicting interests between the parties, were more amenable to negotiation as a way of identifying and capturing the value-creating opportunities.

IMPORTANCE OF RELATIONSHIP. Finally, you should examine whether relationship, service, and/or deal execution are important aspects of what is being bought or sold. If so, you should prefer negotiations over auction-like mechanisms. This is the primary reason that *both* buyers and suppliers have moved away from e-auctions in the procurement context, as discussed earlier in this chapter. In a world where vertical "partnerships" are perceived to be best practice in supply chain management, auctions go in the opposite direction. Auctions signal that the buyer is indifferent among suppliers, other than the price received. Procurement officers have come to learn that these signals can have negative consequences when foreseen and unforeseen problems arise down the road.

As an illustration outside the procurement context, consider the recent case of Edward, a Boston-area homeowner looking to renovate a bathroom in his house. Many homeowners would conduct an implicit auction among general contractors, letting each bidder know about the same-side-of-the-table competition as a way of ensuring a fair price. Instead, Edward picked Dave solely on the basis of word-of-mouth recommendation. In their initial meeting, Edward told Dave, "I've heard great things about your work and I'm really looking forward to working with you. For this reason I'm not shopping around. But in exchange I hope and expect that you'll give me a fair price, and that we'll work together to see this project through to a favorable completion."

Sure enough, the project was on time and on budget. But toward the very end, just as Dave was putting the finishing touches on the bathroom, disaster struck. Dave's plumber came to the house to do some work in the basement, and he turned the water off in order to do so. Soon thereafter, the cleaning person came to the house, opened the bathroom faucet, discovered no water running, and inadvertently left it on while she cleaned the rest of the house. The plumber finished his work, turned the water back on, and left the house. When Edward returned home a couple hours later, he discovered a foot of water in his newly renovated second-floor bathroom, and water damage throughout the rest of the house.

Naturally distraught, Edward called Dave and explained the situation. Both parties implicitly understood the legal backdrop, in which a court would have to apportion fault between Edward's cleaning person and Dave's plumber. But rather than engaging in this complex and indeterminate inquiry, Dave took on the problem, repaired the water damage, and finished the project at no extra charge. In doing so, he remembered his initial encounter with Edward, and the trust that Edward had expressed in not shopping around. Would Dave have done the same thing if Edward had held an auction for the initial business? There is no definitive answer to this counterfactual, but my conversations with Dave afterward suggest that it would have been less likely.

The general point is that when relationship and deal execution matter, you should stay clear of auction-like mechanisms, which signal the opposite. The benefit is often a more favorable resolution of problems down the road.

3. Seller's Profile

The third factor to consider in determining whether to auction or negotiate is your own profile, as the seller of the asset. Two elements here are typically in tension with each other: speed and risk. Auctions can happen far more quickly than negotiations, so if speed is important, an auction is a better mechanism. But faster processes are also riskier, because you have less time to adjust to new information along the way. Let's look at these two competing points in more detail.

IMPORTANCE OF SPEED. Most of the moves in private negotiations—such as exploring interests, generating options, and identifying value-creating moves—take time. Moreover, negotiations usually happen sequentially, not simultaneously as in auctions, because you can't be negotiating with two different counterparties at exactly the same time. In some situations, you don't have this time—there is a window of opportunity to sell, or the asset is deteriorating in your hands as time passes. In these cases, auction-like mechanisms dispense with the benefits of value creation in exchange for speed of sale.

Bankruptcy law implicitly recognizes this point. In the United States, bankrupt companies can sell assets in two distinct ways: under a traditional plan of reorganization, enacted under Chapter 11 of the Bankruptcy Code; or in an auction process under Chapter 3. Chapter 11 reorganizations are known to be the "Wild West" of corporate deal-making. Separate creditor classes, each with certain rights and all with a certain amount of veto power over management's turnaround efforts, jostle among themselves for advantageous positioning over the firm's existing and future cash flows. As this description suggests, a Chapter 11 reorganization is often a long and arduous negotiation. Companies use it when there is a good chance of reorganizing the claims in a way that sustains the company while addressing the creditors' various interests, thereby creating value overall.

In contrast, auctions conducted under Chapter 3 of the Bankruptcy Code are quick and painless. They are known as "363 sales," after the section of the Bankruptcy Code that permits them. The congressional intent behind Section 363 makes clear that the provision is intended for use when the company is in a hurry. In fact, Section 363 is often referred to as a "rotting fish" provision. The term comes from the image of a bankrupt fish merchant, who is best served by immediately converting his inventory into cash rather than letting it rot while lengthy Chapter 11 proceedings unfold. If you've been wondering why the bankers and lawyers who sold Cable & Wireless America in the Introduction went on with their auction for thirty-four hours straight, the reason is that CWA was being sold under Section 363. At the time of the auction, CWA was hemorrhaging more than $300,000 in cash each day.

TOLERANCE FOR RISK. Auctions are well understood to be faster than negotiations, but with speed also comes more risk. You could end up with a "busted auction," in which nobody shows up; or, even worse, you could hold an auction to which only one bidder shows up. In contrast, negotiations move more slowly, enabling you to test the waters as you make your way to a better outcome.

Consider the case of a privately held dot-com that was contemplating a buyout of its minority shareholders in early 2008. Another Harvard Business School professor and I were asked to advise the company on how to execute this so-called freeze-out transaction. One proposal was to hold a reverse auction, in which minority shareholders would specify the price at which they would be willing to sell their shares and the company would buy back the shares from lowest price to highest price until its funds for the buyback were extinguished.

We advised against this approach because it was too risky. There was some chance that no one would be willing to sell at any reasonable price, in the hopes that the company's valuation would return to the sky-high levels of the early 2000s. The result would be either a busted auction or an extremely unattractive clearing price. Even if the minority shareholders played more rationally, these shareholders would be trying to figure out the bids of others while making their bids. In game theoretic terms, the reverse auction was not "strategy-proof." In view of these considerations, the results of a reverse auction were difficult to predict with any certainty, and potentially disastrous.

The company decided to negotiate privately with its major shareholders. The management team quickly homed in on two of the larger minority shareholders—call them John and Fred. John came to the table first and offered to sell his stake for $12.00 per share, a sky-high number that was based on a valuation of the company at the peak of the Internet bubble. The company countered with $1.50 per share, which had been the offer price in the first round of financing back in the late 1990s. It was a big gap, but the counteroffer from the company had the effect of defusing John's unrealistic valuation. The company came up a bit, to $3.00; John came down significantly, to $3.31; and the company quickly closed the deal at $3.31.

So far, textbook negotiations as described in Chapter 2: John made an aggressive anchor and the company did a nice job of defusing the anchor, responding with an aggressive counteroffer, and signaling the end of the road—all of which led to a very good deal for the company. But the private negotiation had another beneficial effect. Fred, the other large minority shareholder, was also on the board of directors for the dot-com. In the board meeting to approve the deal to buy out John, Fred became very emotional. As a director with fiduciary duties, he felt compelled to approve this great deal for the company, but he understood that the $3.31 price had just set a powerful, and unfavorable, precedent for him in his negotiations with the company to sell back his own shares.

In short, the company's sequencing move allowed it to gain significant leverage against Fred. More generally, the company's choice to negotiate rather than auction minimized risk for the company and allowed it to work its way to a very good deal.

4. Contextual Factors

Finally, in determining whether you should auction or negotiate, you should look at two contextual factors: the need for secrecy and the need for transparency.

NEED FOR SECRECY. Broad-based processes like auctions are difficult to keep secret. Even if you require all bidders to sign confidentiality agreements, the chance of leaks increases as you shop the asset. So if secrecy is important, you should consider negotiating privately with one or more buyers.

This is a frequent concern in M&A deals. As one practitioner put it to me, "Auctioning is not something that works for most companies. It has huge internal risks with the employee base."[30] If it becomes known that the company is for sale, employees will start looking for new jobs, and the value of the company will deteriorate while it is being shopped. In my research I regularly find instances of boards that resist a broader-based search process in the sale of their company, on the concern that a broader process will damage the very asset they are trying to sell.[31]

To see how this risk can play out, consider the sale of the Pittsburgh Steelers, one of the most legendary franchises in the history of the National Football League (NFL). The cigar-chomping Hall of Famer Art Rooney bought the team in 1933 for $2,500. Rooney's Steelers then helped transform the NFL from a grassroots organization to the largest and most profitable professional sports league in the United States. In the 1970s, the Steelers won four Super Bowls under coach Chuck Noll and with star players Terry Bradshaw, Lynn Swann, and Franco Harris, among others. The team was widely loved through Pittsburgh's economic ups and downs during this time.

By 2007, Art Rooney had passed away and his five sons owned 80 percent of the team. (The McGinley family, the Rooneys' cousins, owned the remaining 20 percent.) Each of the five Rooney sons would owe more than $50 million in estate taxes upon their death—money that most of the brothers did not have. Dan Rooney, the oldest brother, quietly hired Société Générale SA, the French investment bank, to make an offer to buy out the four brothers and their cousins. The terms of the offer aren't publicly known, but whatever they were, the four younger brothers weren't satisfied. The younger brothers then hired Goldman Sachs to estimate the value of the team in a potential sale to a third party. Working in tight secrecy under the code name "Project Newcastle," Goldman's bankers valued the Steelers at somewhere between $800 million and $1.2 billion. Encouraged by this valuation, the brothers authorized Goldman to quietly begin looking for a third-party buyer.

The story broke on July 8, 2008. Under the headline "Pittsburgh's Rooneys Quietly Shop the Steelers," the *Wall Street Journal* reported, "The Pittsburgh Steelers—owned for 75 years by the same local family—is secretly being shopped to potential buyers as the five sons of the football team's founder and their heirs spar over the storied franchise's future."[32] Not so secretly after a front page *Journal* story.

For some assets, secrecy is not terribly important. But for the Pittsburgh Steelers, the revelation caused an outpouring of negative fan sentiment. "I'm having a hard time breathing," posted one fan on a Steelers website. "This is a dark, dark day in Steelers history," wrote another. Steelers President Art Rooney II hurried to reassure fans that "there is no reason to believe" that discussions about ownership would impact fans. But his reassurance didn't stop another fan from writing, "I, along with most of Steeler Nation, seem to be in a state of shock."[33]

Despite the best efforts of the Rooney brothers and Goldman Sachs, the broader search process that the younger brothers had initiated quickly exposed the deal to public scrutiny. It's possible that the negotiations had sufficiently broken down with Dan, the oldest brother, that the broader process was necessary in order to ensure that the younger brothers would receive the highest possible price. But the more open process also put the Rooney brothers on the defensive, trying to shore up an asset that had been a crown jewel of the Pittsburgh community for decades.

Unfortunately for the younger brothers, the global financial crisis broke in the middle of Goldman's search. The one potential buyer turned up by the market canvass, billionaire Stanley Druckenmiller, walked away at the last minute, and the younger brothers came back to their older brother to negotiate a deal. On November 15, 2008, Dan Rooney agreed to buy out his younger brothers in a deal that valued the team at $800 million—a number at the bottom of Goldman's valuation range. Commentators reported that the younger brothers were hurried into the deal by the prospect of higher estate taxes in the imminent Obama administration.[34]

The younger brothers were clearly unlucky to sell the team in the middle of a financial meltdown, so we can't fault the auction process for the price that they received. Still, it's clear that their auction process increased the likelihood that the deal would become public, and also signaled the brothers' willingness to sell the team outside the family. Even though it was ultimately unsuccessful, this move damaged the franchise among devoted Steelers fans.

Of course, in professional sports all is forgiven for those who win—and in January 2009 the Steelers won their sixth Super Bowl, a record among NFL teams. So the Rooneys' flawed deal process may have been saved by spectacular on-field performance. The general point nevertheless remains: broader-based auction-like processes increase the likelihood that the deal will become public. In some cases, like the sale of the Pittsburgh Steelers, this is another important consideration in determining whether to auction or negotiate.

IMPORTANCE OF TRANSPARENCY. A second contextual factor is the importance of transparency, by which I mean the appearance of a level playing field among bidders. Auctions are more transparent processes than private negotiations, so if transparency is important, an auction is better. This is the reason that most public procurement contracts (i.e., government as buyer) and government privatizations (government as seller) are done through auctions, particularly when the government is looking to defuse criticisms of corruption or favoritism. (The Peruvian government's sale of the Antamina copper mine described in the next chapter is an example.)

Consider the TARP auction case study that opened this chapter. Secretary Paulson may have been attracted to a reverse auction for buying toxic assets at least in part for transparency reasons. Section 119 of the EESA severely limits the ability to obtain judicial review of the Treasury's TARP spending decisions. With such sweeping power comes the responsibility to deploy the capital wisely, and in a way that is perceived to be fair. Secretary Paulson is, famously, the former CEO of Goldman Sachs. Goldman is one of the troubled banks that holds toxic assets that could be sold into the TARP. Any whiff of favoritism toward Goldman in a privately negotiated purchase of toxic assets under the TARP would immediately raise a public outcry. Hence the need for a transparent process.

It might be argued that Secretary Paulson wouldn't have been directly involved in any private negotiations to buy up toxic assets, and we therefore shouldn't assume favoritism toward Goldman just because Goldman might have gotten one or two good deals under the TARP. True enough. The actual administration of the TARP in the Bush administration was delegated to a longtime Paulson aide, Neel Kashkari. Kashkari was the head of the Office of Financial Stability (OFS), and a former vice president at—you guessed it—Goldman Sachs.

Putting aside Goldman, however, there are hundreds of lower-level OFS officials who will be deploying the TARP assets in the Obama administration. These people might have skewed incentives if they are contemplating potential jobs at the troubled financial institutions down the road. Transparency, then, is vitally important in the TARP, and this concern points toward holding a reverse auction. In my view, it does not outweigh the factors against a reverse auction that I discussed in the introduction to this chapter. But in many cases, such as privatizations in developing economies, transparency can be critical and sometimes dispositive on the question of whether to auction or negotiate.

Figure 6 summarizes the factors discussed in this chapter. The acronym BASC—look to the *b*idders, *a*sset characteristics, *s*eller profile, and *c*ontextual factors in determining whether to auction or negotiate— is a useful moniker for this framework. It's a long way from Bulow and Klemperer's stylized model of auctions and negotiations, but in my view it pinpoints the factors that you should think through in order to make a decision on this basic process choice.

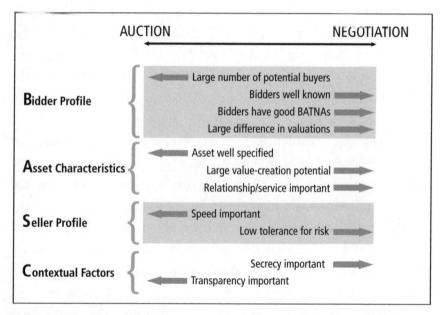

Figure 6. When to Auction, When to Negotiate?—The BASC Framework

What if you work through the various factors and conclude that an auction is the best way to go? In the next chapter, I assume that the process setter has correctly chosen to hold an auction, and I explore the various types of auction mechanisms, and when to use each.

CHOOSING THE RIGHT KIND OF AUCTION

Robert Barnett is a senior partner at the prestigious law firm of Williams & Connolly in Washington, DC. He spends 90 percent of his professional time doing litigation and corporate work for major companies such as McDonald's and Toyota, but that is not why he is ranked number one on *Washingtonian* magazine's list of "Washington's Best Lawyers." That accolade stems from a self-professed "side business" representing authors in securing book contracts. And not just any authors. Barnett's client list is a who's who of politicians and other statesmen from around the world. His web page at Williams & Connolly lists his book-publishing clients as Bill and Hillary, of course, but also Tony Blair, Alan Greenspan, Barack Obama, Laura Bush, "several" former US secretaries of state, "numerous" US senators, Queen Noor of Jordan, and the late Benazir Bhutto of Pakistan, among others.

Barnett doesn't need to convince publishing houses that his clients' books will sell. On the contrary, these houses fall over themselves to sign up his can't-miss authors, not only for the potential profitability, but also for the reputational benefits that a big political name brings to their brand. In some unusual cases, Barnett will negotiate a book deal with a single publisher—for example, Bill Clinton wanted to work with a certain editor at Knopf, so Barnett negotiated the former President's deal privately with that publishing house. In most situations, however, Barnett will parade his superstar client around to the major publishing houses in New York City, his client will describe the book to the swooning editors, and Barnett will leave the hopeful bidder with a letter describing how the process will work.

Barnett has spent more than three decades at Williams & Connolly cultivating a reputation as a straight shooter, and his letter describing the rules of the auction reflects that fact. In it, the name and date change but the other text is always the same:

> If you are interested in acquiring the rights to [author's] book . . . please submit your offer in writing to me at my office no later than [date]. We would like to know as many details as possible, i.e., what rights do you wish to purchase, what is the amount of the advance, what will the schedule for payment of the advance be, what royalty levels and splits of proceeds you are offering, what is your monetary commitment to advertising and promotion, what bonuses, if any, do you propose, etc. . . . We ask . . . that all offers and all subsequent discussions remain confidential . . .
>
> On [date], I will call the low offeror and ask if he/she will top the high offeror. That process will continue for as long as necessary.
>
> [Author] reserves the right to reject all bids, to accept less than the highest bid, and to take into account all factors, including, for example, all aspects of the offer, the capabilities of the publishing house, and the experience of the editor.

Does this process maximize value for the author? Should Barnett not tell the low bidder the number to beat in order to stay in the game? Should he just conduct a single-round sealed-bid auction rather than a multi-round process? Barnett is a lawyer, not an auction theorist or an economist, so he doesn't pretend to know for sure whether his process maximizes value for his clients. When he comes to my Corporate Deal-making class at Harvard, my students often ask him why he uses the process he does. His answer: "Because it is fair."

In the previous chapter I provided a framework to help you determine whether to hold a more open (auction-like) process or a more closed (negotiation-like) process. In this chapter I now turn to the question of what kind of auction to use, assuming that you (like Barnett) are the "process setter" and have determined that an auction is the right way to go. After reviewing the various factors to consider, I revisit the political book auction scenario to examine and evaluate the process choices that Barnett made.

OPEN OUTCRY OR SEALED BID?

The first fork in the road is whether to hold an open-outcry auction or a sealed-bid auction. In a *sealed-bid auction*, bidders submit written bids and do not know what others bid, or (often) how many bidders there are, before the winner is revealed. In many cases the number of bidders and range of bids is not disclosed even after the winner has been announced. The standard RFQ (request for quote) process at most companies is usually a sealed-bid auction. This auction type contrasts with an *open-outcry auction*, in which bidders know the high bid at all times, and have the option of beating it. Typically, bidders in an open-outcry auction know the identity of the high bidder in addition to the amount that is being bid.

Although the question of sealed bid versus open outcry is often portrayed as a dichotomous choice, in fact sealed-bid auctions can look a lot like open-outcry auctions if there are multiple rounds. In Robert Barnett's book auction, the request for sealed bids by the bid deadline date makes it seem like a sealed-bid auction (naturally enough). But recall that the high bid does not automatically win—Barnett tells the low bidder the high bid and gives the low bidder the option to beat it. This process is analytically identical to an open-outcry auction, so later in this chapter we will analyze the book auction as an open-outcry auction, even though the bids are all technically sealed bids.

Then there are the middle-ground cases. Consider a two-round sealed-bid auction with ten bidders, in which six bidders will be eliminated after the first round, the high bid will be announced, and the four remaining bidders will be invited to participate in a "best and final" round. Is this an open-outcry auction or a sealed-bid auction? The answer is that it has features of both. In what follows, we will treat open-outcry and sealed-bid auctions as discrete process choices in order to provide clear costs and benefits of each, with the understanding that in certain situations these mechanisms can be intertwined to reap some of the benefits of each mechanism on its own.

With this simplifying assumption in place, there are four factors you should consider in determining whether to hold an open-outcry auction or a sealed-bid auction. In roughly descending order of importance, they are: (1) the number of potential bidders; (2) the degree to which bidders' valuations are "affiliated"; (3) the degree of bidder risk aversion; and (4) the need to deter collusion among bidders.

Number of Potential Bidders

The most important factor in determining whether to hold a sealed-bid auction or an open-outcry auction is the number of potential bidders. In the previous chapter we saw that when you have more bidders, you should lean toward using an auction-like mechanism, all else equal. Once you have decided to hold an auction, you should revisit this factor to determine what kind of auction to use. Because an open-outcry auction is a more transparent process, an open-outcry auction makes sense when you expect several potential bidders to show up. The minimum number of initial bidders in an open-outcry auction is thought to be in the range of five to six, though this number could be higher if there are weak bidders in the mix, or lower if all of the bidders are strong and committed to "going the distance." Fierce competition among these bidders should drive up the price to a desirable level. In contrast, a sealed-bid auction makes sense when the number of potential bidders is fewer than five or six. The non-transparency of the process invites the possibility that bidders will bid against themselves.

There is a caveat for repeat-player process setters, such as investment bankers who regularly sell companies. If you develop a reputation for always holding an open-outcry auction when you have many bidders and always holding a sealed-bid auction when you have just a few bidders, then over time bidders will know approximately how many bidders there are just by knowing which mechanism you have chosen. To avoid this problem, you should mix things up from auction to auction—for example, sometimes use a sealed-bid auction even though you have several bidders—or simply commit to a sealed-bid auction mechanism regardless of how many bidders you have.

In the extreme case, an open-outcry auction simply won't work if you have only one bidder. In that situation you should hold a sealed-bid auction. Even the possibility of one bidder should drive you strongly toward a sealed-bid process. Unlike an open-outcry process, a sealed-bid process enables you to create the perception of competition when there isn't any. As a senior investment banker once told me:

> We have run many auctions where we have one bidder. We never let the bidder into the central room, so the one bidder thinks they are bidding against somebody else. And we don't lie to them, we just say, "You'll be in this room, and we'll come back to you periodically." And we never lie. We're never untruthful. But we keep them guessing about who else there is. Because if anybody ever senses that there is no other competition, then you're in trouble.

As a variation on this tactic, consider the example of an investment banker trying to sell a division of a company in the late 1990s. Three bidders were rumored to be interested, but when the banker called around, only one of them expressed interest in inspecting the asset further—known in the industry as *due diligence*. Undaunted, the banker calmly informed his one interested buyer that due diligence would have to be conducted over the weekend, with a firm bid due on Monday morning. No problem, said the buyer. How about we come into the "data room" (where confidential company information is located) on Saturday at 12:00 p.m.? Sorry, the banker said, that slot is taken. Saturday at 5:00 p.m.? Taken. Sunday at 5:00 p.m.? Taken.

The only slot that was still available, according to the banker, was Sunday morning at 8:00 a.m. Even in the nonstop investment banking world this was a painful slot, but the interested buyer grudgingly accepted it. The buyer's team went to bed early on Saturday night and showed up at the appointed time on Sunday morning, only to find empty Chinese food boxes piled high in the trash cans around the data room—a ploy by the banker to create the impression that another team had been there the night before.

The tactic worked. The unsuspecting buyer took out the trash, conducted its due diligence, and made a blockbuster bid. After some further haggling over details just to keep up the charade, the seller's banker quickly accepted the offer. This outcome wouldn't have been possible in an open-outcry auction.

This story raises the natural question, was the Chinese food tactic legal? It is clear that auctions and negotiauctions raise unique and important legal questions, and I return to these questions in the final chapter of this book. For now, note simply that the Chinese food tactic was likely legal because there was no overt misrepresentation by the seller—just the strong suggestion that competing bidders had been there the night before.

As a legal matter, the words that were actually said or the actions that were actually taken matter a lot, even if the message that was received is not the same as the message that was sent. As a humorous example of this point, a London-based investment banker recounted to me an auction he helped conduct a few years ago. Because there was some possibility of a single bidder, the banker decided to use a sealed-bid process. Sure enough, on the day of the auction just one bidder showed up. After soliciting a first bid, the banker calmly cabined his one bidder in a conference room and approached him with the following carefully worded line:

"I'm not going to lie to you. But you are the low bidder right now."

The bid went up nicely, and the banker quickly closed the deal.

We return to the legality of this tactic in Chapter 11. For now, the important point is that sealed-bid processes allow you to create the perception of competition when competition might not actually exist. Remember, though, that it's important to mix things up if you're a repeat-player process setter.

Affiliation of Bidder Signals

A second factor to consider in determining whether to hold a sealed-bid auction or an open-outcry auction is the degree to which bidders' signals are "affiliated." In a classic theoretical paper from the early 1980s, Professors Paul Milgrom and Robert Weber demonstrate that an open-outcry auction is more desirable for the seller when bidders' valuations should be influenced by others' bids—a phenomenon that they call "affiliated signals," which, as we will see in the next chapter, is related to "common value."[1] The intuition is that a bidder will walk into the auction with a certain valuation—say, $100—but when the bidders around him are comfortably bidding in the $120–$130 range, his own reservation value should go up—not because of irrational escalation, but because he is learning from the moves of others.

In the next chapter we discuss when you should "rationally update" your reservation value as a bidder. But the point here is that as a seller, you should make use of an open-outcry auction in situations where bidders are likely to learn from others' bids and adjust their own valuations accordingly. As Milgrom and Weber demonstrate, the extra information gained by observing competitors' bidding behavior leads to more aggressive bidding in open-cry auctions, resulting in a higher price for the seller than what a sealed-bid auction would provide. Thus, if bidders' valuations depend on each other, an open-outcry auction will maximize the price for the seller.

Bidder Risk Aversion

In the previous chapter we saw that sellers who want to avoid risk should be more likely to negotiate rather than auction. Now we consider risk aversion on the part of the bidder. When bidders exhibit risk aversion, consider holding a sealed-bid auction to take advantage of it. Sealed-bid auctions are risky propositions for bidders; open-outcry auctions contain no inherent risk. Risk-averse bidders in a sealed-bid auction will shade their bids less, benefiting the seller.

To see this point, imagine the young sales representative who is instructed to bid on a new client's business in a sealed-bid auction. If the business goes for less than his reservation value (recall that this is a reverse auction), then he didn't want the business anyway. No harm done, other than the lost time. His worst fear, though, is that the business goes for more than his reservation value but he bid too aggressively. As he becomes more risk-averse (i.e., more and more scared about losing the business in this scenario), he will shade his bid less in the sealed-bid auction. The risk inherent in the sealed-bid auction induces him to pay more. So when bidders are risk-averse, use a sealed-bid auction to take advantage of it.

Bidder Collusion

The final factor to consider in determining whether to hold a sealed-bid auction or an open-outcry auction—preventing collusion—is not important in most auctions, and for this reason it is last on the list. But when collusion is a factor, it is usually the most important factor and should drive the process setter strongly toward a sealed-bid auction. To see why, imagine two bidders—Bo and Luke—who have identical high valuations for the asset being auctioned. Bo and Luke strike a deal, agreeing that only Bo will bid; then, after Bo wins the auction, Bo and Luke will split the profits. Without collusion, the seller would have gotten Bo's (or Luke's) full valuation and both bidders would have made zero profit. With collusion, the seller gets a lower price, and both Bo and Luke make money.

I address the legality of this arrangement in Chapter 11. For now, the question is how the process setter can avoid the negative effects of collusion without resorting to litigation against the two buyers. The answer is a sealed-bid auction. In a sealed-bid auction, Luke has an incentive to renege on his agreement with Bo, bid just a little bit more than Bo's bid, and keep all the profits for himself. By the time Bo has discovered Luke's betrayal, it's too late—the envelopes have been opened, and Luke has walked away with the prize.

Contrast this outcome to an open-outcry situation. Luke reneges, but this time Bo quickly sees what is happening and realizes that his deal with Luke is off. Bo responds with a higher bid, and the bidding contest is under way. The seller gets Bo's (or Luke's) full valuation, just as if there had been no collusion.

Now imagine the initial conversation between Bo and Luke as they are setting up their collusive scheme. If the process setter has established an open-outcry auction, Bo and Luke are confident that their agreement will stick. The implicit threat is that if Luke breaks the deal, Bo will know immediately and can retaliate, and vice versa. Neither bidder has an incentive to break the deal, and the collusive agreement holds. If instead the process setter has established a sealed-bid auction, Bo and Luke have a real concern that their deal won't stick, because neither can retaliate immediately. Bidders are thus less likely to attempt collusive agreements in a sealed-bid auction, because the collusion is more difficult to enforce.[2]

Figure 7 summarizes the four factors you should consider in determining whether to hold an open-outcry auction or a sealed-bid auction. To see this framework in action, return to Robert Barnett's book auction. As described earlier, even though bidders are technically submitting sealed bids in this auction, Barnett tells the low bidder the high price and invites a topping bid, thereby replicating the fundamental dynamics of an open-outcry auction.

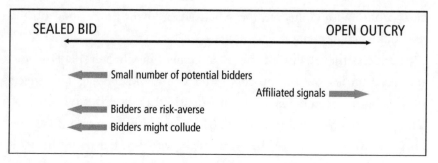

SEALED BID   OPEN OUTCRY

Small number of potential bidders

Affiliated signals

Bidders are risk-averse

Bidders might collude

Figure 7. Sealed-Bid or Open-Outcry Auction?: Four Factors to Consider

The framework that I have described supports Barnett's design choice:

1. The number of potential buyers is high.

2. There are affiliated signals. For example, Simon & Schuster is willing to pay more when it learns that its archrival Knopf is willing to pay more.

3. Bidder risk aversion is low. In fact, publishers are notorious for "taking a flier" on high-risk books that appeal to their gut rather than relying on financial projections.[3]

4. Bidder collusion is virtually unheard of in this world, because of the large number of potential bidders and the reputational consequences of detection. (For the one known exception in the publishing world, skip ahead to the story of Barnett's auction for two colluding authors, James Carville and Mary Matalin, described in Chapter 9.)

In short, all of the factors in the framework point in the direction of an open-outcry auction, which is where Barnett's intuition and concern for fairness take him as well.

OPEN-OUTCRY AUCTIONS: SOME DESIGN CHOICES

Suppose you have reviewed the four factors described in the preceding section and have concluded that you want to run an open-outcry auction. Let's peel back another layer of the onion to discuss process choices within the category of open-outcry auctions. When most people think about open-outcry auctions, they envision what auction theorists would call an *English auction*: the price starts low, bidders raise their hands, and the bidding continues until only one bidder is left standing. English auctions are by far the most common type of open-outcry auction.

In an English auction an important design question is the *minimum bid increment*—that is, the minimum amount by which each subsequent bid must increase. If the minimum bid increment is $10, then bidding can proceed as follows: $55, $65, $80 (more than the increment, but not less), $90, $100, and so on. Although there is no hard science to answer this question, it is a good idea to start with larger bid increments and decrease them over the course of the auction. Large bid increments at the outset keep the momentum going and signal that you are expecting far more than the opening bid.

As a rule of thumb, professional auctioneers often start with an opening bid that is half the lowest possible price that they expect in the auction, but couple it with a large bid increment. The low starting price gets lots of people interested, but the large bid increment keeps the momentum going.[4] As the auction proceeds, however, skilled auctioneers reduce the bid increment in order to extract full value from the high-value bidder. Going back to the simple example in the previous paragraph, if the current high bid is $100 and the minimum bid increment remains $10, a bidder who values the asset at $108 will be unable to bid, and the seller leaves value on the table. By this point in the auction, the auctioneer should be using a smaller bid increment—say, $2—in order to squeeze full value out of the high bidder.

If these points all sound intuitive, return to the sale of Cable &

Wireless America, in which most of these rules were violated. The initial bid in the CWA auction was $50 million, as set by the stalking-horse process. The sell-side investment bankers set a minimum bid increment of $1.5 million, which in retrospect would have required seventy-five bids to reach the eventual purchase price of $168.3 million. Because a bidder typically reruns its financial model each time it makes a new bid, this small bid increment meant an extremely time-consuming auction. And it was. Perhaps realizing the mistake, the sell-side bankers *increased* the bid increment twenty hours into the process—from $1.5 million to $2.0 million—continuing a painful slog toward the eventual purchase price of $168.3 million.

The small bid increments had another, more subtle effect as well. As described by Phil Mindlin, a partner at Wachtell, Lipton, Rosen & Katz who was involved in the CWA auction,

> As a buyer, you're conditioned by the behavior of other buyers. And if increments are small . . . you get the sense that the target price is within sight. And so no one thinks if you're bidding $60 million and the increments are $250,000 that you'll ever get to $100 million . . . Because it's like being in a car that's slowing down.[5]

Therefore, bid increments are an important factor to get right in an open-outcry ascending auction.

Another kind of open-outcry auction is the *Dutch auction*. In a Dutch auction the bidding starts at a high number and declines until one bidder is willing to bid. Dutch auctions are often confused with reverse auctions, in which the buyer is the process setter and potential sellers are the bidders. (A procurement auction is the paradigmatic reverse auction.) In both Dutch auctions and reverse auctions the price starts high and goes down. But the analytics of reverse auctions are identical to those of the standard English auction—just with the roles of buyer and seller flipped. So it is better to think about reverse auctions as a category of English auction rather than as equivalent to Dutch auctions.

When should you use a Dutch auction instead of the more conventional English auction? By far the most important reason is when speed matters. Take the most famous Dutch auction of all: the sale of flowers in the Netherlands. (Indeed, this is why Dutch auctions have their name.) The auctions have taken place at Aalsmeer, a small town near Amsterdam, ever since 1911. According to one report, "At Aalsmeer . . . the three keys to the flower industry are quick, quick, quick."[6] Flowers arrive in the middle of the night from nurseries around the world, and the customers (mostly exporters and wholesalers) are in their offices by 5:00 a.m. to survey the merchandise and prepare for bidding. The auction officially begins at 6:30 a.m. Potential buyers gather in one of five auction rooms, sitting around desks and listening to the auctioneer with headsets. A screen displays the picture of the particular flower up for sale, along with statistical information such as environmental factors, quality, and the grower's logo.

The sale process is governed by a clock, which displays the price of a single flower. The auctioneer sets the starting price and the clock lights up to show the price dropping at breakneck speed—faster than the second hand of a clock—until a bidder presses a button on his desk. This bidder then decides the quantity of flowers to purchase at the price shown on the clock. The clock is then reset, and the price falls again until another bidder (which could be a previous winning bidder) hits the button. The procedure is repeated until the entire lot of flowers is purchased. In this manner, 2.1 million cut flowers and plants are sold each day, yielding revenue of more than $20 billion per year. According to one commentator, "A rose sold under the clock in the morning can be gracing a dinner table the same evening in Paris, Rome, or New York."[7]

Beginning in 1989, the Sydney Fish Market has also been run using a Dutch auction process. Seafood arrives at the market by 3:00 p.m., and potential buyers have until 4:30 the next morning to inspect the crates. Just as in Aalsmeer, a clock is set at a high price, the auction starts, and the price drops until a bidder places a bid. Once the bidder selects the desired quantity from the lot, the remaining fish are reauctioned. The Sydney Fish Market sells nearly a thousand crates of fish per hour using this process, every day.[8]

These examples illustrate that when speed is important, a Dutch auction can get the job done. Another reason to use a Dutch auction is that it reintroduces risk into the auction, which works to the seller's benefit if the bidders are risk-averse. Consider the flower auction again. When the clock is above your reservation value as a bidder, you rest easy—if another bidder pushes his button it doesn't matter, because you aren't willing to pay that price anyway. But once the clock goes below your reservation value, you start to sweat. Every second that you wait, you increase your profits from the deal but also increase the risk that someone else will push his button first. If you are risk-neutral, you simply make your best guess as to when the next-highest bidder will jump in, and press your button a little bit before that. As you become more risk-averse, you build in a bigger and bigger cushion, causing you to press your button earlier and increasing the price you pay relative to an English auction.

Another open-outcry variant is the *Japanese auction*. In a Japanese auction, the price starts low and goes up as in an English auction. The twist is that *all* bidders are required to signal their willingness to bid at each new bid amount, and any bidder who drops out cannot reenter the bidding. A Japanese auction is sometimes called a "button auction" because one way to operationalize a Japanese auction is with buttons. Like a Dutch auction, each bidder gets a button; but this time the bidders have to hold their buttons down, signaling their willingness to bid as the clock hand goes up in price. When bidders take their hand off the button, they are out of the auction. As in an English auction, the last person with a hand on the button wins the auction.

The Japanese auction is not very common in practice, but it does have some desirable features that make it a reasonable process choice in some situations.[9] Like an English auction, which it resembles in some key respects, a Japanese auction benefits sellers if the highest and second-highest valuations are close to each other. If the valuations are close, the second-highest bidder will hold the button almost as long as the highest bidder does, forcing the highest bidder to pay close to his full valuation.

Like the Dutch auction, a Japanese auction is quick. In a Dutch auction the clock starts high and goes down; in a Japanese auction the clock starts low and goes up. Either way, it's quicker than the English auction. Speed can have substantive effects of its own; for example, it makes it more difficult for bidders to update their reservation values, which may induce experts to participate (good for the seller) but may dampen reservation-value updating by bidders (bad for the seller). These effects are discussed in more detail in the next chapter.

SEALED-BID AUCTIONS: SOME DESIGN CHOICES

I now turn to some design choices in sealed-bid auctions. One option that is much discussed in academia but rarely considered in practice is the choice between a first-price and a second-price auction. A first-price sealed-bid auction is the one that we're all used to: the high bidder wins the asset and pays the price that he or she bid. A second-price sealed-bid auction has a twist: the high bidder wins the asset but pays only the second-highest bid.

Why would any seller want to deliberately let the high bidder off the hook for some portion of what the bidder is willing to pay? The answer is that a second-price auction eliminates the strategizing and guesswork that otherwise accompanies a sealed-bid situation. As we will see in more detail in the next chapter, the bidders in a first-price sealed-bid auction are all trying to guess what the next-highest bid will be, so that they can bid just a bit more. No one bids their full reservation value in a first-price auction because if they win under those circumstances, they make zero profit. In contrast, in a second-price auction all bidders should simply bid their full reservation value.

Consider an example. You value an asset at $100, which you assume to be the highest reservation value in the auction, and your best guess is that the next-highest bid will be $60. In a first-price auction, you would bid something just a bit higher than $60—high enough to make sure you win but low enough to maximize your profits from the deal. In a second-price auction, all the guesswork is eliminated and you simply bid your full reservation value of $100. If you win at $100, you pay only the next-highest bid, which you predict to be about $60. If you lose, the winning bidder valued the asset more than you did, so you didn't want it at that price anyway.

Consider an alternative bid—say, $90. If you win, you will still pay the next-highest reservation value, which is about $60. But suppose you lose at $90 and the winning bid is $95—you would have preferred to bid $96 and win. Anytime you bid lower than your full reservation value in a second-price auction, there is some chance that the asset will go to someone else for less than you would have paid, and in those cases you would have wanted to bid higher.

Now consider another alternative bid—say, $110. Here the possible downside is much easier to see: you win the auction, and the second-highest bid turns out to be $105. Oops. For every bid that is higher than your full reservation value, there is some chance that you will pay more for the asset than the value you assigned to it.

Because your bid in a second-price auction determines only whether you win or lose and not the actual amount you pay, the dominant strategy is to bid your full reservation value. All the strategizing that is part of a first-price sealed-bid process is gone. This makes life simpler for bidders and might benefit the seller by stimulating greater competition for the asset. The seller in a second-price sealed-bid auction should receive the second-highest reservation value—exactly the same as what sellers receive, on average, in first-price sealed-bid auctions.

Although second-price auctions are intellectually interesting, in practice they are rare. Economists have come up with several reasons to explain why,[10] but the biggest reason might simply be that it is difficult to explain to practitioners why the dominant strategy in a second-price auction is to bid your full reservation value. Unless they are sophisticated and/or well-versed in auction theory, bidders in a second-price auction will shade their bids anyway, resulting in a lower price for the seller.

Another important reason that second-price auctions are so uncommon might be fear of cheating by the seller. In an open-outcry auction, the bidder can observe the proceedings and her competitors' behaviors and drop out of the auction if she feels she is being shortchanged by the others. In a sealed-bid auction, bids are "blind," and the seller could "adjust" the second-highest bid in order to achieve a higher price.[11] The second-highest bidder doesn't mind (he wasn't going to win anyway), and the highest bidder may never know.

A third reason that second-price auctions are rare is that bidders might be wary of revealing their full reservation value to the seller, believing that their truthfulness will hurt them. This may be a valid concern in situations where there are negotiations after the auction is over.[12]

To see this point, imagine selling your house by second-price sealed-bid auction. The high bid is $600,000, and the next-highest bids are $500,000 and $475,000. Under the rules of the second-price auction, the winning bidder pays $500,000—a great price for the winner, who valued the house at $100,000 more. Now the winning bidder conducts the usual inspection of the house and comes up with significant problems that would normally dictate a reduction in the purchase price. Will you make concessions in the purchase price? Very unlikely. You know that the winning bidder values the house at $600,000, so you would reasonably say, "This is a great deal for you, so take your inspection issues out of your profits." Envisioning this problem in advance, bidders will shade their bids in the auction, despite the process choice that was intended to extract their full reservation values.

By far the biggest natural experiment with second-price auctions is eBay, the well-known online auction website. From its inception, eBay has employed a second-price auction mechanism, much to the delight of auction theorists who believe that this elegant mechanism is underutilized in practice. Because the second-price feature is different from the first-price mechanisms that people are used to, eBay instructs its users on how to bid in its "proxy bidding system":

> Decide on the maximum amount you want to pay for the item before you bid. Then enter that amount as your maximum bid. A maximum bid must be higher than the current minimum bid for the listing. eBay automatically bids on your behalf, based on pre-set increments, but only up to your maximum bid. When others bid, your bid is increased automatically until you are the current high bidder once again. You will be outbid only if another bidder places a higher maximum bid than you.[13]

Thus, eBay has constructed a second-price auction: you bid the maximum that you're willing to pay, but you pay only a bit more than the second-highest bid. The analysis that I sketched out already suggests that the best approach to this kind of auction is to enter your full reservation value as your maximum bid and then forget about the auction—either you will win and pay something less than your bid, or the asset will be sold to someone else for more than your reservation value.

In fact, eBay used to explicitly advise its bidders as such, "encourag[ing] all members to use the proxy bidding system that is in place to bid the absolute maximum they are willing to pay for an item right from the start and let the proxy bidding system work for them."[14] But this wasn't what bidders actually did. In one study, Professors Axel Ockenfels and Al Roth found that the average bidder bid nearly twice (1.89 times) in an eBay auction, usually in the last few seconds of the auction. Ockenfels and Roth note that a "number of observers have expressed surprise and puzzlement at these patterns of late and multiple bidding in Internet auctions that arise despite advice from auctioneers that bidders should simply submit their maximum willingness to pay, once, early in the auction."[15]

In the next chapter, I provide some explanations for this buy-side behavior, based on Ockenfels and Roth's findings among others. For now, the point is that although the second-price mechanism is elegant in theory, real bidders don't play as the theory would predict. This disconnect might explain, at least in part, why second-price auctions aren't used very much in practice.

The more important process choice in a sealed-bid auction is the number of rounds to hold. One important consideration is the cost of bidding. If it takes a lot of time and money for a bidder to figure out what to bid, even high-value bidders might be deterred by the prospect of making a big investment in the due diligence process but walking away empty-handed. To address this legitimate concern, hold a preliminary round in which bidders can make nonbinding "expressions of interest." This is sometimes called an "indicative round" of bidding, in which bidders indicate a rough ballpark idea of their bid. Bidders can make such bids with substantially less due diligence; the result is more participation than you would get in a single-round sealed-bid auction.

Once you've received indications of interest, you can winnow the field to the most promising four to eight bidders. You then invite these bidders to conduct more thorough due diligence, with the goal of obtaining "serious" (binding) offers. These bidders can invest more in due diligence because their chances of winning are now higher than at the outset.

An indicative round followed by a binding round encourages bidders to participate when the costs of a serious bid are high, such as when the asset is difficult to value. In this scenario, an indicative round followed by a binding round gets you more participation and a higher sale price than you would get from a single-round sealed-bid auction.

One simple approach for getting from the indicative round to the final winner is to just hold a single, "best and final" round, but you might be disappointed with the bids you receive. You minimize this risk by holding several sealed-bid rounds and kicking people out along the way. This route is less risky but takes longer. Moreover, it requires something of a balancing act: On the one hand you want to keep kicking bidders out of the process as a way of keeping the momentum going. But on the other hand, you don't want to unknowingly kick out the high-value bidder, who might have made a misstep in one particular round by bidding too low.

As you feel your way through multiple rounds, you must "show bidders the finish line." This is a well-known phrase among practitioners, and the metaphor is apt. If you've ever been a spectator at the finish line of a long race, you'll notice that runners often sprint at the end. This is especially true among the top runners if the race is close, but even runners way back in the pack will sprint to the finish line to get the best possible time. What's going on? Why don't they just pace themselves along the way? We understand that runners typically hold something back, which they draw on for the finish-line sprint.

Now imagine a race in which the organizer doesn't tell the runners how long the race will be—just that the runners should start running, and at some point the organizer will stop the race and the person in front will be declared the winner. Sound crazy? Then you see the problem with a sealed-bid auction that has no end in sight, and no clear process rules to determine the winner. Bidders will be frustrated, for sure, but they will also hold something back with the expectation that they will need it for a future round. The result is that they don't put their best foot forward, thus hurting the seller.

Consider the example of an American retailer that was rapidly expanding its store locations a few years ago. The retailer held an e-auction to select the local general contractor who would build each of its new stores. The retailer was clear that price was important but not the sole criterion—reputation, timetable for completion, and other factors would also carry weight in the decision. The retailer also announced an additional rule: once the winning bidder was picked, there would be a thirty-day window during which the unsuccessful bidders would have an opportunity to view the winning bidder's bid and submit a better bid, if they wanted.

This added rule sounds unobjectionable, at first—what could be wrong with adding a little more competition to the mix? The retailer's experience with the post-auction round also appeared to validate this view: new bids flew in from several of the unsuccessful bidders, often with significant price reductions relative to the "winning" bidder from the formal e-auction. As experience and thinking developed further, however, the retailer realized what was going on: because the auction process didn't show bidders the finish line, bidders were not putting forth their best offer during the formal e-auction. They knew they could always come back again during the post-auction process.

Logic eventually prevailed, and the retailer stopped using its two-stage process. Now, general contractors submit sealed bids, the retailer picks the best bid, and there is no further opportunity to bid again. The retailer loses the post-auction competition but gains the big benefit of having bidders make their best offer in the auction itself. By showing bidders the finish line, the retailer eliminated gaming among the bidders, and likely got itself comparable or better pricing than it had gotten with its two-stage process.

The retailer auction highlights one general point, which is a useful way of closing this chapter: in sealed-bid auctions, the process setter needs to think very carefully about process choices. Minor differences in the rules of the game can have big implications for bidders' strategies. In some sealed-bid situations, the rules of the auction can create unintended, unforeseen, and perverse bidder incentives.

Consider the case of Antamina, a Peruvian copper and zinc mine.[16] In June 1996, Centromin, the state-owned mining company, decided to sell the mine through a sealed-bid auction process. Forty bidders initially expressed interest and twelve visited the data room; but as the bid deadline approached, only three were expected to make formal bids: Noranda, a large mining company based in Toronto, Canada; Rio Algom/Inmet, a joint venture between two other Canadian companies; and RTZ-CRA, the world's largest mining group, with operations spread around the world.

Centromin specified that each bid would consist of two parts: an initial payment, which would be payable at the closing; and an "investment commitment," which the winning bidder would need to spend over the five years after the closing. Bidders had to bid at least $17.5

million in the initial payment and $135 million in the investment commitment. Bids would be valued as the initial payment plus 30 percent of the investment commitment.

After two years, the winning bidder could return the mine to Centromin, as long as it had spent at least $13.5 million on exploration and development. If it didn't return the mine at the two-year mark, the winning bidder would pay a 30 percent penalty on any shortfall in the investment commitment at the five-year point. For example, if the winning bidder committed to spending $1 billion, didn't give the mine back to Centromin after two years, and had spent only $500 million after five years, it would owe Centromin $150 million (30 percent of $1 billion minus $500 million).

Complicated, no doubt, but these rules had a purpose. The ability to give the mine back to the government protected all bidders against downside risk. If a bidder won the auction and discovered that the mine was a dud, it could simply walk away at the two-year point. This feature attracted bidders into the auction, which was extremely useful for a government that had experienced two busted auctions in trying to sell the same assets over the prior two years.

The other important objective for the government—to promote investment in the mine—was achieved through the investment commitment process. According to one Centromin official, "We obviously want to sell at an interesting price, but the principal objective is to maintain and develop the sector by attracting quality companies."[17] Another spokesperson said, "Our main concern is for the amounts that the new owners will invest to promote, modernize or expand" the mine.[18] The rules reflected this interest, with the investment commitment valued at 30 cents on the dollar in calculating bid values. The 30 percent penalty imposed after five years for any shortfall would ensure that the winning bidder would take the investment commitment seriously.

The lurking problem was that these two goals—protecting bidders against downside risk and promoting investment—were in tension with each other. To see this point, start with the optimal mix between the initial payment and the investment commitment, from the perspective of the potential bidders. A cost/benefit analysis reveals that the optimal strategy is to make the minimum possible initial payment ($17.5 million), and to load all of the value of your bid into the development commitment. One dollar loaded into the initial payment is worth $1 in terms of bid points, and it costs the bidder $1 if the bid is successful. In contrast, $1 loaded into the investment commitment is worth 30 cents in terms of bid points, and it costs the bidder—at worst—30 cents in five years. Bidders get more bang for the buck in the investment commitment than in the initial payment, which means that all bidders should minimize the initial payment and maximize the investment commitment in making their bids.

So far so good, you might say, because the government's main goal is to have the winning bidder develop the mine, and a large development commitment does precisely that. But the winning bidder in the Antamina auction had a choice at the two-year point: give the mine back to the government, or go forward and be on the hook for any investment shortfall. What kind of bidder would be most likely to give the mine back to the government at the two-year point? The one with a big investment commitment if it went forward. And what kind of bidder would be most likely to win the auction? The one with the biggest investment commitment.

Thus, the auction rules created a situation in which the winning bidder would be the one who was *most* likely to walk away from the mine at the two-year point. And if the winning bidder walked away, Centromin would be in the difficult position of trying to resell a mine that would be perceived as "damaged goods."

Three bids came in on July 12, 1996. RTZ-CRA bid $17.5 million up front and a $900 million investment commitment. Noranda bid $17.5 million up front and a $1.9 billion investment commitment. And the winning bidder was Rio Algom/Inmet, which bid $20 million up front and a staggering $2.52 billion investment commitment. In a press conference that day, a Rio Algom spokesman made it clear that the consortium would be perfectly happy walking away after two years: "If it does not prove viable, we just lose our up-front investment."[19]

The deal closed two months later, in September 1996. On February 26, 1997, Rio Algom/Inmet announced that geological work had revealed approximately 400 million tons of ore at Antamina—well beyond their expectations.[20] As a result, the consortium declined to exercise its option to walk away in September 1998, thereby signing on to the $2.52 billion investment commitment.[21] The consortium completed the Antamina project in late 2001, ahead of schedule and under budget. The final capital expenditure was $2.148 billion—$372 million below the consortium's development commitment.

This result reveals the illusory nature of Rio Algom/Inmet's development commitment, since even a blockbuster ore discovery did not justify spending the full commitment that the consortium had signed onto. Pursuant to its contract, Rio Algom/Inmet paid a 30 percent penalty on the difference, or $111.6 million.[22] In the end, the consortium did well and the government got the development it wanted out of the mine, but the government's process rules had not facilitated this outcome.

As the retailer reverse auction and Antamina examples illustrate, the rules of a sealed-bid auction can have big effects on bidder behavior. The key is to think things through from the bidder's perspective in designing the auction. In the next chapter, we visit this topic squarely: accepting the process as given, and describing the best way to play the game as the "process taker."

CHAPTER 5

PLAYING THE GAME AS PROCESS TAKER

When I teach about auctions to executive groups at Harvard Business School, I sometimes begin the class session by auctioning off a jar of US coins. (This classic game was invented by Professors Max Bazerman and William Samuelson in the 1980s.)[1] Participants have a chance to look at the jar and shake it, and then, if they wish, they can write down their bid. I explain that I know the value contained in the jar, and the high bidder will win the value in the jar (*not* the jar of coins itself—that would be too difficult to get through airport security on the way home) in exchange for their bid. I offer an example to make sure everyone understands the rules: "If you bid $20 and it is the highest bid, and there is $25 worth of coins in the jar, then we will just net it out and I will pay you $5. But if you bid $30 and it is the highest bid, and there is $25 in the jar, then you owe me $5." I further clarify that this is a real auction, and real money will change hands one direction or the other.

Participants write down their bids and show them to a neighbor to bind themselves, and then I ask for a show of hands: "Who here bid more than $10?" Already there are some concerned looks in the room. $10? Didn't he just say there was $25 in the jar? I privately marvel at the power of anchoring, even though I had made it abundantly clear that my example was solely for illustration purposes.

The purpose of the exercise, however, is not to demonstrate anchoring. I ask participants to keep their hands up if they bid more than $15. A few hands go down. More than $20? A few more. More than $25? Now there are about ten hands left in the air, and the participants begin to look at each other nervously. More than $30? Now there are usually two or three hands up, so I stop and ask for their bids: "$32," says one. "$35," says another. And with deep concern, the high bidder says, "$38.50."

The interesting part comes next. Before I reveal how much is actually in the jar, I ask the winning bidder how he feels. (It is almost always a he.) "Not so good." Why? "Because apparently I guessed higher than everyone else in the room." The remarkable aspect of this comment is that it comes *before* I reveal how much is in the jar. The winner knows that he has very likely overpaid from the simple fact that he is the high bidder. This is the well-known but little-understood *winner's curse* problem. Sure enough, in my ten years of using this exercise at Harvard, the high bidder has always been subject to the winner's curse. My two jars at Harvard Law School and Harvard Business School contain $15.88 and $15.67, respectively. The high bid is always higher than these amounts and typically in the mid-$30s. I joke with the participants that if I didn't have a job as a professor I could make a decent living auctioning off jars of coins on street corners.

BEFORE YOU ENTER: CONSIDER ALL COSTS AND BENEFITS IN SETTING YOUR RESERVATION VALUE

I will return to the winner's curse problem and how to solve it, but I start with the first step in playing the game as process taker: determining your reservation value. Recall that in a negotiation, your reservation value is defined as your full valuation for the asset, which then determines your bottom line in the negotiation. It's not what you hope to get, or hope to pay, but the reservation value does indicate whether you are creating value in the deal at the table. Your reservation value is determined by your BATNA (best alternative to a negotiated agreement). In the *Frasier* example presented in Chapter 1, Paramount's reservation value for the TV show was somewhere around $5.25 million per episode, which reflected its BATNA of selling the show to CBS.

Things get more complicated in auctions because you need to reflect *all* the costs and benefits of winning or losing the auction in calculating your reservation value, and in many cases these costs and benefits are subtle. First, losing the auction sometimes costs you something; that is, your BATNA in the auction is not the status quo, but something worse than the status quo. A few years ago a European private-equity firm was selling one of its portfolio companies in what amounted to an open-outcry ascending auction. The bidders were the two customers of the portfolio company, and it was clear to all participants that the winning bidder would be a stronger competitor and the losing bidder would be a weaker competitor in the marketplace as a result.

How should each of the bidders think about their reservation value in this auction? The answer starts with their full valuation of the asset but also includes the costs that they would bear if they lost. If a bidder valued the company at $100 but would suffer a $20 loss if it didn't win, its reservation value should be $120. As counterintuitive as it seems, the bidder is better off winning the auction at $119 and overpaying by $19, than losing the auction and suffering a $20 loss.

As this analysis would predict, the private-equity firm got an astronomical price for its portfolio company. Each bidder, desperately concerned that its competitor would get the target company, continued bidding well beyond its stand-alone valuations for the company. In the end, the winning bidder overpaid, and the losing bidder suffered in the marketplace. Auction theorists call these kinds of auctions *all-pay auctions*, because all bidders must pay something, regardless of whether they win the prize. All-pay auctions are bad for bidders and great for sellers.

Consider the irony of the situation. Typically, we think that having ten bidders is better than having two. But if there had been ten downstream customers, then each losing bidder would have suffered only one-ninth of the market share loss to the winning bidder. The all-pay feature would have been smaller, and the winning bidder would have paid less. With two bidders, the losing bidder suffered the full cost of the market share loss. The all-pay feature was severe, and the bidding went up accordingly. For the private-equity firm, having two interested bidders was better than having ten.

All-pay features are common in real auctions, and often overlooked. Consider this account of an online procurement auction from a recent *Harvard Business Review* article:

> Before the bidding ended, the VP had bid well below his previously calculated, rational limit. Luckily, the company lost the auction. The VP later admitted that he had stopped when he did only because he was unsure who the remaining rival was; had he known it was his company's biggest competitor, he said, he probably would have continued to bid.[2]

The article's authors present this case as an example of "competitive arousal" in bidding situations. In their analysis, the VP was tempted to bid more by the irrational unwillingness to lose to his biggest competitor. Competitive arousal may have been a factor in pushing the VP below his reservation value. It could also be highly rational for the VP to bid more aggressively (lower) against his biggest competitor—for example, in a situation where his firm would suffer if his competitor got the business. In an all-pay situation, it is not only rational but essential to include *all* the costs associated with your BATNA in determining your reservation value in the auction. If you don't do this, you will walk away too soon.

It is important to distinguish rational all-pay features from competitive arousal. Consider again the *Frasier* negotiation described in Chapter 1. In the negotiauction between CBS and NBC to acquire the show, NBC lead negotiator Marc Graboff was confident that NBC valued the show more than CBS did on a stand-alone basis, but he was concerned that CBS would pay significantly more than its break-even value just to get the show away from NBC. From the other side of the table, Kerry McCluggage confirmed that this is how CBS would have looked at the show:

> Not only do they [CBS] get a show that they can promote and sell, and presumably launch other hit comedies, but their competitor loses. So there is value in that to the new network, because they are gaining a hit show and their competitor is losing one.

Sellers love all-pay structures because bidders who are playing rationally will bid well beyond the actual value of the asset. Therefore, sellers should look for all-pay features or make bidders aware of all-pay features that exist. The outcome of all-pay auctions is of course unsatisfying for all the bidders, even if (in fact, especially if) they are playing rationally. The winning bidder overpays for the asset but avoids the cost of losing the auction; the other bidders avoid overpaying for the asset but bear the cost of losing. Recall that this is exactly what happened in the *Frasier* negotiation.

Game-changing moves, which I discuss in Part II, can help you bid effectively in all-pay auctions. For now, though, the main idea is that bidders should recognize the all-pay feature of an auction before it is too late and incorporate these costs when calculating their reservation values.

In determining your reservation value in an auction, it is important not only to incorporate costs but to consider all the potential benefits of winning and losing. Consider a partnership agreement between two partners—Ernie and Bert—that specifies that upon dissolution by either partner, the partnership will be sold by open-outcry, ascending auction to the highest bidder, and the proceeds from the sale will be distributed equally to the two partners. This is a common dissolution provision in partnership agreements. Usually, when such a provision is triggered the partnership is sold to one of the partners, who then becomes the continuing sole owner.

Certainly the partners should determine the value of the firm as a starting point for their bidding strategy, but the strategy also changes because the losing partner receives a benefit, in the form of 50 percent of the sale proceeds. Imagine that Ernie values the partnership at $100. Should he bid up to $100 and then quit, as simple auction theory would predict? Not necessarily, because of the benefit he receives from being the losing bidder. Consider the extreme scenario in which Ernie knows with great confidence that Bert values the enterprise at $200. In this case, Ernie should bid all the way up to $198 to maximize the value he receives from the sale. An interesting twist arises if Bert knows with equal confidence that Ernie values the partnership at only $100. In this case Bert is likely to call Ernie's bluff. The partnership will be sold to Ernie for an amount higher than Ernie is willing to pay, and both partners know it. The likely outcome is that Ernie and Bert then renegotiate in the ZOPA (zone of possible agreement) between $100 and $200.[3]

Real situations get far more complex because each partner is trying to guess the reservation value of the other partner and bid up to that point. If the partner guesses incorrectly, there might be an after-the-fact renegotiation. Always consider the costs and benefits of both winning and losing in order to set your reservation value in an open-outcry ascending auction. As the examples here illustrate, this analysis can become quite complex.

THE WINNER'S CURSE PROBLEM: WHAT IT IS, WHEN IT APPLIES, AND HOW TO OVERCOME IT

Determining your reservation value for an auction isn't finished until you have determined whether the winner's curse applies and, if so, adjusted your reservation value to account for it. The winner's curse problem doesn't apply just in coin jar auctions—it applies in just about every sealed-bid auction that has ever been run, from bidding for professional athletes to the sale of oil tracts in Oklahoma. Nevertheless, the winner's curse problem is frequently misunderstood, because most people do not grasp where it comes from, or when it applies.

Many people assume that rational people won't succumb to the winner's curse problem. You avoid it by "keeping your head about you." This interpretation confuses the winner's curse with another well-known bidding problem, sometimes known as "auction fever" or "bidding frenzy," in which bidders irrationally trump each other in the heat of battle, only to discover that the winning bidder has significantly overpaid when the auction is over.

Even though both auction fever and the winner's curse lead to bidder overpayment, they are based on different phenomena. Auction fever is indeed based on irrational escalation and emotional attachment. (I will talk about ways to overcome irrational escalation in open-outcry auctions later in this chapter.) In contrast, the winner's curse problem is devoid of emotional content. Consider the coin jar auction described at the beginning of this chapter. No one has any (obvious) emotional attachment to the jar of coins. There is no bidding frenzy or irrational escalation of bids. All the participants are trying to guess the same thing: how much is in the jar.

A long line of experimental research shows that the *average* estimate among a roomful of people is likely to be remarkably close to the actual value in the jar.[4] But this average estimate does not win—the high bid does. Putting these two facts together, the winning bidder is likely to have overpaid.

In the coin jar situation, bidders should look forward and reason back as follows: "When I am the high bidder (the only scenario that matters), what do I know that I don't know now?" The answer is that everyone else in the room guessed lower than I did. "Would I feel comfortable making this bid, knowing that fact?"

The answer could be yes. Some bidders have expertise that gives them an "edge" over others; that is, they are able to assess value better than anyone else can. Imagine a situation in which ExxonMobil and Bob's Oil & Gas Company are the only bidders for the right to drill for oil on a particular tract. ExxonMobil's highly sophisticated exploration equipment indicates likely reserves worth $300 million. Should Exxon be concerned when it wins with a $200 million sealed bid and discovers that Bob bid only $150 million? Almost certainly not. Exxon has a significant edge with its deep experience base and high-tech equipment, and therefore can be comfortable with its winning bid, even though Bob bid significantly less.

In a coin jar auction, it's unlikely that any bidder has an edge based on expertise. In fact, although I have never collected systematic data on this point, the winner of the coin jar in my Harvard Business School executive education classes is often a non-US participant. It's possible that people outside the United States (or at least those people who come to US executive education programs) are more willing to bid aggressively than are US participants. A more plausible explanation, I think, is that non-US participants are at a systematic *dis*advantage because they aren't as familiar with US currency; therefore, they are more likely than American participants to guess either very high or very low. Very low isn't problematic, but very high is. Knowing that the game is tilted against them, non-US students should decline to participate in the coin jar auction. Even US students should be wary of playing, because they lack an edge. The question in its simplest form is this: "What do I know that no one else knows?" If the answer is "nothing," then winner's curse concerns apply in full force.

Another way to overcome the winner's curse comes from synergies, or private value in the asset. Your company may have special value that no one else has, safely enabling you to bid higher than others. Consider again the bidding contest for the oil-drilling rights. If ExxonMobil owns land adjacent to the tract that is under consideration while Bob's Oil & Gas does not, ExxonMobil will use its existing drilling equipment on the adjacent land to explore this site also. This lower cost to explore is a source of private value for ExxonMobil, mitigating the winner's curse problem. (Very likely, the adjacency also gives ExxonMobil better insights into the reserves in the tract.)

A coin jar auction is unlikely to provide private value to any of the bidders. Sometimes the winning bidder will joke that he is a connoisseur of coin jars, thereby providing private value that justifies his bid. This explanation doesn't hold up, though, because the rules state that the winning bidder gets the value contained in the jar, not the jar itself. Instead, a coin jar auction is a classic *common value* situation in which all bidders are trying to guess the same thing—how much is in the jar? No one has an edge, and no one has synergies that might yield private value.

The winner's curse is a ubiquitous phenomenon in real-world auctions. For an example, return to Robert Barnett's book auctions. In December 2000, then-Senator-elect Hillary Clinton retained Barnett to find a publisher for her memoirs from her eight years as First Lady— a book that would eventually be called *Living History*. Barnett ran an auction using the process described at the beginning of Chapter 4. Eight publishers showed up for the auction, all big names from the New York City publishing world. Simon & Schuster was the winning bidder, with an $8 million advance and a 15 percent royalty rate.[5] This was the third-highest advance ever offered for a public figure's memoir, behind President Bill Clinton's $15 million advance and Pope John Paul II's $8.75 million advance. (This latter fact apparently relieved Senator Clinton, who wanted to stay on the good side of her Catholic constituents in New York.)

David Rosenthal is the executive vice president at Simon & Schuster who called the shots in bidding for Hillary Clinton's book. After winning, he told the press, "I haven't heard of the winner's curse, but there's an old publishing dictum—'The only thing worse than not getting a book is getting a book.' There's a reason publishers tend not to like auctions."[6] It's a little strange that Rosenthal, who participates in dozens of book auctions each year, claims not to have heard of the winner's curse. But even if he hasn't, his "old publishing dictum" is certainly consistent with the theory's underlying logic.

In the Hillary Clinton book auction, all of the publishers were trying to guess the same thing: how many copies would the book sell, in hardcover, paperback, overseas, audio, and so on? In making this assessment, some publishers had sources of private value—for example, expertise with political memoirs, or better distribution capability in certain parts of the world, or better marketing or editing talent. But the Hillary Clinton book auction was primarily a common-value auction. Among big-name New York City publishing houses, no bidder had a meaningful edge in guessing how many copies the book would sell, or any significant edge in making the book sell more.

The common-value nature of the auction meant that the winner's curse applied in full force, and Rosenthal's comments reflected this point. The Hillary Clinton book auction also illustrates another important aspect of the winner's curse problem. Contrary to popular perception, it is not the case that when the winner's curse applies, the winning bidder always loses. *Living History* did fabulously for Simon & Schuster, making big bucks for the publishing house and royalty payments well in excess of the $8 million advance for Hillary Clinton.[7] The winner's curse problem tells us only that the winning bidder will lose, on average, unless bidders adjust their strategy to reflect the problem. It does not say that the winning bidder will lose every time the winner's curse applies.

Bidders must be aware of the winner's curse problem and adjust for it in their bidding strategy before it is too late. Return to the oil-drilling rights example—a pure common-value situation. In the 1950s, new technology allowed companies to drill for oil offshore, making drilling rights in the Gulf of Mexico suddenly valuable. The US federal government auctioned off the rights, and the bidding proved fierce.[8] Over time, the winning bidders discovered that they were, on average, losing money on their offshore drilling investments. What was going on? The problem was that no one knew with any confidence what the tracts were worth. The new technology had created the ability to drill offshore, but the methods for determining how much oil was actually in the ocean were still being developed. Everyone was trying to guess the same thing—how much oil was in the ocean tract?—but the guesses were all over the place. In an empirical study of the situation published in the early 1970s, researchers found that three factors made the winner's curse problem particularly severe in the case of offshore drilling rights: (1) very little information, (2) high uncertainty about valuations, and (3) a large number of bidders.[9] This is indeed a "sweet spot" where the winner's curse will be the most severe.

What can be done to compensate for the winner's curse? A few years ago, the students in my Dealmaking class examined the December 2003 sale of *New York* magazine. The seller was Primedia, a publishing conglomerate, which in turn was owned by private-equity powerhouse Kohlberg Kravis Roberts (KKR). Four parties expressed serious interest in buying the magazine: two news magazine companies (American Media and CurtCo Media Labs), a consortium headed by writer Michael Wolff and billionaire Mort Zuckerman, and famed investment banker (and also billionaire) Bruce Wasserstein. Final bids came in on Thursday, December 11, at 5:00 p.m.: $40 million from American Media, $44 million from Zuckerman's group, $52.5 million from CurtCo, and $55 million from Bruce Wasserstein. Wasserstein sealed the deal in the ensuing few days and owns the magazine today.

Wasserstein came to my Dealmaking class in April 2007 to discuss his bidding strategy in the *New York* magazine auction. At one point in the discussion a student asked him whether he was concerned about the winner's curse problem, in view of the significant common-value element that the asset seemed to have. Wasserstein responded:

> Let's say you have ten bidders. The "reasonable person" is the person within the standard deviation, right? So, whatever the standard deviation is, it's number three to seven who are the "smart guys." They never buy anything, though. So you have to have some comparative advantage . . .
>
> Often you have a group of people sitting around a room, and they all say, "Aren't you smart, you got the discount rate of 11.23 percent and you projected this, and you did that . . ." And you have a book that weighs a ton, and everyone looks at each other, but they haven't bought anything . . .

Now, it may be a good idea to buy something, or it may be a terrible idea to buy something. And the question is, Do you have a vision, an investment thesis, a hypothesis, a business plan, why this is going to work for us? . . . So that's what we did, but I think it's the winner's *dilemma* more than curse, meaning that anytime you're the buyer, you wonder why the nine other guys didn't want it.

Wasserstein clearly knows his auction theory. His "investment thesis" is the equivalent of the question of "edge" presented earlier in this chapter. That edge can come from expertise in valuing the asset, sources of value that others don't have, or both. In the auction for *New York* magazine, Wasserstein felt that he had operational expertise that would squeeze more value out of the magazine than his competitors could—an important source of private value. In addition, there were personal elements of private value in the deal. As a longtime resident of Manhattan, Wasserstein undoubtedly considered the "trophy value" that comes from owning *New York* magazine. Wasserstein also considered himself to be something of a journalist, working for the student newspaper while in college and writing well-received books during his investment-banking career. For Wasserstein, this edge enabled him to overcome the winner's curse problem in the bidding for *New York* magazine.

To summarize, with an edge you can bid comfortably; without an edge you should either shade your bid or consider one of the game-changing moves that will be discussed in detail in Part II. More specifically, the flowchart in Figure 8 describes the steps you should take to adjust for the winner's curse.

The first question to ask is whether the auction has a common-value element. In some cases the answer is no and the asset is purely private value, but these cases are few and far between. Consider a Monet painting, a classic example of an allegedly pure private-value asset. If you and all the other bidders are bidding on the Monet in order to hang it over your fireplace at home, then the value to you is theoretically entirely independent of the value to anyone else. So what if the other bidder values it at $2 million? If you gain $3 million of value looking at the painting every day, then you should feel comfortable winning it with a $2.9 million bid—you have created $100,000 of value—even though the other bidder valued it at significantly less.

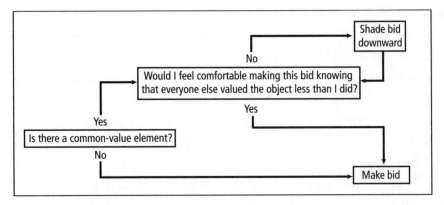

Figure 8. Adjusting for the Winner's Curse—Flowchart

Even with a seemingly pure private-value asset, there is a significant common-value element. In the real world, you (or your heirs) will want to sell the Monet painting someday, and when that day comes you will be troubled to discover that the market value of the painting is actually only $2 million. All bidders are trying to guess the same thing: what is the market value of the painting down the road? The answer is not relevant for the pleasure you get from looking at it every day, but the answer is relevant for resale later.

If the asset is truly a private-value asset, then the flowchart indicates that you can make your bid without any consideration of the winner's curse problem. That almost never happens—virtually all assets have *some* common-value element, so the inquiry proceeds to the next question: would you feel comfortable making your bid knowing that everyone else valued the object less than you did? If you have an edge, as described earlier, then maybe the answer is yes—and if so, then you should go ahead and make your bid. If your answer is no, you should keep shading your bid downward until you can answer the question in the affirmative.

BIDDING IN SEALED-BID SITUATIONS

In sealed-bid situations, adjusting for the winner's curse is just part of your challenge. Anyone who has ever won in a sealed-bid auction knows that five seconds after the euphoria of winning comes the worry of having paid more than was necessary. Not paying more than the value of the asset (that's the winner's curse, which you've presumably adjusted for), but paying significantly more than the second-highest bidder.

As a dramatic illustration of this phenomenon, consider the auction for baseball's superstar shortstop Alex Rodriguez.[10] In November 2000, "A-Rod" became a free agent, meaning that his considerable talents would be available to the highest bidder. He was represented by Scott Boras, the A-Rod of sports agents, who was well known in the industry for extracting astronomical salaries for his clients. Boras ran a "blind auction" for A-Rod, with teams invited to submit bids without knowing who else had bid, or what the high bid was. Boras assured the press that a substantial bidding war was on for A-Rod; in fact, according to Boras, one club was so interested in Rodriguez that it had faxed an offer to Boras's office a few minutes after the signing period began at midnight on November 11.

On December 9, during the four-day free-agent auction in Dallas, Texas, Boras announced that he was narrowing the field from eight teams to four finalists. Some observers questioned Boras's math, considering that only Texas, Atlanta, and Seattle had shown up for the weekend bidding, and only Chicago, Colorado, and Pittsburgh had been mentioned as peripheral contenders. In the end, Boras received offers from only two teams, the Texas Rangers and A-Rod's incumbent team, the Seattle Mariners. The Rangers' offer was $225 million over twelve years. Boras then met with Tom Hicks, the owner of the Rangers and CEO of the buyout firm Hicks, Muse, Tate & Furst. The pair negotiated all day on Sunday, December 10. At 4:00 a.m. on Monday, the Rangers closed a $252 million, ten-year deal for Rodriguez.

The competing offer from the Mariners? A five-year deal, with only the first three years guaranteed, for a total salary of $92 million. Kudos flowed to Scott Boras, and Tom Hicks was for some time the laughingstock of the baseball intelligentsia. James Surowiecki wrote in *The New Yorker*:

> Rumors swirled, but Rodriguez's agent, Scott Boras, kept everyone in the dark about who was in the hunt and how much anyone was willing to pay. So Tom Hicks had to decide how much Rodriguez was worth without any real sense of what other teams were thinking. In the end, he concluded that Rodriguez was worth a quarter billion over ten years, which was, oh, just a hundred million dollars more than anyone else was willing to pay.[11]

New York Daily News columnist Bill Madden told *60 Minutes*: "It's amazing that these people have made millions and millions of dollars in their private lives, and as soon as these people come into baseball, they turn into idiots . . . [Tom Hicks] was bidding against himself. [The other owners] were not even close."[12]

Three years later, Hicks traded Rodriguez to the New York Yankees. The Rangers would pay A-Rod $67 million, spread out over the next ten to twelve years, to get out of their $252 million contract. In exchange for Rodriguez, the Rangers picked up second baseman Alfonso Soriano and another player, to be determined later (eventually, Joaquin Arias).[13] The Yankees would pay A-Rod $16 million per year.[14] The Rangers unloaded a star player who was clearly too big for the Texas market. Tom Hicks paid dearly for his unwise blind bid.

Hicks is not alone. When I teach executives, I frequently ask them how they determine what to bid in sealed-bid situations. Even when millions of dollars are at stake, the response is usually some version of "winging it": "Well, we start with our full valuation, and then we shade it downward to build in some profit, on the basis of how many other bidders we think there will be, and how strong we think they are."

Admittedly, there is a lot of art to the process of making a sealed bid, and the practitioners' approaches reflect this unavoidable reality. But there are analytical tools that can be brought to bear as well. The core challenge in any sealed-bid situation is to bid high enough that you win, but low enough that you preserve as much profit as possible from the deal. Experienced dealmakers in a sealed-bid situation balance the probability of winning against the profits from winning.

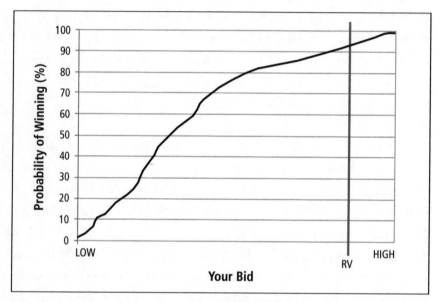

Figure 9. Bidding in Sealed-Bid Situations—MBOO Illustration

How do you do this? A useful starting point is Professor Howard Raiffa's *maximum bid of others* (or *MBOO*, pronounced "maboo") analysis, which captures the fundamental trade-off in graphical form.[15] The first step in a MBOO analysis is determining how your chance of winning increases as your bid increases. As the graph in Figure 9 indicates, if you make a low bid your chance of winning is very low, and if you bid your full reservation value your chance of winning is (typically) very high. Reflecting most real situations, the graph is drawn so that even if you bid your full reservation value, it's not 100 percent certain that you will get the deal. In other words, in most bidding situations you're not 100 percent sure that you are the highest-value bidder.

Between a low bid and a high bid, all you know is that your chance of winning increases as your bid increases, but you don't know exactly how. Getting comfortable with the contours of this curve requires some trial and error and iteration. You can get some traction by comparing the subjective probabilities that you are trying to assess with objective probabilities, like balls in an urn. For example, ask yourself which you would rather bet on: winning with a sealed bid of $100, or drawing a black ball out of an urn containing sixty black balls and forty white balls. If the two bets are equally appealing, then you can plot one of the dots on your MBOO curve: 60 percent chance of winning with a bid of $100.

Other techniques are also available in putting together a MBOO analysis. For example, in a residential real estate transaction that I describe more fully in Chapter 8, two buyers were asked to make sealed bids in a best and final round. One bid was the result of three separate MBOO analyses: one by the husband, one by the wife, and one by their real estate broker. Even though they worked independently, the three drew similar MBOO curves, and that fact assured the couple that they were in the right ballpark in making their bid.

Drawing the MBOO curve is the hard part. Once you have reasonable confidence in the shape of the curve, most of what remains is just a math problem of multiplying the probability of winning by the profits from winning. For example, consider a relatively low bid, as illustrated in Figure 10. This bid has only a 20 percent chance of winning, but if it does win your profits are very large.

Now compare this bid to a relatively high bid (Figure 11), where the chance of winning is about 70 percent but the profits from winning are smaller. The straightforward task is to maximize the area of the shaded box. To put it in more concrete terms, all you are doing with this analysis is maximizing the expected profits from your bid.

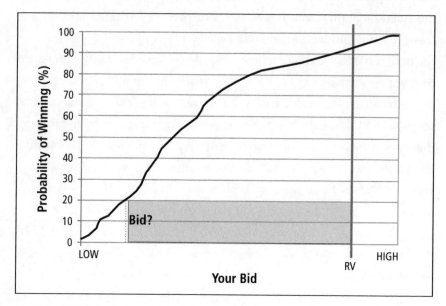

Figure 10. MBOO Analysis—Low-Bid Illustration

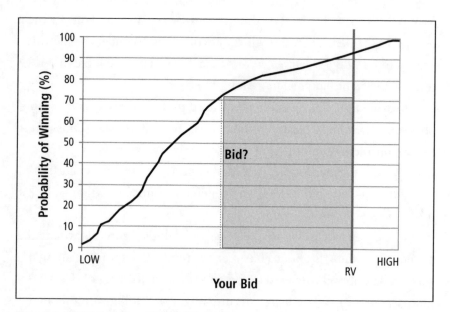

Figure 11. MBOO Analysis—High-Bid Illustration

MBOO analysis is a useful tool for organizing your thinking around the fundamental trade-off between probability of winning and profits from winning. Of course, you should adjust this analysis to account for the context of the deal. For example, you should shade your bid upward to reflect regret you might feel if you don't win.

Without a formal tool to guide them, many people "wing it" in sealed-bid situations. When they do, typically they bid too much—increasing their chance of winning but reducing their profits. Consider the wisdom from Roe Stamps, a veteran of the private-equity industry who founded the hugely successful private-equity firm Summit Partners. In his courtly southern drawl, he told me:

> I sit in meetings sometimes with the younger guys and they get all worked up about a situation. "Bid whatever it takes," they'll say. I tell them to calm down, because deals are like buses: if you miss this one, there's another one coming around the corner.[16]

Recently a colleague of mine was working with sales reps and business managers from a manufacturing company on improving their negotiating skills. The sales reps from this company regularly participated in sealed-bid auctions. And how did they decide what to bid in these auctions? My colleague asked them to imagine a simple case in which the manufacturing cost for a particular customer order would be $500. Then he asked the group to consider three hypothetical bids for the business:

$600, which would have a 90 percent chance of success
$800, which would have a 50 percent chance of success
$1,000, which would have a 10 percent chance of success

Without hesitation the sales reps responded that they would bid $600, because that bid would maximize their chance of getting the business. The business managers in the room went bananas. The reason was the expected value of each bid, which the business managers had mentally calculated:

$600 bid = 90 percent chance of $100 profit = $90 in expected value

$800 bid = 50 percent chance of $300 profit = $150 in expected value

$1,000 bid = 10 percent chance of $500 profit = $50 in expected value

Why, the business managers asked, were the sales reps submitting a bid that had a $90 expected value when they could submit a bid that had a $150 expected value? MBOO analysis revealed that the sales reps were systematically destroying value by bidding too low, which increased their chance of winning the business but reduced the profits to the company—exactly the same instinct that Roe Stamps was cautioning his younger colleagues against.

To bid in a disciplined way, you trade the likelihood of winning against the profits from winning. Some sophisticated dealmakers do this instinctively. If you're not one of them, MBOO analysis can help.

BIDDING IN OPEN-OUTCRY SITUATIONS

Bidding in open-outcry situations is considerably simpler than bidding in sealed-bid situations—at least, at the start. There is no need to worry about predicting the likely bids of others, and no need to engage in MBOO analysis. Even the winner's curse problem is typically quite small because the pool of remaining bidders is visible, so you can realize, before it is too late, that you value the asset more than virtually everyone else in the room.

The strategy in an open-outcry auction is relatively straightforward. You determine your full reservation value for the asset. The auction begins, and you stay in the bidding as long as the price is below this number. If the price exceeds your value, you drop out. If instead you are the sole bidder standing, you pay slightly more than the second-highest bidder and make a profit from the deal.

Simple enough, for starters. But there are important nuances. Suppose you have fully examined all the costs and benefits of winning and losing and firmly established your reservation value. In an open-outcry ascending auction, the story doesn't end here. Whenever common value plays a role, bidders should rationally "update" their reservation values during the course of the bidding, on the basis of who the remaining bidders are and what they are bidding. This is another important way in which expert bidders influence auctions. In Chapter 4, I discussed the design choices that process setters face when they are trying to convince experts to participate. If a process setter has chosen an open-outcry auction, non-experts can take their cue from the experts in determining their reservation value.

This factor is one likely explanation for why bidders in an eBay auction bid more than once: they are learning from the moves of others. To dampen this effect, bidders with expertise often choose to "snipe," or bid at the last minute. As explained on one website:

> The greatest advantage of sniping is it affords you anonymity among the other bidders. If you're a long-time bidder, others who bid on the same items as you will recognize your user ID. Some might even "ride your coattails," performing site searches on what you're bidding on, then perhaps bidding against you. If you choose to snipe, the other bidders won't know where you'll strike next, and that can mean more wins and frequently better prices for you.[17]

Consistent with this advice, but inconsistent with second-price auction theory, Professors Roth and Ockenfels find a significant amount of sniping in online auctions with a "hard close" (i.e., a fixed deadline for all bids), such as eBay auctions.[18] This empirical finding makes sense only if bidders are concerned that others will react to their bids.

To see another example of this point, consider the bidding contest for Revlon, the well-known cosmetics company, in the mid-1980s. The public contest began in August 1985, when noted takeover artist Ron Perelman made a hostile all-cash offer for Revlon at $47.50 per share. The Revlon board rejected the offer and installed takeover defenses that prevented Perelman from going forward. But Perelman just kept coming: he raised his offer to $50, $53, and finally to $56.25 per share, with the promise of even more if the Revlon board would negotiate with him. The Revlon board persuaded buyout mogul Ted Forstmann of Forstmann Little to enter the auction with a $57.25 bid, but Perelman promptly increased his offer to $58 per share.

The sale of Revlon was a seminal event in corporate dealmaking, and twenty-five years later I did a retrospective case study on the deal, interviewing key participants on all sides. The Revlon board strongly preferred Ted Forstmann to Ron Perelman, but Perelman knew his auction theory well and was able to use the legal rules to learn from Forstmann's bids. According to Steve Fraidin, a lawyer who represented Ted Forstmann in the deal:

> At one point there was a negotiation between the parties to try to settle the situation, and my client tells Perelman, "We have a big advantage—we have confidential information, you don't have any. We know what to bid and you do not." Perelman, who is a smart man, said, "Actually, I have even better information than you have because I know what you're bidding. And once I know what you're bidding and I know how smart you are and I know that you have all the confidential information, I know I can bid a nickel more and still have a good deal." And he was absolutely right.[19]

In the end, the Delaware Supreme Court ruled that the Revlon board of directors had unfairly tilted the auction to favor Ted Forstmann, and it awarded the company to Ron Perelman at the blockbuster price of $58 per share (representing a 132 percent premium over the pre-deal trading price of $25 per share). Ron Perelman owns the cosmetics company to this day.

It's clear that Perelman won by updating his reservation value on the basis of bids from an informed, inside bidder. In the Revlon case, this move made the difference between getting the deal and not getting the deal. However, there is also a dark side to going beyond your reservation value, which we all know well. You're at a charity auction for your local church or school. The wine is flowing freely. You have bought a table, so your spouse and six of your closest friends are there. An item comes up that you have some vague interest in—say, a yachting trip off Cape Cod for four people. You mentally conjure up a reservation value of $1,500. The bidding starts at $500, and you jump into the fray. The bidding moves quickly—$750, $900, $1,200, $1,400. Suddenly it's you and one other guy on the other side of the room. "Fifteen hundred dollars," you say emphatically. "Sixteen hundred," comes the all-too-quick response.

The adrenaline is flowing, your friends are watching, and suddenly nothing is more important to you than winning this auction. The irony is evident only in retrospect. Ten minutes ago you had no interest in wasting a day on a yacht off Cape Cod. Now you are willing to pay anything to get it. "Seventeen hundred," you respond. And it's off to the races.

For anyone who doubts the ability of auctioneers to extract a higher price in this way, consider this account from an experienced auctioneer at a major international auction house:

> As an auctioneer, you've got to have a relationship with the people in the room and really understand where they are coming from. So for example, you can tell when a couple is at their first auction, they've targeted the item that they want, and they have a firm limit in mind. They will sit quietly near the front for most of the auction, then when their item comes up they will spring to life. There is sometimes the moment when they have to decide, quickly, whether to break through their limit. [Depending on specific factors that I can read,] I know I can get the bid up.[20]

The phenomenon has several names—"irrational escalation," "competitive arousal," "bidding frenzy"—but the basic point is that rationality has gone out the window. The end result is just like the Revlon auction—you blow through your previously set reservation value in order to win—but the driver is emotion rather than an updated reservation value based on new information.

The difference matters. Perelman didn't overpay for Revlon. His winning bid of $58 was squarely in the $50–$60 range that analysts estimated as the breakup value of Revlon before the bidding contest, and this range didn't include the value of the operational improvements that Perelman could realize by *not* breaking up the company.[21] But you have almost certainly overpaid for your Cape Cod yachting trip. Professor Deepak Malhotra and colleagues identify three factors that fuel what they call "competitive arousal": intense rivalry among bidders, time pressure, and the presence of an audience (the "spotlight effect").[22] All three factors are present in the fictitious but not unrealistic charity auction example that I just described.

Some psychologists suggest that you should slow the pace of the auction to avoid irrational escalation, on the theory that taking a step back will allow your emotions to come back into check. This is good advice, but of course in some cases (like the charity auction) you don't have the luxury of slowing down. In these situations, be explicit about the reasons for exceeding your reservation value.

The first step in this process is to calculate your reservation value for the auction and *write it down*. Research in social psychology shows that the simple act of writing something down can be an effective commitment device.[23] When you write down a number, it becomes more difficult to convince yourself later that you actually planned to pay $2,000 for the yachting trip. Writing down a number also sharpens the moment of truth, when you are forced to either cross your reservation value or drop out of the auction.

When you arrive at the moment of truth, ask yourself, "What do I know now that I didn't know at the beginning of the auction?" In Perelman's case, it's easy—he knew that Ted Forstmann thought the company was worth at least that much. In the yachting example, you might have an answer as well. Your boss is sitting at your table and seems unusually enthusiastic about the possibility of your winning (and taking him with you on the trip). This new information certainly has value that you should factor into your reservation value. Indeed, it would be foolish not to.

If you have new information, update your reservation value and, again, write it down. The new value should reflect the new information you have. But if you don't have new information that would justify exceeding your previously determined reservation value, you should drop out of the auction. The same auctioneer who told me that he can extract more from first-time bidders had this to say about experienced dealers: "In contrast [to first-time bidders], there are the dealers, who typically stand at the back of the room. I would never try to persuade a dealer to break through his or her limit, because the dealers know what they are willing to pay and they're not going to pay any more than that."[24] Disciplined bidders know when to walk away.

As another example of disciplined bidding, consider the famous takeover battle between bitter rivals Sumner Redstone (chairman and CEO of Viacom) and Barry Diller (chairman and CEO of QVC) to acquire Paramount in late 1993.[25] Viacom was the initial bidder at $70 per share; QVC entered the fray at $80; Viacom went to $85; QVC went to $90. At this point, the parties went into major litigation in the Delaware Supreme Court, the result of which was a continuation of the auction.

The Paramount board announced that Viacom and QVC should submit their best offers by 4:00 p.m. on December 20, 1993.[26] Shareholders would "vote" for the competing offers by tendering their shares to one or the other bidder, and the auction would end when one bidder got 51 percent of Paramount's shares.[27] Both bidders could change their offers at any time, and Paramount shareholders could accordingly change their votes. But the absolute final deadline for bids and counterbids was February 1, 1994.[28]

QVC was the high bidder on December 20, with a $92 bid. But

because Paramount's process did not "show bidders the finish line," it's not surprising that Viacom came back with more—$105, and then $107 per share. (If this post-deadline bidding behavior sounds familiar, recall the experience of the American retailer reverse auction described in Chapter 4.) According to *Time* magazine:

> Diller had packed up 10 lbs. of Paramount documents and hauled them along on a year-end Caribbean vacation. Running the numbers while onboard the rented yacht *Midnight Saga* as he cruised off St. Barts, Diller decided that Paramount was not worth a penny more than the $10 billion in cash and stock that QVC was bidding. "When I came back on Jan. 3," he recalls, "I said, 'We're not going to exceed our offer . . .' It would have been irresponsible, I thought, and I held to that belief."[29]

Diller clung to his existing offer and lost to Viacom's $107 bid. A clinical study of the deal several years later estimated that Viacom had overpaid by more than $2 billion, and that QVC would have overpaid by $688 million, had it won.[30] Disciplined analysis on the *Midnight Saga* saved Diller from winning the auction and not wanting the prize.

CHAPTER 6

THE LIMITS OF EXISTING THEORY

In the spring of 2005, I first offered a course focused on corporate dealmaking at the Harvard Law School (HLS). The idea was to dig deeply into a series of recent real-world deals, with the main dealmakers present for the class discussion, in order to derive principles that could guide dealmakers more generally. After a couple years at HLS, I began offering the course jointly with my colleague Jim Sebenius at the Harvard Business School (HBS). Half of the ninety seats each year were reserved for HLS students, and half for HBS students, and the class sessions were held equally at the two schools.

In putting together my syllabus each year, I was deliberately unsystematic—picking deals from the newspaper or personal experience that I considered to be interesting not for their dollar value but for the dynamics that they presented. I then asked, "Who is the practitioner—lawyer, banker, CEO, etc.—at the very center of this deal?" Sometimes I was involved as an expert witness or adviser, which gave me firsthand evidence to answer the question. In most cases I called around to ask whom I should invite to discuss the deal. After the first couple years of teaching the course, I also got calls from former students, as well as practitioners, with recommendations on whom I should invite to the class.

The terms of engagement were demanding. For each deal, a student team consisting of five or six MBA and JD students would prepare background materials for the other students, which would be based on public reports on the deal and a pre-class conference call with the practitioner. We then spent two hours in class examining the deal: The first hour was a conversation among the students and faculty, with the practitioner interjecting only selectively. The second hour was the practitioner's, to comment on our discussion and to offer his or her further perspectives on the deal. Several of the examples and illustrations that I offer in this book come from deals that we discussed in the course.

Although I was not looking for it, what became apparent to me over the course of this teaching experiment was that existing negotiation theory is mostly of second-order importance for sophisticated and experienced real-world dealmakers. For example, I cannot recall a single instance in which a BATNA analysis or the Negotiator's Dilemma generated non-obvious insights about the case. Nor can I recall an instance in which an understanding of behavioral effects in negotiations "unlocked" our diagnosis of the negotiation situation, either descriptively or prescriptively. This is not to say that such factors were not possibly important in these real-world, high-stakes deals—just that they were less centrally important than the negotiation literature would suggest. This is admittedly a strong claim, so I take the rest of this chapter to explain why.

SHORTFALLS IN NEGOTIATION THEORY

I begin with the most bedrock principle in negotiation theory: BATNA, or best alternative to a negotiated agreement. The concept makes a lot of sense in the dispute resolution context, where the BATNA is typically to go to court. Lawyers, along with their clients, carefully assess the BATNA of a trial in order to determine their reservation value in settlement negotiations with the other side. Sometimes the concept translates reasonably well to dealmaking. In the *Frasier* case study, for example,

NBC's BATNA was to buy another show to fill the time slot, and Paramount's BATNA was to sell the show to CBS. In these kinds of deals, it's not that the BATNA concept is wrong; it's just that dealmakers with some reasonable analytical abilities, and not laden with the emotional baggage that often exists in disputes, think them through instinctively.

Moving beyond *Frasier*, there are other dealmaking contexts in which the BATNA concept is less helpful. Imagine you are trying to sell a product to a potential customer. This is a classic negotiation. What is your BATNA? You might gamely respond, "The possibility of some other deal." In fact, this BATNA is not an *alternative* to your negotiated agreement; in most cases, you can do the alternative deal *and* the deal at the table. The BATNA concept implicitly assumes that the alternative away from the table is mutually exclusive of the deal at the table. This makes a lot of sense in the dispute resolution world, where you can either settle the case *or* go to court. In many dealmaking situations, however, the BATNA concept breaks down because deals are not mutually exclusive. You can sell to zero, one, two, or thirty customers. The BATNA concept is not wrong—clearly you should think about your BATNA before entering any negotiation—but it's less helpful for more sophisticated dealmakers because it fails to go beyond the obvious.

The Negotiator's Dilemma is another central concept in negotiation theory that is less relevant for real dealmakers than the negotiation literature would suggest. One of the unstated but core assumptions in the Negotiator's Dilemma is that the parties will make a deal. This point is implicit in the fact that Stone and Ward (the hypothetical negotiators in the classic Lax and Sebenius formulation discussed in Chapter 2) will each accept even a "terrible" deal, meaning that such a deal must be better than their BATNA. In the real world, dealmakers will not accept "terrible" deals; or, more precisely, the likelihood that dealmakers will accept a deal increases with the profits from doing so. In some of my empirical work on so-called freeze-out transactions (buyouts by controlling shareholders), I found that the implications for negotiation strategy change dramatically when we move away from the assumption that dealmakers will accept deals that are just better than their BATNA to the more realistic and nuanced assumption that the likelihood the other side will say yes increases with the incentive to do so.[1]

To see how the removal of this assumption changes things, take another look at the Lax and Sebenius formulation of the Negotiator's Dilemma, but this time with probabilities (in brackets) that the deal will actually happen (Figure 12). Consider Ward's choice: If he plays Claim, he faces either a possible mediocre outcome or an unlikely great outcome. If he plays Create, he faces either a likely Good outcome or an unlikely Terrible outcome. Stone faces the same choice, with the same payoffs. Injecting some chance of no deal moves us away from the dominant strategy of Claim/Claim to what game theorists would call a "mixed strategy" that combines Create and Claim moves. In fact, if we rule out the possibility that Ward or Stone will ever accept Terrible outcomes (that is, if we assign a 0 percent probability to "unlikely" outcomes), the dominant strategy becomes Create/Create.

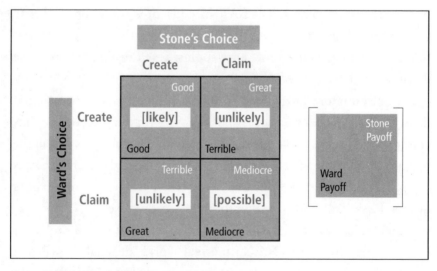

Figure 12. Negotiator's Dilemma Revisited

In the real world, the incentive to be guarded and deceptive in the dealmaking context is more muted than the Negotiator's Dilemma suggests, because the Claim strategy increases the likelihood of no deal. Consider the *Frasier* negotiation. When the parties reached an impasse, NBC offered development commitments in an effort to salvage the deal. Graboff truthfully told Paramount that development commitments were cheaper for NBC to give than dollars per episode. Paramount could have bluffed by devaluing the development commitments, as the Negotiator's Dilemma predicts, but McCluggage and his colleagues understood that if they did so, they risked losing the deal entirely. The result was a relatively truthful exchange on both sides, inconsistent with the Negotiator's Dilemma but readily explainable by the more realistic model developed here.

Once we inject one simple but highly realistic assumption—that the likelihood of a deal increases with the profit from the deal—the Negotiator's Dilemma becomes a significantly smaller problem. In fact, with the right probabilities associated with the different quadrants, a Negotiator's Dilemma–style analysis might actually flip to provide a dominant strategy of Create/Create.

This flip becomes particularly likely in situations with significant same-side-of-the-table competition. For example, consider the contest between Microsoft and Netscape to become the internal browser provider for accounting giant KPMG back in 1997. After hearing pitches from both sides, Roger Siboni, deputy chairman of KPMG, called Netscape CEO Jim Barksdale to tell him that Netscape had won the business, but that he needed a week to break the news to Jeff Raikes, one of Bill Gates's chief lieutenants at Microsoft. According to the *Wall Street Journal*, Raikes went into overdrive when he heard:

> During the next two weeks, Mr. Raikes repeatedly escalated Microsoft's earlier offers and concessions. To satisfy KPMG's concerns about the timetable for Microsoft's software, Mr. Raikes agreed to include KPMG in a "rapid deployment" program to give the firm early access to Microsoft's software, accelerating the schedule by a full eight months, and promised to speed up work on the Macintosh versions of its programs . . . Mr. Raikes also offered deep dis-

counts on other software if KPMG agreed to deploy Microsoft's technology globally . . . That still wasn't enough to seal the deal. "I e-mailed him and said, 'Here are my ideas,'" Mr. Raikes says. "He wrote back, 'Let's talk on the phone.'"[2]

Microsoft—not known for its warm-and-fuzzy approach to business—was making textbook value-creating moves in order to maximize the likelihood of getting the deal. Raikes's "here are my ideas" comes straight out of the playbook for open and forthcoming negotiations. Ultimately, Microsoft's strategy was successful—KPMG reneged on its oral commitment to Netscape and went with Microsoft instead. "Don't call me and say I got the business and then go back to the next guy," a frustrated Barksdale told the *Journal*.[3]

The general point is that when there is significant same-side-of-the-table competition, the dominant strategy for parties on that side of the table often becomes a relentless search for value-creating opportunities in order to maximize the likelihood of getting the deal. As a result, one or more parties are extremely forthcoming with their interests. Same-side-of-the-table competition represents an important qualification to the predictions of the Negotiator's Dilemma.

SHORTFALLS IN EMPIRICAL STUDIES OF NEGOTIATIONS

Thus far I have described why core concepts from negotiation theory such as BATNA and the Negotiator's Dilemma are less central to deal-making than the conventional wisdom would suggest. There is also a vast and growing literature in social psychology and behavioral economics on negotiations. Is it possible that these empirical studies are useful to real dealmakers? If so, these studies would be quite important for practitioners to know about in order to effectively carve up the ZOPA (zone of possible agreement).

To answer this question, we need to dig into the way most empirical work in negotiations is conducted. Negotiation scholars tend not to examine real-world negotiations empirically because data on real deals is hard to come by; and even when it is available, it is difficult to control for the numerous factors that influence these negotiations so as to be able to compare deals in a meaningful way. (The M&A world often provides an exception to this point.) Instead, most empirical studies of negotiations use data from undergraduate classes. One recent article surveys all of the empirical studies of negotiations published in top-tier, peer-reviewed journals between 1990 and 2005 and finds that two-thirds of these studies use classroom data.[4]

Economists tend to ignore classroom data because the experimental "subjects" typically have no financial incentives at stake. Sometimes the subjects have other incentives to do well, such as grades or reputational standing in the class, but these incentives are idiosyncratic in ways that are likely to make the results difficult to interpret.

Instead of using classroom subjects, most economists who study negotiations do so in a laboratory, where the factors that we believe influence the negotiation, including the incentives of the participants, can be carefully controlled and measured. In fact, the Harvard Business School has one of the most sophisticated labs of this kind in the country: the Computer Lab for Experimental Research (often called, admittedly redundantly, the "CLER Lab"). Subjects show up at the lab and perform tasks that are intended to generate insights on how negotiations work. According to the CLER Lab website, subjects typically receive a $10 show-up fee, plus an additional $10–$15 based on performance in the exercise. One study reports that the average CLER Lab participant earns $23.80 in a session.[5]

HBS is not an easy campus to get to via public transportation—it is either a twenty-minute walk from the Harvard Square subway stop or a shorter walk from a local but slow bus route. CLER Lab studies usually last one to two hours. So when one considers the commute to and from HBS, as well as the time spent in the study itself, subjects are implicitly valuing their time at something like $8–$10 per hour if they assume they will receive the average payout.

Not surprisingly, the vast majority of CLER Lab participants are students at local schools. So the participant group is the same as in the classroom studies, but the difference is that the subjects receive financial compensation in the experimental lab. The question is whether such small monetary payments are sufficient to create incentives to do well. An equally important question is whether the small monetary payments might actually attract less sophisticated subjects than the ones who participate in classroom experiments for course credit.

Even within the severely self-selected group of lab study participants, there are biases. Approximately 40 percent of those who sign up for CLER Lab studies don't show up for the experiment.[6] Among those who show up, most do so repeatedly. One study reports that over a two-year period, the average CLER Lab subject had participated in more than six prior studies.[7] If these repeat customers are different from the subjects who don't show up, or (more importantly) different from real-world negotiators, we have what economists would call a "selection bias" problem.

In a recent article entitled "Too Many Studies Use College Students as Their Guinea Pigs," the *Wall Street Journal* noted:

> Many of the numbers that make news about how we feel, think and behave are derived from studying a narrow population: college students. It's cheap for social scientists to tap into the on-campus research pool—everyone from psychology majors who must participate in studies for course credit to students who respond to posters promising a few bucks if they sign up.[8]

The natural question is, what inferences can be drawn from these classroom and laboratory experiments for real-world negotiations? This is a basic question in virtually all scientific endeavor. Consider, for example, new drugs that are demonstrated to be effective with mice or monkeys in laboratory experiments. Before these drugs can be offered to the public, hundreds of person-years are devoted to the question of translatability—will humans react the same way as mice and monkeys? Clearly, the stakes are far higher with new drugs than they are with new insights about negotiations, but as academics we spend surprisingly little time or effort investigating whether the outcomes from low-stakes experiments done with college students can be translated to high-stakes, real-world dealmaking. Experimental studies might be useful for shedding light on very basic negotiation points, such as the anchoring effect or the midpoint rule, but as the studies get more removed from core phenomena, there needs to be more exploration of the translatability question before we draw inferences for real-world negotiations.

To see the dangers of deriving prescriptions for real-world negotiations without assessing the translatability question first, consider a "classic" study from the late 1970s examining the power of justifications. The experimenters waited at a table in the graduate center of the City University of New York (CUNY) within eyeshot of the copier machine. When a subject approached the copier and there was no line of people waiting, one of the experimenters quickly approached the copier and asked to "cut" in front. With the control group the experimenter asked, "Excuse me, I have five pages to copy. May I use the Xerox machine?" With the experimental group the experimenter asked, "Excuse me, I have five pages. May I use the Xerox machine, because I have to make some copies?"[9]

Of course, the explanation offered in the experimental group would seem self-evident for the control group. Yet the study authors reported starkly different results: 60 percent of the control-group subjects allowed the experimenter to cut in front to use the copier machine, but a remarkable 93 percent of the experimental group allowed the experimenter to cut in front.[10] The study concluded, "If a reason was presented to the subject, he or she was more likely to comply than if no reason was presented, even if the reason conveyed no information."[11]

Several recent negotiation books have latched onto the study to demonstrate the power of meaningless justifications. The problem is that these prescriptions are unwarranted. One concern with the "famous"[12] and "widely cited"[13] photocopier study is that the difference goes away entirely when a "big" request is made, where big requests are those in which the experimenter had more pages to copy than the subject had.

So the more accurate conclusion is that when the request is trivial, any reason will do; but when the request is non-trivial, meaningless reasons don't have an impact.

Even if the results held for "big" requests, negotiation scholars have not explored the translatability question. Does an effect among CUNY students standing around the photocopier translate to high-stakes, real-world negotiations? The answer is uncertain at best. And the burden would seem to be on those who propose such counterintuitive negotiation tactics to demonstrate that translatability does in fact hold.

In legal practice, a standard move among litigators is to poke holes in opposing counsel's arguments, even if those arguments are not central. Poking holes in non-central arguments will cast doubt on central arguments too, even if those arguments are in fact solid. As a result, litigators are careful not to overextend and make weak arguments if strong arguments are available.

The same lesson would seem to hold in negotiations. Meaningless reasons might actually have a negative impact in high-stakes negotiations, because sophisticated dealmakers will jump on any logical flaws in your arguments in a way that is likely to put you on the defensive more generally. Contrary to the results from the photocopier study, but consistent with what you learned in the eighth grade, the quality of your justifications matters.

There are other questions about the methodologies and inferences from experimental studies, but I will not belabor the point here. Instead, I turn to a more subtle problem with the way in which most negotiation research is conducted. Experimental studies of negotiations typically use "static BATNAs"—that is, well-defined BATNAs that are the outcome if the subjects reach no deal. Occasionally, experimental studies will permit "dynamic BATNAs," but usually in a precisely defined way; for example, "if Subject #1 chooses to break off negotiations with Subject #2 and instead negotiate with Subject #3, Subject #1 will incur a cost of $1."

The problem is that the real world is far messier than these well-specified processes suggest. As one senior manager put it to me recently,

"As we negotiate with our customers, we often fail to find their BATNA, in large part, I believe, because they are working with other vendors simultaneously, and haven't yet struck an agreement with anyone, leaving their BATNA in flux."[14]

To take a stark but well-known example, consider negotiating to supply Wal-Mart. You are placed in one of the famous (or infamous) cubicles in Bentonville, Arkansas, with your biggest competitor in a cubicle on one side, and a private label supplier in a cubicle on the other side. Or maybe not. The point is, you don't know. Price pressure is coming across the table from the Wal-Mart "buyer" for sure, but it is also coming from known, unknown, and potential competitors who are lurking in the wings. If your buyer leaves the room, you are not sure if she is getting a drink of water or talking to your competitors. (And of course, she might say one thing but do the other.) You are fighting on two fronts, in ways that experimental studies can't possibly capture.

The core of the problem is that experimental studies require precise specification of the negotiation process. But in most complex negotiations the process is murky and messy, itself subject to negotiation, and not conducive to precise specification. Putting these two points together, experimental research in negotiations can't possibly capture the way in which real deals actually are done, or ought to be done.

SHORTFALLS IN AUCTION THEORY

About six months after the sale of Cable & Wireless America, I got a call from an attorney who had been involved in the deal asking me to moderate a panel discussion in New York City. The idea was to convene participants from all sides of the CWA transaction, and to get advice from a well-known auction theorist on how the practitioners could have run the sale process better. I readily agreed, curious to see how this interaction would play out.

The event was held in November 2004. Despite the good turnout and engaging dialogue, the disconnect between the auction theorist and the practitioners in the room was striking. In one exchange, a banker asked the auction theorist what he would have done if he had been advising the practitioners in the Park Avenue conference room at 6:00 a.m. The auction theorist responded that the hard work had already been done by getting seven bidders to show up, and that the competitive bidding process would do the work from there. Based on the practitioners' reaction, it is my impression that this was an unhelpful response. As the group disbanded, I sensed that many felt dissatisfied with what auction theory could offer to guide them in the heat of battle—even though most of the battles they were involved in had significant auction elements.

It was not the auction theorist's fault. The discussion contributed to my growing sense that auction theory has little to say about how most real auctions actually work. In a recent book surveying the auction literature, well-known Oxford economist and auction theorist Paul Klemperer agrees with this stark assessment: "Most of the extensive auction literature . . . is of second-order importance for *practical* auction design" (italics in the original).[15] Professor Klemperer concludes that what really matters in auction design is "mostly good elementary economics": things like discouraging collusive, entry-deterring, and predatory behavior. I find it impressive that an academic who has contributed a great deal to our theoretical and practical understanding of auctions would acknowledge candidly that most of the literature on auctions focuses on things that are not that important for auctions in the real world.

Professor Klemperer's comment is even more striking because he is talking about the kinds of problems that auction theory should be *most* likely to solve: well-defined situations, in which the rules of the game are precisely specified and the only question is optimal strategy for buyers and sellers—situations like the sale of third-generation (3G) cell phone licenses by the UK government in March 2000, for which Klemperer in fact helped design the rules.

Another problem with existing auction theory, not identified by Klemperer but in my view more significant, is that most of the real-world auctions that economists look at to guide their work are pure auctions, such as FCC spectrum license auctions, art auctions at Sotheby's, Dutch flower auctions, and timber auctions, to name a few. These are important cases, and economists tend to focus on them because they have clear rules. Clear rules are what make the auction problems "tractable." But tractable problems are not what real dealmakers have to solve.

Auctions in the real world are messy. The rules are unclear and constantly changing. Price is just one of many terms to be decided. The seller is not a passive participant after establishing the rules of the game. All of these real-world factors violate the fundamental assumptions on which much of auction theory is based.

In the sale of Cable & Wireless America, Mark Gordon, a partner at Wachtell, Lipton, Rosen & Katz who was in the Park Avenue conference room at 6:00 a.m., recounts:

> We really were scratching our heads. I remember somebody uttering the words, "What do we do now?" And I remember thinking, "There should be an answer here. This is not something we should all be figuring out on the fly." How to conduct an auction when you have seven different interested bidders all essentially bidding on the same thing—this is something we should have learned in business school or law school. There should be an answer to it.[16]

In fact, auction theory doesn't provide an answer, because it fails to consider the interplay between auctions and negotiations. The remainder of this book seeks to bring together auction theory and negotiation theory in a way that overcomes the limits of either field on its own.

PART II

Negotiauctions

CHAPTER 7

AN INTRODUCTION TO NEGOTIAUCTIONS

In 2002, as the co–course head for the first-year course on negotiations at the Harvard Business School, I ran a large experiment to test the effectiveness of auctions and negotiations as alternative mechanisms for selling assets. My subjects were all nine hundred first-year MBA students. Eleven sections of eighty to eighty-five students each were divided into twenty-six teams per section. Each team, consisting of three to four students, was given four assets to sell to classmates. Each asset had two, four, six, or thirteen potential buyers, and the number of potential buyers for each asset was known among the teams.

My experimental test focused on the mechanism of sale. *Odd*-numbered teams could only auction their assets. According to my instructions, "Private negotiations with one or more potential buyers are prohibited (even if initiated by potential buyers). This means that odd-numbered teams must announce auctions in order to sell any of their assets." *Even*-numbered teams could only negotiate the sale of their assets. According to my instructions, "Talking to more than one buyer at the same time is prohibited. If these teams want to talk to more than one potential buyer, they must do so sequentially and separately." My hypothesis was that auctions would do better, from the seller's perspective, when the number of potential buyers was higher (six or thirteen) and negotiations would do better, from the seller's perspective, when the number of potential buyers was smaller (two or four).

The experiment was a bust. Despite my efforts to keep the mechanisms pure, auctions regularly devolved into private negotiations with the top two or three buyers; and negotiations regularly culminated with the seller going from buyer to buyer extracting successively higher prices. Even though my students adhered to the letter of my rules, the auctions looked a lot like negotiations, and the negotiations looked a lot like auctions. As you might expect, I found no statistically significant differences in the sale prices between the two mechanisms, for two, four, six, or thirteen buyers.

I was disappointed. Not only was six months of preparation out the window, but I had nothing to report back to nine hundred MBA students who had each invested eighty minutes in my exercise. But despite the lack of a publishable paper, there was a glimmer of an insight from my failed experiment. I had failed because I tried to do two things simultaneously: keep the auction and negotiation mechanisms pure, and also keep the exercise realistic by capturing how people actually transfer assets in the real world. I realized only later that these two goals were at odds with each other. In an effort to maximize value as both buyers and sellers, smart Harvard MBA students, who have good business instincts and a reasonable amount of business experience, will contort auction and negotiation processes in ways that bear only a vague resemblance to the pure models of auctions and negotiations that academics study and write about.

I saw similar patterns in real deals that I was researching. In numerous situations across diverse industries, management of same-side-of-the-table competition and across-the-table competition influenced the terms far more than did anchoring, first offers, patterns of concession, value-creating moves, and strategies of persuasion and influence. That's not to say that these other factors were unimportant; they were just less important than the implicit or explicit auction-like mechanisms on one, both, or all sides of the table. In 2004, Richard Zeckhauser and I used the term *negotiauction* to describe the messy middle ground between auctions and negotiations. In our increasingly complex and competitive global economy, negotiauctions seemed to be the dominant mechanism by which assets were transferred.

To illustrate this point, consider my experience contracting for a new fence around our house. Our old fence was falling down, and I needed to find someone to replace it. As it happened, our neighbor down the street was having his fence rebuilt, and he was very pleased with the work. My neighbor's new fence looked good to me too, so I asked his contractor to give me a bid for my fence.

The offer came in at $12,000. This was much more than I was hoping to pay, so I got two more bids for the fence. These bids came in at $8,000 and $6,500. I then went back to my preferred contractor and informed him that he was the high bidder "by a long shot," but I appreciated he did quality work and I wanted to work with him. After some probing on what my other offers actually were (which I resisted), he said he could do the job for $8,500. Even though he was still the high bidder, I agreed to his revised price, and sure enough he did a great job rebuilding my fence.

Notice what didn't happen in this negotiation. I didn't make my preferred contractor a counteroffer. I didn't try to use strategies of persuasion or influence. I didn't try to think creatively about win-win opportunities between us. Instead, I simply used same-side-of-the-table competition to get to a price that I thought was acceptable. I'm guessing that nothing in my account will surprise you. This is just how deals get done in our world today.

Which brings me to the second part of this book. In Part I, I examined the static mechanisms of auctions and negotiations. Part I tries to advance the ball a little bit, but it also draws extensively from the deep literature in these two fields. The goal throughout is to provide practical insights for playing the auction and negotiation games as effectively as possible, as both buyer and seller.

In Part II we enter the uncharted but more important territory of negotiauctions. This chapter begins the inquiry by defining the negotiauction concept and some other important terms, and offering some general prescriptions for how to play in negotiauctions as both buyer and seller. In subsequent chapters, I discuss three specific kinds of moves that I see repeatedly in negotiauctions: setup moves, rearranging moves, and shut-down moves. In my research, these moves often mean the difference between deal and no deal. It is the relentless pursuit and constant assessment of the viability of these three kinds of moves that distinguishes great dealmakers from just very good dealmakers in negotiauction situations.

NEGOTIAUCTIONS DEFINED

A *negotiauction* is a dealmaking situation in which competitive pressure is coming from both across-the-table competition and same-side-of-the-table competition. As in our discussion of auctions, I generally will assume that the seller is the process setter in the negotiauction, exerting across-the-table pressure, and that same-side-of-the-table competition comes primarily from buyers. The analysis remains unchanged but the "buyer" and "seller" labels are flipped when the roles are reversed.

The common features in negotiauctions are these:

1. *Several (but not too many) potential buyers*, usually somewhere between three and ten. If there are more than ten buyers, then the seller is unlikely to be able to invest seriously in negotiations with more than a few of them. Therefore the mechanism is more likely to be auction-like, although it may still have negotiation features, particularly toward the end.

2. *Asymmetric information*, in which the seller typically knows more about the structure of the situation than the buyers do, at least initially. For example, the seller typically knows more than the buyers about the asset itself. The seller also knows who the interested parties are, though the seller may not know precisely what motivates their interest. The seller also controls the flow of infor-

mation among the participants, at least initially. The seller dictates if, when, and how potential buyers understand the initial structure of the negotiauction situation. As we shall see throughout the remainder of this book, one of the core challenges for buyers in negotiauctions is to overcome this information asymmetry through process moves.

3. *Ambiguity around traditional process setter and process taker roles.* In traditional auctions, the seller is the process setter, and the potential buyers are process takers. But in a negotiauction, *process setter* and *process taker* are just initial classifications. One might even think of these terms as misnomers, because one of the fundamental prescriptive insights for playing effectively in negotiauctions is that the process is itself up for grabs. Therefore, one of the core features of a negotiauction is that the process setter and process taker labels reflect only the initial positions. The roles are highly malleable, and control over deal process can shift over time.

4. *One-on-one meetings that resemble standard negotiations* between the seller and various potential buyers. One of the reasons that negotiauctions depart from the conventional negotiation model is that the seller's BATNA is fluid, not static, because it involves the prospect of negotiations with known, unknown, or potential competitors on the same side of the table as the buyer. Another distinguishing feature, as discussed in Chapter 6, is the mitigation of the Negotiator's Dilemma. If the likelihood of getting the deal increases with the value that is created, the buyers' collective and individual best strategies may be to look for value-creating opportunities and disclose them to the seller.

5. *One or more rounds of bidding and other forms of direct competition among potential buyers in ways that resemble auctions.* Unlike conventional auctions, the rules in these auction rounds are typically murky and subject to potential change, creating both opportunities and challenges for the bidders.

In the remainder of this chapter I provide three general lessons for how to play effectively in negotiauction situations. To do so, I revisit the *Frasier* case study from Chapters 1 and 2. In those chapters we studied the *Frasier* deal using a negotiation lens, focusing on aspects such as first offers, patterns of concession, and value-creating moves. In this chapter we apply a negotiauction lens to the same deal, to illustrate core lessons in the negotiauction arena and to generate insights for understanding the *Frasier* situation itself.

In General, Look Forward and Reason Back to Learn from the Moves of Others

In negotiauctions, some of the most valuable information is contained in the potential moves of others, yet in the "heat of the battle" practitioners often fail to systematically look forward and reason back in a way that enables them to learn from such moves. The *Frasier* case study illustrates the insights that can be gained from doing so. Before the negotiations began on February 1, 2001, NBC sent Paramount a letter describing how the process would work. If the parties didn't reach a deal by the end of their thirty-day exclusive negotiating period, the letter specified that Paramount would submit a "Last Offer" to NBC. If NBC accepted the Last Offer, then they would have a deal. If NBC rejected the Last Offer, Paramount could shop the show to other potential buyers, but NBC would have a "last look" under certain conditions. So in our terms, Paramount's BATNA to a negotiated deal with NBC was a negotiauction for the show. The relevant paragraphs of the letter described the negotiauction rules as follows:

> If there is no agreement reached by March 1, 2001, Paramount will submit its last offer ("Last Offer") to NBC. If NBC rejects said Last Offer, Paramount is free to negotiate with third parties, subject to the matching rights of NBC set forth below.

> If Paramount wants to license the series to a third party (including, without limitation, CBS), on financial terms less favorable to Para-

mount than the Last Offer, NBC has 10 days to match such terms. On the other hand, Paramount is free to license the show to a third party (including, without limitation, CBS) on financial terms equal to or more favorable than the Last Offer, without any further obligation to NBC.[1]

Thus, NBC and Paramount agreed to what is sometimes known as a *one-way match right*: NBC could match anything that Paramount came up with that was *less* than the Last Offer; but NBC didn't have a right to match anything that was *more* than the Last Offer.

How should NBC and Paramount play this complex negotiauction game? The answer requires looking forward and reasoning back. As a starting point, the conventional wisdom is that a match right benefits the right holder, and often this conventional wisdom is correct. (For an explanation and illustration of this point, see KKR's match right in the negotiauction for Toys "R" Us, which is described in Chapter 10.) In the *Frasier* deal, however, looking forward and reasoning back suggests that Paramount, not NBC, was likely to have benefited from NBC's match right.

The reason is that CBS didn't want to trigger NBC's match right. If a CBS offer did trigger the NBC match right, NBC and CBS would then be engaged in a back-and-forth bidding contest, which would be a game that CBS couldn't possibly win. So if CBS ever got a look at the show (i.e., if the exclusive negotiating period ran out), CBS would bid just above the Last Offer, with a "short fuse" on its offer so that Paramount couldn't go back to NBC. (Even though NBC would have no contractual match right in this scenario, Paramount would have strong financial incentives to go back to NBC anyway.) In effect, Paramount's Last Offer to NBC served as a credible ultimatum to CBS: "If you don't bid more than the Last Offer, you will be in a bidding contest with NBC, and you don't want that."

In fact, this is exactly how the one-way match right had played out the previous time Paramount and NBC had negotiated over a *Frasier* renewal, back in 1998. The only difference that time was that the other likely bidder was ABC, not CBS. NBC and Paramount went through an exclusive negotiating period, Paramount made a Last Offer to NBC, and NBC declined the Last Offer. Kerry McCluggage recounts what happened next:

> I called ABC, and said, "Do you want to talk about *Frasier?*" And I said, if you do, don't come over for a meeting unless you're past this [Last Offer] price level. And they said, "We'll meet you at 8:30 in the morning." And at 6:00 a.m. that morning, NBC called at my house, and agreed to all the terms that we had. And I had to call over to ABC and say, "Don't bother coming over, we closed the deal with NBC."[2]

This prior experience illustrates how the one-way match right could actually work to Paramount's advantage in its negotiations with NBC, because the Last Offer process enabled Paramount to credibly commit in its negotiations with CBS. Looking forward and reasoning back, this power to commit with CBS gave Paramount bargaining power in its negotiations with NBC. In an academic paper that uses *Frasier* as a motivating case study, Professors Brit Grosskopf and Alvin Roth develop a theoretical model and construct an experimental test supporting the counterintuitive conclusion that the one-way match right actually worked to Paramount's advantage.[3] The general point is that systematically looking forward and reasoning back to learn from the potential moves of others generates important insights in negotiauction situations.

The lesson is readily generalizable. Speaking in my Dealmaking class at Harvard a few years ago, Steve Munger, chairman of the Global Mergers & Acquisitions Group at Morgan Stanley, spoke of the "fog of war" that can cloud negotiators' ability to make decisions in the heat of the battle. Even experienced negotiators can "walk themselves off a cliff." Munger observed that the role of advisers is to "take things up a level," thinking things through a few moves ahead in high-stakes dealmaking situations.[4]

To be clear, negotiauction strategy is not like grandmaster chess, in which both players are thinking twenty or thirty moves ahead—what will they do, then what will you do, then what will they do, and so on. This kind of analysis would be impossible in the dealmaking world that we live in. But Munger's point is that rigorously thinking through just the first few moves and countermoves can yield insights for the bargaining table that go well beyond what the typical dealmaker, in the heat of the battle, is able to contemplate.

As Process Setter, Use the BASC Framework to Determine How to Apply Competitive Pressure

Recall that a negotiauction is different from a negotiation and an auction because there is competitive pressure both across the table and on the same side of the table. As a process setter in a negotiauction, then, your unique challenge is to determine which source of competitive pressure to utilize, and when. In general, auction-like mechanisms make use of same-side-of-the-table competition, and negotiation-like mechanisms make use of across-the-table competition. Recall that the BASC framework, introduced in Chapter 3 and reproduced here in Figure 13, enumerates the factors to consider in determining whether to auction or negotiate.

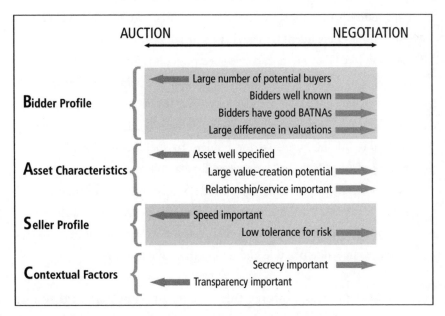

Figure 13. When to Auction, When to Negotiate?—The BASC Framework

The important difference in negotiauctions is that the decision whether to auction or negotiate is no longer a static choice, to be made at the outset of the deal process. Instead, the deal process constantly evolves as the various BASC factors change. You can think about it as a sliding scale on each dimension of the BASC framework. As the factors change, your deal process should adjust accordingly.

The most common evolution is from more auction-like mechanisms to more negotiation-like mechanisms. Three factors from the BASC framework tend to push process setters in this direction: (1) the number of bidders goes down as the process setter winnows the field, (2) the difference in valuations among the remaining bidders becomes relatively more important, and (3) value-creation potential becomes a larger fraction of the remaining value in the deal. Brad Peterson, a partner at the law firm of Mayer Brown and a reader of an early draft of this book, describes the negotiauction process that he typically uses, which follows the auction-then-negotiate trajectory:

> In my job, I help companies hire service providers to provide IT or outsourcing services. These are long term deals and generally commit hundreds of millions of dollars over three to ten years. My client becomes dependent on the service provider for a mission-critical function like IT or finance, so we need to get it right. We start with a field of 4 or 5 service providers and narrow the field to two bidders . . . We then negotiate in parallel for weeks. It's Monday and Tuesday with Bidder 1, Wednesday and Thursday with Bidder 2, and a recap on Friday. It's not unusual for bidders to spend a million dollars in the pursuit. Once we've negotiated away all material issues with both bidders, the client selects a single finalist and we negotiate to final documents. The idea of a negotiauction is powerful because we are both negotiating and auctioning, and we seek to simultaneously leverage same-side-of-table and across-the-table leverage.[5]

This deal process captures the benefits of same-side-of-the-table competition early on and then shifts to negotiation mechanisms to identify value-creation opportunities and build a relationship. So the BASC framework explains why auction-then-negotiate makes a lot of sense for this kind of deal.

The deal process can go in the other direction as well. For example, when you are just starting out to buy a new car, you may have no idea what you want—in BASC terms, the asset is not well specified. So you may spend a lot of time in negotiations with one or more dealers in order to pin down the make, model, and features you want. But once the asset is well specified, the various factors in the BASC framework typically point toward making use of same-side-of-the-table competition through auction-like mechanisms. So car buying is an illustration of when a negotiate-then-auction deal process makes more sense.

These examples make it clear that simply running a pure auction or engaging in a pure negotiation is almost never the best approach, for either the process setter or the process takers. Deal process is more fluid than that and must respond as the deal dynamics change. The critical task for process setters in negotiauction situations is determining when to apply across-the-table pressure, using negotiation-like mechanisms, and when to apply same-side-of-the-table pressure, through auction-like mechanisms. The BASC framework can guide you in answering this question.

To see this framework in action, consider the CWA case study from the Introduction. In our Chapter 3 analysis of the deal process, the uncertainty about the set of possible bidders and the interest in speed pushed toward an auction mechanism; but the large difference in valuations between the two top bidders, Savvis Communications and Gores Technology, pointed toward private negotiations. With the BASC framework, then, an auction-then-negotiate negotiauction would have maximized the likelihood of identifying the top bidder (Savvis) through an auction and then extracting full value from that bidder through a negotiation. Instead, the sellers held a pure auction, with the final few rounds as an open-outcry auction in the main conference room. A more nuanced negotiauction deal process would likely have yielded a better result for the seller.

As Process Taker, Change the Game to Your Advantage through Setup, Rearranging, and Shut-Down Moves

Whereas the critical task for process setters is to determine their optimal deal process, the critical task for process takers is to reshape the deal process, and even take control if they can—so-called *game-changing moves*. The viability of game-changing moves depends significantly on the context. In a legal dispute, for example, you may discover facts that give you leverage in the settlement negotiation, but opportunities to truly change the game are rare. Likewise, you wouldn't want to "change the game" in negotiating with your spouse.

Negotiauctions are at the other end of the spectrum. With multiple issues typically on the table and complex coalitional dynamics, negotiauctions provide fertile ground for game-changing moves. In fact, in my research I find that the relentless pursuit of game-changing moves is what distinguishes great negotiators from just very good negotiators in negotiauctions. As Bruce Wasserstein explained to my Dealmaking students at Harvard:

> It is very rare for the rules of an auction to actually be rules . . . When there are rules, you always have to think of the way you want to play it and what degree of hand you want to show. So I really don't care what rules people purport to have. You have to figure out what works for you, and the power of the situation.[6]

The *Frasier* deal illustrates how game-changing moves can unlock significant value. Networks invested heavily to promote shows, and when these shows became hits, the studios would "hold up" the networks for significantly higher prices in the renewal negotiations. *Frasier* was a prime example of this problem. One might say that this common practice was good for the studios, but bad for the networks. But over time it was bad for the studios too, because the networks were becoming wary about promoting shows too heavily, which would then fuel the holdup problem. The result was that networks would underinvest in promoting shows relative to the "optimal" level of promotion. In the *Frasier* negotiation, for example, Paramount alleged that NBC had moved the show from Thursday night to Tuesday night to weaken the ratings just before the renewal negotiations started, thereby gaining leverage for a lower price.

The situation was bad for both sides in the long run, and the solution was a game-changing move: the introduction of perpetual license fees, in which the network would prenegotiate the fees for new shows based on future performance. In fact, perpetual license fees have become the norm in the industry today. So, as interesting as the negotiation dynamics were, the 2001 *Frasier* deal was the end of an era. A game-changing move made these kinds of renewal negotiations extinct, yielding better deals for the industry overall.

Although illustrations can be helpful, the advice to "seek out game-changing moves" is too general to be useful on its own. What, precisely, are game-changing moves? And how does one go about finding them? It's a lot easier to find something, of course, if you know what you are looking for. In my research over the past ten years, I have found that three types of game-changing moves appear regularly, across industries and across countries: setup moves, rearranging moves, and shut-down moves. Rather than playing passively, the best process takers are constantly assessing the viability of these three kinds of moves in negotiauction situations. A *setup move* establishes your terms of entry into a negotiauction situation. A *rearranging move* reconfigures the assets, the parties, or both, in a way that creates additional value in the deal. And a *shut-down move* cuts off same-side-of-the-table competition.

In the *Frasier* case, NBC and Paramount played the standard negotiation game and got to a three-year deal at $5.4 million per episode. The result, as Marc Graboff described (see Chapter 2), was that "they weren't happy and we weren't happy." In the longer run the networks and studios unlocked value through a rearranging move: a new asset—namely, all future seasons—was added to the mix. This reconfiguration prevented the holdup problem and short-circuited competition from other potential networks when the show became a hit, all of which created value between the parties. A rearranging move changed the game in a way that allowed one or even both parties to be happy.

At McKinsey & Company, the consulting firm where I worked before joining the Harvard faculty, we were constantly asking ourselves whether our framework for thinking about a problem was "MECE"—*m*utually *e*xclusive and *c*ollectively *e*xhaustive. A central claim of this book is that the taxonomy of setup, rearranging, and shut-down moves is MECE. A return to the negotiauction diagram in Figure 1 (see the Introduction) reveals why. Recall that there are two sources of competitive pressure in a negotiauction: one on the same side of the table, the other across the table. As we will see in the remaining chapters, setup and shut-down moves work to dampen same-side-of-the-table competition, while rearranging moves enhance leverage in the across-the-table dynamic. Therefore, the taxonomy of moves offered in this book maps well onto the two sources of competitive pressure that distinguish negotiauctions from both negotiations and auctions. Rather than having to look broadly for game-changing moves in negotiauction situations, the categories of setup moves, rearranging moves, and shut-down moves tell you where to look. The next three chapters explore each of these three kinds of moves in more detail.

CHAPTER 8

SETUP MOVES

> **CAPTAIN'S COVE WATERFRONT JEWEL.** In a waterfront setting of idyllic peace and beauty this brilliant contemporary commands a sweeping vista of Sengekontacket to Vineyard Sound. Entering the tiled foyer through to the fire-placed living room with walls of glass and bleached oak floors, your breath will be taken away by the light-filled splendor. A superb kitchen, separate dining area, large master bedroom with bath and a beautiful view complete the first floor. Ascend the staircase to find an ideal office area framed by a bookcased balcony, a second master suite with view, two additional bedrooms and bath. Custom details abound. This jewel has been professionally sited on a beautifully landscaped lot with terraces and mature gardens. Two car garage, three and a half baths total, Association tennis, saltwater access, direct path to wildlife sanctuary. $1,390,000.

After several months of looking for their dream vacation house on Martha's Vineyard, an island off the coast of Massachusetts, Joe and Alice Townsend thought they had found The One.[1] On June 12, 2005, just days after the property came on the market, the Townsends reviewed their finances and took the plunge. They submitted a somewhat aggressive offer of $1.28 million, 8 percent less than the asking price, and attached several conditions on a rider to their formal offer.

The seller's response was quick and unequivocal. Another bid had just come in at the full asking price, with no conditions other than septic compliance (which was required by state law) and the usual inspection condition. The Townsends would have to bid again, and this time they would have to put full value on the table.

The Townsends wanted the house, but they did not want to be drawn into a protracted bidding contest with another bidder or, even worse, into bidding against themselves if no other bidder existed. After considerable thought, Joe Townsend sent a fax to the seller's broker offering $1.395 million, to demonstrate seriousness, along with the following text:

> I would be willing to participate in [your] process provided I have an express assurance that this would in fact be the final round. This could be achieved, of course, if you and the Seller indicate in writing that the Seller will accept the higher of the two final bids and that there would be no further bidding after this final round.

Consider the seller's choice. Clearly, she would prefer a frothy auction. But if she read the implicit threat in Joe Townsend's fax, she would understand that her choice was either the one-round, sealed-bid auction that the Townsends were proposing, or a reasonable likelihood that the Townsends would disappear and she would be left with a single bidder to negotiate with.

It's not a no-brainer, from the seller's perspective. The other bidder had already demonstrated serious interest in the house by offering the asking price without any conditions. It's possible that that buyer could be pushed to pay more even without a competing bidder, especially if the Townsends' departure from the auction could be kept quiet. Nevertheless, the seller played it safe. A one-round auction would assure her of something beyond the asking price and was better, she thought, than her BATNA of negotiating with the other buyer. The Townsends were informed that final bids from both parties would be due on Wednesday, June 15, by 3:00 p.m.

Joe and Alice now had to come up with The Number. To do this, Joe, Alice, and their broker each did separate MBOO analyses, as described in Chapter 5. The similar results from these separate analyses gave the Townsends considerable comfort. After several iterations, the Townsends decided to bid something in the range of $1.48 million–$1.5 million. Then Alice interjected, "Our anniversary is August 4th, or 8/4. So we should bid $1.484 million."

The suggestion wasn't frivolous. By attaching a couple random digits at the end of their offer, the Townsends ensured that they would not tie with the other bidder. A tie would invite the possibility of further rounds of bidding, thereby erasing all the benefits of the process they had just negotiated hard for. (If they won, the random digits also would provide a nice story to tell the grandkids while swimming in the cove.)

The Townsends sent the bid to their broker with the following cover note:

> Enclosed is our offer. Please put it in a sealed envelope and do not discuss it with anyone. You are authorized to deliver this offer to Barbara Levine [the seller's broker], provided that:
>
> (1) The other interested buyer has in fact submitted a new offer with a precise dollar figure;
> (2) Barbara is prepared to assure you and me that this is the "final round," and that the Seller and her attorney has assured Barbara that the Seller will accept today the higher of the two offers submitted by 3:00 pm today.
>
> Call me if you have any questions or problems. As is obvious, Alice and I have "stretched" to make this offer. I hope we win.

June 15, 3:00 p.m., came and went. At 4:00 p.m. there was still no response from either the Townsends' broker or the seller's broker. Joe called his broker and left a message: "What's going on?" At 5:00 p.m. the broker called back with news: "There may be a problem with the other bidder's bid, possibly in the form of $X higher than the competing bid. After an hour and a half, I'm still on the phone, trying to learn more." Joe pointed out that the "$X higher" bid would violate the first condition in his offer letter.

At 10:00 p.m., the seller's attorney called Joe and offered a redo. The other bid had indeed been in the form of "$X higher," which violated both the spirit of the sealed-bid auction and the explicit condition contained in the Townsends' bid that the other bid must be "a precise dollar figure." Rather than engaging in protracted legal wrangling, Joe and Alice agreed to a redo. Bids would be due at 10:00 a.m. the next morning.

Because the problem with the other bidder's bid had been detected before the envelopes were opened, Joe and Alice felt comfortable submitting the same offer, $1.484 million. At 10:05 a.m. the next day, the Townsends got a call from their broker. They had won. And the other bid? $1.475 million. The Townsends had won by a hair.

At 10:45 a.m. the Townsends' phone rang. It was the other bidder: Would the Townsends accept $1.5 million? After a brief pause, Joe responded, "No way!" The Townsends own the house to this day.

The Townsends' house purchase reveals a series of very impressive *setup moves* in a negotiauction.[2] The most important setup move was agreeing to play only if the second round was the best and final round. To see why, consider what would have happened if the Townsends had simply accepted the seller's process and bid again by the 3:00 p.m. deadline. If the bids were "too close to call," the seller might have told the bidders to bid again in a third round. Or the seller might have called the low bidder first and said, "I'm sorry, you're the low bidder and I'm about to sell the house to the other buyer. Is there anything you would like to tell me before I do that?" The auction would have been off to the races.

In the absence of a setup move, the seller would have gotten something resembling an open-outcry, ascending auction. The Townsends would have paid at least $1.5 million for the house, since we know in retrospect that the other buyer was willing to offer that amount. The setup move got the Townsends their dream house at a lower price than they would have paid by simply being a process taker.

There were other important setup moves that the Townsends made as well. Recall that the Townsends didn't know the identity of the other bidder, or even if the other bidder existed. This would be a very important piece of information, of course, if they could get it. Martha's Vineyard is a relatively small community, so they asked their broker to try to find out, but no luck. Their fear, which is quite common in sealed-bid situations, was that the other bidder didn't exist and that they were bidding against themselves.

Thus, another setup move was a condition to their bid: that the bid be delivered to the seller only if another bid was submitted at the same time. The solution wasn't foolproof—the seller could always simply ask her sister-in-law to submit a bid of $1 to satisfy the condition—but it at least required the seller to come up with a competing bid in order to get the benefit of the Townsends' bid. Note that if no other bidder showed up, the Townsends would not reveal their number to the seller. The Townsends could then sit down in one-on-one negotiations with the seller and get a much better price without the pressure of competition.

Another nice setup move, which proved to be quite critical in retrospect, was the condition that the other bidder "has in fact submitted a new offer with a precise dollar figure." The Townsends asked themselves, "What would be a rational strategy for the other bidder, given these process rules?" The Townsends looked forward and reasoned back, as described in Chapter 7, to understand that they needed to cut off the possibility of a bid in the form of "other guy plus $50,000."

Of course, the other bidder tried to get cute by making a bid of this kind anyway. In the absence of their setup move, the Townsends would have been in a very weak bargaining position, arguing that the other bidder's bid just wasn't fair. The seller would have 50,000 reasons, in the form of dollar bills, not to accept this argument. The Townsends' setup move gave them a strong legal claim against the seller's broker, who had accepted the process condition. From this starting point, the Townsends conceded by agreeing to a redo for the next morning. This redo was far better than what they would have gotten in the absence of their setup move.

A final setup move was in the redo itself. Recall that the Townsends had choreographed the opening of the envelopes very carefully. They instructed their broker to put their bid in a sealed envelope and allow it to be opened only if the setup conditions had been satisfied. Imagine instead if the envelopes had been opened at the same time and the other bidder's trickery was discovered only at that moment. The seller might still offer a redo, but the big difference would be that the other bidder would now know the Townsends' $1.484 million number. The so-called redo would actually be a third round of bidding, in which both bids would have to be higher than $1.484 million. Instead, the Townsends' precise instructions allowed a true redo, in which they simply submitted the same bid again.

The general point is that your entry in a negotiauction can have value. When it does, don't give it away for free; instead, extract concessions for it. There is even a practitioner shorthand for this move: "Pay me to play." In the Martha's Vineyard house purchase, the Townsends' entry had enormous value for the seller because it made the difference between an auction and a one-on-one negotiation. The Townsends understood this point and extracted significant process concessions in exchange for their entry.

Clearly, a setup move cannot be made unilaterally—it almost always requires acceptance by the process setter. A setup move will succeed if, and only if, it is better than the process setter's perceived BATNA. This is a general and obvious point in negotiations, but one specific implication in the negotiauction arena is that setup moves almost always have to be made at the outset. Most of the time, once you've given away your entry it's too late to try to get something for it.

As another example of an impressive setup move, consider the nego-tiauction for NCS HealthCare, a long-term health care provider.[3] After experiencing significant difficulties for most of the 1990s, in July 2001 the NCS board contacted Omnicare, the market leader, to negotiate the sale of the company. NCS asked Omnicare to sign a confidentiality agreement before sitting down for serious discussions. Among other things, this agreement would have prevented Omnicare from soliciting NCS's customers outside the ordinary course of Omnicare's business. Omnicare declined to sign, and negotiations broke down. Unknown to NCS at the time, Omnicare was actually conducting a full-scale assault on NCS's customers—a strategy known within Omnicare as the "NCS Blitz."

After further poor performance, NCS contacted Genesis, another competitor in the long-term health care marketplace. Genesis was interested in buying NCS, but it was terrified of Omnicare, the "800-pound gorilla" in the industry. As a setup move, Genesis demanded an exclusive negotiating period, which NCS accepted.

Omnicare got wind of the NCS-Genesis negotiations and sud-denly became very interested in buying NCS. Why the sudden inter-est? According to the Delaware Supreme Court opinion reviewing the deal (which I discuss in Chapter 11), "Omnicare came to believe that NCS was negotiating a transaction, possibly with Genesis or another of Omnicare's competitors, that would potentially present a competi-tive threat to Omnicare."[4] It was a classic all-pay structure, which we have already seen in Chapter 5. In July and August of 2002, Omnicare repeatedly faxed offers to the NCS board of directors, but the NCS board refused to speak with Omnicare in view of the NCS-Genesis exclusive negotiating period.

Now, however, Genesis had a problem: once its deal to buy NCS was announced, it would have to be approved by the NCS sharehold-ers. In the three-month window between the announcement of the deal and the NCS shareholder vote, Omnicare could publicly announce its offer for NCS. The analysis of all-pay auctions in Chapter 5 sug-gests that both Omnicare and Genesis would rationally bid beyond

NCS's actual value—a game that Genesis couldn't possibly win. Most likely, Genesis's offer would simply open the door to a better offer from Omnicare.

The solution was an impressive setup move: Genesis would pay $42 million to acquire NCS, but as a condition to the deal, the two major NCS shareholders, who were also NCS board members, had to sign written agreements stating that they would vote for the deal with Genesis, even if a better offer appeared before the shareholder vote. Because these two shareholders owned a majority of the shares, it wouldn't matter if all other NCS shareholders voted for an Omnicare offer. It would make the NCS-Genesis deal a *fait accompli*. Genesis could rest comfortably during the three-month window before the shareholder vote, confident that its deal with NCS was unassailable.

The NCS board, of course, didn't like the setup move. Like the seller on Martha's Vineyard, the NCS board would have preferred a frothy auction between Genesis and Omnicare. But Genesis refused to deal on any other terms. On July 27, 2002, the Genesis board set a deadline of midnight, July 28. If the NCS board did not agree to the deal by then, including the two shareholder voting agreements, the deal would be off.

After extensive deliberation, the NCS board voted unanimously to approve the Genesis deal. The NCS CEO signed the merger agreement, and the two major shareholders signed the voting agreements shortly before midnight on July 28. For what happened next, skip ahead to Chapter 11. But for our current purposes the deal illustrates an impressive setup move by Genesis, which short-circuited Omnicare's inevitable counteroffer for NCS.

The Martha's Vineyard case and the NCS deal are illustrations of situations in which setup moves were accepted by the party that would otherwise have been the process setter. Of course, the process setter doesn't always have to accept a setup move. Take Kerzner International, a gaming company that owns and manages high-end resorts around the world. Sol Kerzner, the South African son of Russian Jewish immigrants, founded the company in 1963. By the early 2000s, Kerzner International owned dozens of world-famous high-end resorts, including its flagship resort Atlantis, a 2,300-room hotel and casino on Paradise Island in the Bahamas. The company was traded on the New York Stock Exchange, and Sol Kerzner was a billionaire a couple times over.

On February 3, 2006, Kerzner revealed to his board of directors that he wanted to buy the company—a "management buyout" (MBO) in Wall Street–speak. In order to fulfill its fiduciary duty to get the highest possible price, the Kerzner International board established a committee of independent directors to negotiate with Sol Kerzner. The parties reached a price of $76.00 per share, and the deal was announced on March 20.

Under the terms of the merger agreement, the board then had forty-five days to negotiate with other potential buyers to see if anyone could beat Kerzner's price of $76.00 per share—known on Wall Street as a "go shop" clause. On April 11, twenty-two days into the go-shop period, an unknown bidder (identified in Kerzner's public filings only as "Party A") expressed significant interest in acquiring the company. But the bidder was concerned that Sol Kerzner and his management team had a significant inside track on what the company was worth.

Party A's solution was a setup move: the Kerzner board would have to pay to get Party A to play. Specifically, Party A demanded (1) reimbursement of its expenses in the event that it made a firm offer at $78.00 per share or better; and (2) approximately $100 million more in the event that its bid was the highest outside bid and the Kerzner board did not sign a deal with Party A within ten days of its bid being made. The Kerzner board explained Party A's setup move:

> Due to its concerns that the investor group [led by Mr. Kerzner] had a natural advantage over other bidders from its pre-existing knowledge of the company and established relationships with governmental authorities and joint venture partners, it would require an inducement to complete . . . due diligence and to submit a proposal to acquire the company.[5]

The Kerzner board nevertheless rejected Party A's setup move, and Party A walked away. One might say that the setup move in this case lost Party A the deal, but Party A correctly understood that Sol Kerzner and his team had a big advantage over any outside bidder. If Party A bid and won, it would know that the insiders didn't think the company was worth that much. And if Party A bid and lost, it would have nothing to show for the time and effort it had invested. Under these conditions, Party A needed significant inducements in order to play. So rather than the setup move losing the deal, the better interpretation is that the setup move avoided a situation that Party A couldn't possibly win.[6]

To summarize, setup moves are a vital tool to keep in the repertoire for complex negotiauctions. In some situations, when the setup move is better than the process setter's perceived BATNA, the move can shape the game to your advantage. In the Martha's Vineyard example, the Townsends got the house, and they got it at a better price than they would have otherwise, through a number of effective setup moves. In other situations, where the setup move is not better than the process setter's perceived BATNA, the setup move protects you against entanglement in a negotiauction where you can't possibly win. In the Kerzner situation, for example, Party A needed significant "pay to play" concessions in order to make bidding worthwhile. When Party A didn't receive those concessions, it correctly walked away.

In my research on negotiauctions over the past decade, I have regularly seen setup moves, across industries and across contexts. Setup moves shape the game from the outset. In the next two chapters, I turn to moves that can be used once the negotiauction is under way.

CHAPTER 9

REARRANGING MOVES

In the spring of 2008 I was teaching Negotiations ("NEG" for short) to ninety first-year students at the Harvard Business School. Approximately halfway through the course I received the following e-mail from one of my students:

Dear Professor Subramanian:

Hope all is well. Our section charity auction is next week and one of the items will be hotly contested between a ladies' team and a men's team. The item is a dinner/basketball game for 10 at the home of [HBS professor], who as you probably know has strong links to the Venture Capital/Private Equity community. We anticipate that the men will have high willingness to pay and given their backgrounds in VCPE, will have substantial firepower. Our due diligence shows that last year the event went for $3,000.

We women, who have historically been under-represented in the VCPE industry and not for lack of interest or qualification, would like to be a formidable bidder. Taking a play from NEG, we are building a coalition of financial backers to help augment our bid in case the auction escalates. We would structure any sponsorship contingent on a successful bid by the ladies' team and all proceeds will be donated to charity. We would appreciate if you would be willing to consider supporting our bid as part of a contribution to the charity event.

We also kindly request that you keep our coalition plan confidential as any leakage would only increase the men's resolve. Please excuse the lengthy (and unusual) email—thank you for your time and we look forward to your thoughts.

Best regards,

Ten Ladies of Section C

I happily contributed $250 to the women's war chest, pleased to help the apparent underdog in a charitable cause, and doubly pleased that the Ten Ladies were "taking a play" from my course. Unfortunately, they still lost to the men, who bid the astronomical amount of $3,500 for a ten-person dinner and basketball game. For $350 per person, you could have a very nice dinner at just about any Boston restaurant you wished, and have enough money left over to buy a decent seat at the Celtics game. But maybe that comparison misses the point.

In any case, although it occurred in a pure auction context, the women's clever idea reminded me of a negotiauction from about a year earlier, in which a similar maneuver had more success. On March 19, 2007, ABN AMRO, the Dutch bank founded in 1824, announced that it was in exclusive discussions with Barclays, the British bank founded in 1690, about a potential combination.[1] The announcement took the banking world by surprise and sent the CEOs of several major European institutions scrambling to assess their strategic positions. One such CEO was Sir Fred Goodwin of the Royal Bank of Scotland (RBS). Goodwin had his eye on ABN's US operations but had less interest in the assets in Europe, Latin America, and Asia. He reached out to

Alfredo Abad, CEO of Spanish banking heavyweight Banco Santander. RBS and Santander had a history of working together, and the two CEOs quickly hatched a plan to trump Barclays' bid for ABN: RBS would take ABN's US operations, and Santander would take most of the remaining assets.

There was a problem, however: the two CEOs thought it unlikely that Dutch regulatory authorities would allow the bust-up of a two-hundred-year-old Dutch institution by two foreign banks. Enter Fortis, a smaller Dutch bank. If Fortis acquired ABN AMRO's Dutch operations, Dutch regulators would be more likely to let the deal go through. On March 20, just a day after the initial Barclays-ABN announcement, Merrill Lynch banker Andrea Orcel arranged for Goodwin and Abad to meet with the chairman of Fortis (Count Maurice Lippens) and its CEO (Jean-Paul Votron). According to the *Wall Street Journal*, "Over lunch at the Four Seasons Hotel des Bergues in Geneva, the bank chiefs and Mr. Orcel drank wine and hatched their plan."[2]

The three CEOs created RFS Holdings, held 38.3 percent by RBS, 33.8 percent by Fortis, and 27.9 percent by Santander. According to the *Journal*, "They also formed a crucial pact to keep the group together: The trio would all win or all lose together. If any one party was forced to drop out, they would all drop out."[3] It was a move reminiscent of the Three Musketeers' famous cry, "All for one and one for all."

Just like the Ten Ladies of Section C, the RFS consortium had rearranged the players in the negotiauction in a way that gave it tremendous firepower in the negotiauction that was shaping up. And just like the Ten Ladies, who requested confidentiality to avoid "increasing the men's resolve," the RFS consortium thought carefully about the challenges that lay ahead and addressed them with its Three Musketeers compact.

Meanwhile, ABN AMRO made rearranging moves of its own. On April 22, ABN AMRO carved out LaSalle Bank, its main US subsidiary, from the Barclays deal and presold it to Bank of America for $21 billion—by all accounts an astronomical price. One day later, ABN AMRO announced a stock-for-stock deal with Barclays for the remainder of the bank, valued at €36.25 per ABN share or $91 billion in total value.

RBS wanted to go after LaSalle aggressively, but the other RFS consortium members were less willing to go toe-to-toe with Bank of America. The consortium compromised by making a lukewarm bid for LaSalle, which was quickly rejected by the ABN AMRO board as inferior to the Bank of America offer.

Although the key US assets had left the fold, RBS was still interested in going after the remaining pieces of ABN AMRO. The consortium made an offer of €38.40 per ABN AMRO share, with more than 90 percent of the value in cash. Barclays responded with an offer of approximately €35.73 per share, with one-third in cash and the remainder in Barclays stock.

On July 30, 2007, the ABN AMRO board said the bids were too close to call, issuing a statement that it was no longer in a position to recommend either bid to its shareholders. But the ABN AMRO shareholders had no difficulty determining which bid was worth more. By the October 5 deadline for tendering shares, 0.4 percent of ABN AMRO shareholders had tendered into Barclays' offer, and 86 percent had accepted the consortium's bid. The deal closed in late 2007. At approximately $100 billion in total value, it was the largest deal in the history of the financial services industry.

In negotiauction situations, effective players are constantly assessing the viability of *rearranging moves*, which I define as moves that reconfigure the assets or the parties, or both, in ways that create additional value in the deal. Rearranging moves can be made at the outset of a negotiauction, but unlike setup moves, rearranging moves can also arise after the negotiauction is under way.

The ABN AMRO deal has not been kind to two of the three members of the winning consortium. RBS fell prey to the global credit crisis, and after a £20 billion capital injection from the British government, RBS CEO Fred Goodwin resigned in October 2008. Fortis's stock price dropped 63 percent in the one year after the acquisition, and CEO Jean-Paul Votron resigned in July 2008. For both banks, many commentators blamed the ABN AMRO deal, at least in part.[4] Only Santander has emerged unscathed, selling the Italian network soon after the deal and retaining the Brazilian operations, which have been generally successful.

In retrospect, the big winner was Andrea Orcel, the Merrill Lynch banker who brought the consortium together. Merrill Lynch is said to have earned $179 million in advisory fees from the ABN AMRO deal. (Merrill earned an additional $150 million for helping to arrange the financing.)[5] Orcel himself took home a $34 million bonus that year in cash and stock. Goldman Sachs, a regular adviser to both RBS and Santander, didn't identify the rearranging move but still played a part in the deal. Goldman's fee: $500,000. Barclays' advisers (Citigroup, Deutsche Bank, Credit Suisse, Lazard, and JP Morgan Cazenove) are reported to have walked away with just their expenses covered.[6] The contrast illustrates that rearranging moves require a deep understanding of the structure of the situation. The person who understands the structure first can extract significant value, even when others may lose.

To see another example of a powerful rearranging move, return to Robert Barnett's auctions for political memoirs (discussed in Chapter 4). In February 1993, James Carville (the "Ragin' Cajun" who masterminded Bill Clinton's presidential campaign) and his then-girlfriend (now wife) Mary Matalin (the political director for the Bush-Quayle campaign) hired Barnett to sell their joint memoir from the 1992 presidential campaign. Barnett paraded his dynamite duo through what Carville began to call the "Twelve Stations of the Publishing Cross." According to Barnett, the pair began arguing in some of these meetings, since nerves were still raw from the election, in which Carville's candidate had won and Matalin's candidate had lost. The publishers nevertheless gushed at the prospect of publishing the "Hepburn and Tracy" of Washington politics.

All publishers received Barnett's usual letter describing the auction rules, as described in Chapter 4. The auction began on February 4, 2003, and the first few rounds proceeded with little incident. But momentum began to build, and a week into the auction the bidding was getting frothy.

Then something unprecedented happened. Richard Snyder, the chairman of Simon & Schuster, ran into Harold Evans, head of the Random House adult trade division, at a party. Snyder suggested a rearranging move in the Carville-Matalin auction that was under way: why not bid together? Evans took the idea back to his people and got their support, and Snyder and Evans then jointly took their idea to Barnett.

Barnett loved it. In addition to combining the horsepower of two heavyweight publishing houses, Barnett reasoned that the free publicity would create additional interest in the book. On February 22, the deal was announced. Simon & Schuster and Random House would jointly pay Carville and Matalin a blockbuster (but undisclosed) amount for the right to publish their memoir of the 1992 campaign. The book would bear the logos of both publishing houses, with all decisions made jointly by the two publishing houses and all profits and losses split equally. "It's like the Hatfields and the McCoys publishing the Montagues and the Capulets," Barnett told the *New York Times*.[7]

Other publishers applauded the rearranging move, with a "why didn't we think of that?" undertone to their comments. "It's unexpected and unprecedented," said the HarperCollins bidder who had lost in the auction for the book. "In terms of hype, copublishing is perfect for this particular project." Said another bidder, "I would certainly say this is creative. In my 16 years in publishing, I've not heard of this type of arrangement before."[8]

All's Fair: Love, War, and Running for President was published in the spring of 1994 and spent eight weeks on the *New York Times* bestseller list. Just as Barnett had predicted, the joint publication arrangement generated additional free publicity for the book and likely led to higher sales. A rearranging move orchestrated over drinks at a cocktail party transformed an otherwise standard auction into a negotiauction, and led to significant value creation overall.

Rearranging moves can have claiming implications as well. Consider the sale of the John Hancock Tower, the tallest skyscraper in New England. The sixty-story building is a Boston landmark, located in the heart of the city's swanky Back Bay area and home to many of the city's biggest names in finance. In December 2006, Broadway Partners bought the building for $1.3 billion. But when the financial crisis struck, occupancy and rents fell on the 1.76 million square feet of office space, Broadway Partners defaulted on its loan, and the building went on the auction block in March 2009. One analyst estimated that the building would fetch somewhere between $650 million and $750 million;[9] another estimated somewhere between $700 million and $900 million.[10]

The auction was held at 10:00 a.m. on March 31, 2009, in the New York City offices of powerhouse law firm Skadden, Arps, Slate, Meagher & Flom. The *Boston Globe* describes what happened next:

> A young man with jet black hair stepped behind a lectern and called for offers from a crowd of stone-faced lawyers and real estate investors. From the front row, Jeffrey Gronning, an executive with Normandy Real Estate Partners, quickly raised a paddle in the air, bidding $20.1 million with a flick of the wrist. The auctioneer began darting glances and pointing fingers. "I have $20 million, 100,000. Do I hear 20.2?" The crowd was silent and still. The auctioneer followed with the familiar call, going once, twice, "fair warning?" Again, nothing.
>
> In less than 60 seconds, Boston's most storied office building was sold, for $20.1 million plus $640.5 million in preexisting debt, putting the total value of the building at $660.6 million . . . The event ended before many of the executives had taken off their suit jackets.[11]

Afterward, blog commentators noted that the $640.5 million mortgage carried a below-market interest rate of 5.6 percent. A Morgan Stanley analyst estimated that the value of being able to get 5.6 percent financing on a 97 percent loan-to-value commercial real estate mortgage in March 2009 was worth about $190 million.[12] So if you include this source of value, the actual purchase price was something in the neighborhood of $470 million, well below the low end of what the building's already dismal valuation would have suggested.

How did Normandy Partners do it? (Were the other bidders asleep?) The answer is a combination of impressive rearranging moves. Normandy was not bidding just for itself in Skadden's Times Square offices; it had formed a partnership with Five Mile Capital Partners, another real estate investment firm. In August 2008, the Normandy/Five Mile partnership began assembling a controlling interest in the "mezzanine debt" that Broadway Partners was using to bridge the gap between its $640 million mortgage and its equity in the building. Normandy/Five Mile bought the mezzanine debt at deep discounts, less than 40 cents on the dollar.[13] According to the "terms of public sale" that governed the auction, owners of the mezzanine debt could count the *face value* of the debt that they owned toward their bid, which meant that Normandy/Five Mile was bidding with 40-cent dollars. So when Gronning raised his paddle to bid $20.1 million, he was using less than $8 million of actual cash. The playing field was tilted so far in his favor that other bidders didn't even bother to bid once he did.

Kevin O'Shea is the managing partner of Allen & Overy's New York City office and served as chief legal counsel to the Normandy/Five Mile partnership in the Hancock Tower auction. When I asked him why others didn't pursue the same strategy as his clients had, he responded, "A strategy like this takes foresight, strategic thinking, willingness to take risk, and a little bit of luck. But the reward can be huge. So I think some others are waking up to this strategy."[14]

The real puzzle isn't why Normandy got the building for such a low price—rather, the question is why the other bidders bothered staying in the room once Normandy arrived. (Luckily, they didn't have to wait very long.) Normandy's rearranging move eight months before the auction had stacked the cards significantly in its favor. The result was an auction that was over before it began.

Stepping back from these case studies, we see that rearranging moves in negotiauctions can have distributional consequences among the parties (i.e., claiming aspects) as well as value-creation aspects. On the claiming side, buy-side rearranging moves gave the Ten Ladies of Section C and Normandy Partners more firepower than they otherwise would have had. On the creating side, rearranging moves unlocked significant sources of value in the Carville/Matalin book memoir and in ABN AMRO. Consider the *Wall Street Journal*'s description of ABN AMRO: "The consortium bid allows companies to pay a higher price by uniting and allocating pieces of the target to buyers that most want those assets."[15] Textbook value creation, through a rearranging move.

When a rearranging move creates value, there is still a question of who gets that value. The answer depends in part on whether the rearranging move is initiated by the process setter or by the process taker. In general, the party that initiates the rearranging move will capture most of the value that arises as a result. To see this point, let's examine the sale of two well-known retailers, both of which occurred through negotiauction processes in early 2005.

In March 2005, Toys "R" Us, the well-known toy retailer, retained Credit Suisse First Boston (CSFB) to sell the company. CSFB contacted twenty-nine buyers, nine made preliminary bids, and eventually the field was narrowed to four bidders. All of these final four bidders were well-known private-equity firms: a consortium of six private-equity firms led by Cerberus; Apollo, along with one other (unspecified) private-equity firm; Kohlberg Kravis Roberts (KKR); and a Bain Capital/Vornado club.

Just before the best and final round, KKR made a rearranging move, agreeing to bid only if it could join the Bain/Vornado club. Toys "R" Us was unusual among retailers in that it owned most of the land where its stores were located. A key source of value in the deal came from the chance to optimize and rationalize the company's land holdings. Vornado had real estate expertise; Bain and KKR brought operational skill and financing capability. KKR argued that it could make a stronger bid if it could "club" with these two other private-equity firms.

The Toys "R" Us board agreed to KKR's demand. Final bids then came in: the Apollo club bid $24–$26 per share, conditional on further due diligence; Cerberus bid $25.25; and the KKR/Bain/Vornado consortium made by all accounts a blockbuster offer of $26.75, winning the negotiauction. The $6.6 billion deal closed a few months later.

At almost exactly the same time, Neiman Marcus, the well-known high-end retailer, retained Goldman Sachs to sell the company. Goldman contacted thirty-two bidders, and this time eight made preliminary bids. As with the Toys "R" Us deal, and reflecting the massive pools of private-equity capital at the time, all eight bidders were well-known private-equity firms.

Now came the rearranging move. Before the final few rounds, Neiman's bankers grouped the remaining bidders into teams of two to increase their firepower: Warburg Pincus paired with Texas Pacific Group (TPG); KKR paired with Thomas H. Lee Partners; and the Blackstone Group paired with Bain Capital. In the end, the Warburg Pincus/TPG club won, paying $100 per share, or $5.1 billion total, to take Neiman Marcus private.

The rearranging moves used in the Neiman Marcus and Toys "R" Us deals show an important difference: in the Toys deal, the rearranging move was initiated by KKR on the buy-side; in the Neiman Marcus deal, the rearranging move was initiated by Neiman's bankers on the sell-side. Both approaches have potential costs and benefits that should be weighed carefully in any negotiauction.

Controlling the rearranging moves as the process setter has the benefit of optimizing the bidding groups from the process setter's perspective. So, for example, Neiman's bankers tried to create equally matched teams to drive the bidding up. If instead the bidders could talk to each other, the strong bidders could collude with a joint bid that would have to just beat the much weaker next-highest bid. So shifting to a *hub-and-spoke* process, with the process setter acting as intermediary for the flow of all information up to the point that the bidding groups are formed, can be an effective rearranging move for process setters who are confident that they know who the high and low bidders are and where the sources of value lie.

If instead the process setter is less sure about who the high-value bidders are for each of the pieces and the whole, the process setters should consider allowing the "spokes" to talk with each other. This is the opposite of a hub-and-spoke process, often called a *peer-to-peer* approach—in effect what the Toys "R" Us board allowed KKR to do with Bain/Vornado. The peer-to-peer approach increases the chances that value-creation opportunities will be identified, because it eliminates the intermediary of the process setter. For example, if Bidder #1 values certain assets and Bidder #2 values other assets in a negotiauction, neither is likely to disclose its interests to the process setter, but the two bidders are quite likely to discover that information between themselves. The cost, of course, is that Bidder #1 and Bidder #2 are likely to extract a good part of the value that they create, by making a joint bid.

The bottom line is this: If you are confident about the "structure" of the negotiauction—who the high bidders are, how much they are willing to pay, and which bidders might want certain pieces—you should consider making rearranging moves in which you control the flow of information (a hub-and-spoke system). This is how Neiman's bankers ran their negotiauction. If you are not confident about the structure of the situation, you should invite others to make rearranging moves. They will identify the value-creation opportunities, but it's likely that more of the value will go to them. The amount of value extracted by the rearranging group is constrained by the existence of other bidders. In the Toys "R" Us deal, the Bain/Vornado/KKR consortium created a lot of value, but the presence of other bidders forced the group to give a reasonable share of it to the Toys "R" Us shareholders.

As an illustration of who captures the value from rearranging moves, return to the Cable & Wireless example in the Introduction. Recall that Savvis Communications, the winning bidder, promptly executed a sale-and-leaseback transaction for five data centers with DuPont Fabros, a competing bidder, soon after the initial deal had closed. How did Savvis and DuPont Fabros identify each other? The CWA bankers initially chose a hub-and-spoke system to run the negotiauction, which, according to the analysis presented in this chapter, would require CWA to identify the possible side deal between Savvis and Dupont Fabros.

In the introductory meeting, the seller's banker told the assembled bidders that each team should stay in its conference room, with no roaming in the hallways allowed. Anyone who violated these rules would be thrown out. This is a classic hub-and-spoke situation, with CWA controlling all information flows. But twenty hours later, the seller's banker shifted to a peer-to-peer approach. Bidders could talk to each other, as long as they were escorted between conference rooms by the seller's representatives.

This process shift made it far more likely that Savvis and DuPont Fabros would identify the opportunity for value creation between them, but it also increased the likelihood that Savvis and DuPont Fabros, rather than CWA, would capture that value. This is particularly true because the second-highest bidder, Gores Technology, valued the CWA assets significantly less than Savvis did.

I now turn to the third, and in my view most powerful, game-changing move in negotiauctions. The ordering is roughly chronological: setup moves (covered in the previous chapter) typically occur at the beginning of a negotiauction, rearranging moves (this chapter) typically arise while a negotiauction is under way, and shut-down moves (the next chapter) end the negotiauction prematurely—often (if done well) in ways that benefit both buyer and seller.

CHAPTER 10

SHUT-DOWN MOVES

In 2004, my wife wanted to buy me a fancy new car to commemorate a professional milestone, so four years later I relented, sold my ten-year-old Toyota 4Runner (which I loved), and went shopping for a new car. I eventually homed in on a particular make and model, went to Edmunds.com, clicked on the options I wanted, and entered my zip code and desired color.

I discovered that the manufacturer's suggested retail price (MSRP) for my car was $57,975, and the invoice price was $54,615. The MSRP is a hard number—it's the "rack rate" for the car, which the manufacturer calculates by starting with a base price for the car and adding in the MSRPs for the various options. In contrast, the invoice price is a softer number—it represents the nominal cost of the car to the dealership based on the factory invoice price, but it doesn't include things like dealer "holdbacks" that can reduce the actual cost of the car to the dealership. I aspired to pay right around the invoice price, on the assumption that the holdbacks would assure the dealership of a reasonable profit from the sale.

Armed with this information, I turned to deal execution. Negotiate or auction? I had done enough research to pin down the features I wanted, and I knew that there were four dealerships in the Boston area, so the factors discussed in Chapter 3 pointed to an auction: four potential "bidders" (the sellers), a commodity product, and a deal that was all about price. Edmunds.com makes running an auction incredibly easy: with the click of a few buttons, I entered the options I wanted, announced my interest to all four dealerships, and requested quotes. I then sat back, ready to watch the bids roll in.

It was not to be so easy. Dealer #1, which was closest to our house, never got back to me. Dealer #2 called but refused to give me a quote over the phone. "Our best deals are reserved for customers who come to the showroom," the sales rep assured me. "Come on in and we'll give you a great price." This dealer was about thirty miles away, making its proposal a non-starter for me.

Dealer #3 was willing to play ball, sort of. After an initial e-mail exchange in which the salesman urged me to come to the dealership and discovered that I wouldn't, he shifted his game: "If we can make you a great deal now, will you place the order with us today?" "Sure," I replied. Then came the offer: $57,975, exactly the MSRP. I e-mailed back: "Can you do any better?" In answer to this question came the following e-mail, this time from the sales manager:

> Can we do better than MSRP? . . . Absolutely!! John was just looking for a commitment from you to buy, rather than just through [sic] a number out to never hear from you again. It sounded like you had some numbers that you were trying to beat but would not give them to him for some reason???? . . . Like he said, there is no better price than in the showroom, so if you want a spectacular deal, please come in . . . when are you available to visit?

This was déjà vu all over again, as Yogi Berra would say. I crossed Dealer #3 off my list.

I had the most interesting exchange with Dealer #4. A salesman— call him Chris—called me to confirm the model and options that I had requested in my Internet application. Chris then called me back with a price of $41,650.

$41,650?!? More than $10,000 less than invoice? I accepted the offer on the spot. Chris told me that I would need to come to the dealership to sign the paperwork. I told him I would be happy to come in to sign the paperwork but I'd like the offer in writing, with itemization of the various options, faxed to me first.

Twenty-four hours passed, and no word from Chris. I called and left a message, and eventually got a phone call back: Sorry, there had been a mistake—Chris had quoted a price on a much less expensive model. Oops.

I did not believe that there had been a mistake. My hunch is that Chris was trying to do what Dealers #2 and #3 were trying to do, which was to get me into the showroom in order to short-circuit the negotiauction. I understand that car salespeople hate auctions, and I appreciate the tactics that Dealers #2 and #3 had used to try to get me to come to their respective dealerships. But in my view, Chris crossed the line into unethical behavior by trying to lure me to a dealership twenty miles away with a lowball offer. The fact that he even attempted such a tactic suggests that other customers fall for it, racing to the dealership to grab the once-in-a-lifetime offer before the dealer comes to his senses, only to discover that the price was illusory. (And in case you're wondering what recourse the jilted buyer would have, the answer is none, because no contract was formed in the e-mail exchange.)

Once we had clarified (again) the model I was interested in buying, I e-mailed Chris again: "Please let me know correct price along with breakdown of options we might want to switch in/out. We would like to move quickly." I never heard from Chris again.

All of this left me with a busted auction and no car, so I decided I would have to switch tactics and go to a dealership. I reasoned that Dealer #1 would be the most promising place to start, because it was the closest to our house and I had a good experience with them back in 2003 buying my wife's car. I also thought that this dealer's non-response to my request for an offer indicated that it was too busy selling to showroom customers, which seemed a good sign.

I went in on a weekday afternoon and was met by a pleasant-looking guy—call him Andy. We talked through the various options, I confirmed the package I wanted, and we sat down at his desk to talk price.

Andy explained to me that the 2008 model had just come out, it was an extremely hot car, and people were buying it for even higher than MSRP. When I looked at him incredulously, he opened his desk drawer and pulled out a few invoices, with names hidden but dates revealed, showing customers who had bought the same model in the previous few weeks at significantly more than MSRP. I thought to myself that either these customers were complete idiots, they were indifferent to price, the invoices were rigged, or some combination thereof. Whatever the explanation, I was not going to go for it. I sought to forcefully disable Andy's aggressive anchor: "If you think I am going to pay anything close to MSRP, this is a waste of both of our time and I will just leave right now."

Andy relented. He went to "run some numbers" and came back with his first offer: $57,975—exactly MSRP. This was getting tiresome. Andy was writing down his offers as we went (see Figure 14), which is what car salespeople are taught to do in order to improve clarity and show progress on concessions. Unfortunately, I wasn't similarly trained, so I don't recall my counteroffer. But after some further haggling, Andy came back with his "best and final" offer: $55,885, a $2,090 reduction from MSRP. Now we were getting somewhere, I thought. I would have been happy buying the car at that price, particularly since I had already dealt with the other three Boston-area dealerships. I could have gone back to Dealers #2 and #3, but I would have been in a severely weakened bargaining position if I had done so.

Nevertheless, I persisted. Andy made the classic "going back to the manager" move and came back with the "absolute best I can do" figure of $55,350, representing an additional reduction of $535. Mentally I congratulated Andy on making smaller and smaller concessions, as Chapter 2 advises. What Chapter 2 doesn't teach you, but car salesman school does, is to write this final concession in the middle of the page, as illustrated in Figure 14, in order to convince the customer that it really is the final offer.

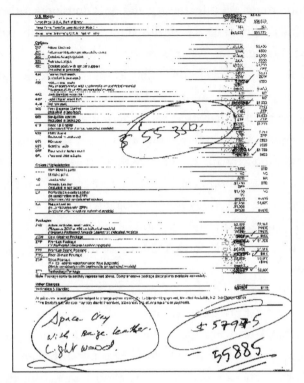

Figure 14. Negotiating the Price of a New Car

I then played the card that I had been reserving until this moment: "Thanks very much for your time," I told Andy. "Let me talk this over with my wife, and I'll get back to you tomorrow."

Of course, by leaving the dealership I opened up the possibility of shifting what had been a one-on-one negotiation into a competitive bidding situation. With all the features now pinned down, the car was a commodity that I could easily shop around to three or four other dealerships.

Andy tried a soft shut-down move: "Why don't you call your wife now? I can wait."

I was prepared for this: "My wife has a very busy job, so I try not to bother her during the workday unless there is an emergency."

Andy then came back with a hard shut-down move: "What would it take for you to sign the papers now, without talking to your wife?"

The truth was that it would be my car, and my wife didn't particularly care about what features it did or didn't have (other than the color). So I was willing to accept this shut-down move in exchange for a final price concession. What was the value to Andy from shutting down the negotiauction? Andy didn't know that the actual value to him was zero, because I couldn't go back to the other dealers that I had already talked to. But there was certainly some perceived value.

If I were gutsy, I would have gone all the way to the invoice price of $54,615, but I didn't want any chance that I had aimed too low, Andy would tell me to go shop around for that price, and I would be back in his dealership the next day in a seriously weakened bargaining position. So I played it cautiously: "$55,000 even." It would be a $350 final price reduction, and $385 more than my goal of invoice price.

Andy went back to his manager again (or so he said), and came back five minutes later: "Deal." I accepted Andy's shut-down move in exchange for a final price concession.

To be clear, I have no idea whether I got a good deal or a bad deal. (In fact, it's quite possible that Andy is using the same story right now with other car salespeople, for a good laugh.) But the car purchase example does illustrate how a shut-down move can create value between the parties. I got a better deal than I otherwise would have gotten, and the salesman got to shut down the competition.

I define a *shut-down move* as a move that prematurely cuts off same-side-of-the-table competition. In ten years of researching negotiauctions, I have seen effective use of shut-down moves in many different contexts. Consider the 2003 sale of *New York* magazine, discussed already in Chapter 5 as a pure auction. Bruce Wasserstein initially disavowed interest in Primedia's auction for the magazine, then made a stealth bid just minutes before the deadline. Wasserstein explained afterward, "It is like flying planes at a low altitude . . . You escape the radar."[1] Billionaire media mogul Mort Zuckerman was the other major contender in the negotiauction. According to a Zuckerman insider, "By 11 a.m. Tuesday, we heard that Wasserstein was [negotiating] and we thought, 'Uh oh, there's a wrinkle—we're going to have to pay more.' By 2 p.m. it started looking bleak. By 2:30 it was over. We were screwed."[2]

Wasserstein was able to effectively shut down the negotiauction by leveraging his long-standing relationship with Henry Kravis, cofounder of KKR and indirect owner of *New York* magazine. Zuckerman and others appealed to Kravis to let the bidding continue, but these efforts were unsuccessful. According to Zuckerman, "We made it clear that we were willing to put more money on the table, but after they had a handshake, they were not willing to entertain other offers. It was inconsistent with the normal bidding process."[3] David Pecker, chairman of American Media, had a similar experience as a bidder for *New York* magazine: "We had more money on the table, but never had the opportunity to put in the second bid."[4]

The shut-down move in the *New York* magazine deal illustrates another solution to the winner's curse problem identified in Chapter 5. Recall that one important process step to avoid the winner's curse is to ask yourself, "What's my edge?" Wasserstein had certain operational and editorial expertise that gave him an edge, which created private value that enabled him to bid comfortably in the auction. In addition, Wasserstein used a shut-down move to short-circuit the auction process. When you have no edge, a game-changing move may be the only way to win the auction without succumbing to the winner's curse.

Roll the tape back fifteen years. In one of the most famous negotiauctions of all time, the management group at RJR Nabisco, led by CEO Ross Johnson, is trying to buy the company from the public shareholders. The RJR Nabisco board has set up a process to evaluate bids, and Johnson's group seems to be in command. Suddenly, a bid comes in from nowhere that appears to shut down the negotiauction. Steven Goldstone (a partner at Davis Polk & Wardwell and counsel for the management group) appeals to Peter Atkins (a partner at Skadden, Arps) to keep the bidding open. According to the classic account in *Barbarians at the Gate*,

"We're not done!" Goldstone insisted . . . "Peter, we're willing to bid more. We'll bid more! What is this nonsense about starting an auction and shutting it down an hour later? There are no rules governing these procedures. We put in a bid saying we'll bid more, and we will. How can you do this? It's not fair!" Atkins tried to calm the feverish lawyer but got nowhere. "Peter you've got to keep the bidding open. You've got to keep the bidding open as long as people are willing to bid."[5]

The stealth bidder? Henry Kravis at KKR, in the deal that put his firm on the map. And one of his main advisers was Bruce Wasserstein, then a young investment banker who had just opened up a firm called Wasserstein Perella. Wasserstein, it seems, has been perfecting the art of the shut-down move for more than two decades.

KEYS TO SUCCESS

Shut-down moves work only when they are better than the process setter's perceived BATNA. Imagine if one of the bidding groups in the Cable & Wireless situation had shown up on January 21 at 8:30 a.m. and announced, "Here is an offer for $80 million, but if you don't accept it in the next fifteen minutes we are gone." The bankers who were running the process would have laughed—they had six other bidders sitting eagerly in their conference rooms, waiting for the negotiauction to begin. Twenty hours later, however, the same statement would have been far more likely to succeed.

The difference is CWA's perceived BATNA—at 8:30 a.m., the imminent negotiauction among the six other bidders is expected to be frothy; but at 6:00 a.m. the next morning, when the auction is stalled in the mid–$60 millions, an $80 million offer is extremely attractive. Effective players in negotiauctions are constantly assessing the viability of shut-down moves on the basis of the process setter's perceived BATNA at the moment.

A related point is that the shut-down move itself must be choreographed properly to influence the seller's perception of its BATNA. In the CWA deal, imagine that the buyer had gotten the timing of the shut-down move right (6:00 a.m.) but, instead of offering the language just described, had said this: "Here is an offer for $80 million, and you need to accept it in the next fifteen minutes."

The natural question is, "Or else what?" If the process setter perceives that the buyer will not drop out and the BATNA is simply a continuation of the negotiauction, the process setter is unlikely to accept the offer. Instead, the process setter will now use the $80 million "bird in hand" to extract more from the other bidders. The shut-down maneuver has backfired against the buyer, actually reigniting the auction.

Any shut-down move must be coupled with a credible threat that weakens the perceived BATNA and therefore increases the likelihood that the move will be accepted. The ideal shut-down move in the CWA deal comes at 6:00 a.m., overcoat on (recall that this is January in New York City), briefcase in hand, and goes like this: "Here is $80 million. We are happy to sit down with you now and work out the details. But if anyone leaves the room, the offer is off the table and we are going home."

Would it have worked? In the world of negotiauctions we can only talk probabilities, not certainties. In hindsight, it seems clear that the chance of a deal at $80 million would have been better than the actual outcome of no deal for six of the bidders. After all the dust had settled, the seller's main banker commented on how shut-down moves can play out in negotiauction situations:

> I've seen bidders come into an auction and announce to the entire world, "Here's an offer, it's substantially above where everybody else is, and it's only good for 30 minutes." And that causes pandemonium among the bidders, and if the banker running the auction doesn't keep their head about them, the auctions will sort of run away from them and others will be controlling the auction.[6]

To see what happens when a shut-down move is not accompanied by a threat that worsens the process setter's perceived BATNA, consider the negotiauction to find a publisher for this book. Unlike many authors, I chose not to use a book agent, so that I could spend more time working on the substance and less time positioning the book to make it attractive for potential publishers. I did send my book proposal to what I considered to be the very best academic and trade presses—eight altogether. Not missing the irony of the situation, I was hoping for a negotiauction for this book.

A few days after sending out the proposal, I received an e-mail from an editor at a top-tier university press informing me that he would like to make a "classic shut-down move" by securing approval for publication within two weeks. If the publisher had requested exclusivity during this two-week period, I would have been forced into a difficult choice, but he did not. I notified the other potential publishers of this interest and requested expedited reviews from them. Offers began to come in quickly. Analytically, the interest from the top-tier university press served as a positive signal to other bidders, who became more interested as a result.

Ten days later, I informed the university press editor about the other offers I had received. The editor exited with a gracious e-mail indicating that the negotiauction had gotten too rich for him to compete. Rather than shutting down the negotiauction, his self-proclaimed shut-down move had unintentionally fueled it.

As a counterexample, consider the sale of HUB International, a US/Canadian insurance brokerage, in 2006. Apax Partners, a London-based private-equity firm, made a shut-down move that was later described in the proxy statement to shareholders as follows:

> Representatives of Apax explained that they did not want to participate in an auction process . . . At the end of the meeting, representatives of Apax advised Mr. Hughes [the CEO of HUB International] that, subject to further due diligence, they were prepared to present Hub a proposal within ten business days. In addition, Apax requested that for the remainder of the week, Mr. Hughes not contact any other party regarding a potential transaction. Mr. Hughes

agreed that he would not make any such solicitations with the view that this would improve Apax's proposal.[7]

The university press would have done well to follow Apax's blueprint for an effective shut-down move.

These examples show that an effective shut-down move must be timed properly, must influence the process setter's perceived BATNA, and must be credible. On this last point, consider the negotiauction of MCI, the well-known telecommunications company.[8] In July 2002, WorldCom filed for bankruptcy in the aftermath of the largest corporate fraud in US history. CEO Bernie Ebbers and his CFO, Mark Swartz, went to jail for their roles in orchestrating massive accounting violations. WorldCom (renamed MCI) emerged from bankruptcy protection in April 2004, and the new CEO, Michael Capellas, quickly concluded that the company could not remain independent in the consolidating telecommunications marketplace.

By July 2004, MCI had received "indications of interest" from several of the RBOCs—the Regional Bell Operating Companies, or "Baby Bells," which had sprung forth from the breakup of AT&T in the mid-1980s. In February 2005, Verizon, one of these RBOCs, offered $20.75 per share in cash and stock, and the offer was accepted by the MCI board. Analysts predicted that Qwest, another RBOC, would likely make a bid; one commented that the deal was "attractive for Verizon— a MUST HAVE for Qwest."[9] According to this analyst, a deal was "absolutely necessary for [Qwest] if it ever expects to begin paying down its onerous $17 billion debt load, which it likely could not do on its own."[10] The situation was quickly shaping up to be a multibillion-dollar negotiauction between Verizon and Qwest to acquire MCI.

Sure enough, the bidding took off. On February 24, ten days after the initial Verizon offer, Qwest offered $24.60 in cash and stock. When this offer was rejected by the MCI board, Qwest came back again on March 16 with $25.60. Verizon responded on March 28 with a $23.10 bid. Qwest came back with $27.50 on March 31.

The MCI board had to decide which offer it considered to be "superior" for its shareholders. The answer was not self-evident, because both offers consisted of cash and stock, and there was a serious question as to what the stock portion of each bid would be worth nine to twelve months later, after all the regulatory hurdles had been overcome and the MCI shareholders would actually receive payment.

Verizon claimed, and most analysts agreed, that it had the more stable stock. In Verizon's view, its $23.10 offer was worth more than Qwest's $27.50 offer. On April 4, while the MCI board was trying to decide which offer to recommend to shareholders, Verizon issued a press release that read as follows:

> Qwest has submitted what we believe to be an inferior offer. If the MCI board, capitulating to Qwest's artificial deadline, declares this bid to be "superior," it would seem to us that the decision-making process is being driven by the interests of short-term investors rather than the company's long-term strength and viability. Should this occur, we would no longer be interested in participating in such a process.

Every word of this press release had been carefully scripted by Verizon's public relations advisers and lawyers. The idea was a classic shut-down move: $23.10 is our best and final offer, and if MCI doesn't accept it we are not going to bid any more.

It didn't work. Phillip Mills is a senior partner at Davis Polk & Wardwell and was lead outside counsel to MCI's board of directors. According to Mills, "When I saw Verizon's April 4th press release, I laughed . . . It told me that Verizon was in for the long haul."

But didn't Verizon's press release say "we would no longer be interested in participating?" It did—and that was the problem. According to Mills,

> Verizon knew how to say "We're out of here," but they didn't. Instead they said "We would no longer be interested in participating in your process." What does that mean? The ambiguity told me

that we could continue to use Qwest as a stalking horse to extract more from Verizon, without risking that Verizon was going to walk away. Instead of telling me that we were about to lose Verizon, it told me just the opposite.

On April 6, MCI declared Verizon's offer still superior but issued a press release stating that it "remain[ed] open to the possibility of further discussions" with Qwest. On April 21, Qwest accepted the invitation by offering $30 per share. This time MCI declared Qwest's bid to be superior, confident that Verizon was "in for the long haul." MCI brazenly gave Verizon a May 3 deadline to submit a new bid.

Contrary to its April 4 press release but consistent with Mills's prediction, Verizon didn't walk away. On April 29, Verizon came back with $26 per share, conditioned on MCI's disclosure that "a large number of its most important business customers had recently expressed concerns about a transaction between MCI and Qwest." Verizon was forcing MCI to renounce Qwest as a suitor in order to have the benefit of Verizon's blockbuster bid.

This time the shut-down move worked. MCI accepted Verizon's offer, Qwest dropped out, and the Verizon-MCI deal closed in January 2006. The failed effort to shut down the negotiauction on April 4 had cost Verizon an extra $3.00 per MCI share, or $970 million more for MCI's 323 million shares.

In hindsight, it seems clear that Verizon should have committed more forcefully to walking away in its April 4 press release. A more credible commitment to walking away would have been taken very seriously by the MCI side because Verizon was the buyer capable of paying the best price. The MCI board, no stranger to shareholder litigation during its tumultuous history, would be terrified at the prospect of losing its strongest bidder. A firm commitment to walking away, then, would have had a greater chance of shutting down the negotiauction.

Instead, Verizon tried to have it both ways, shutting down the negotiauction but leaving enough ambiguity in the press release so that it could keep bidding if it had to. This was crossing the river halfway—

ineffective in its intended purpose and embarrassing when Verizon in fact came back to the table.

DEGREES OF SHUTTING DOWN

Although shut-down moves should be clear and credible, they need not be absolute; they can also be a matter of degree. Sophisticated players in negotiauctions are constantly looking to dampen same-side-of-the-table competition, even if they can't shut it down completely. Consider the Toys "R" Us negotiauction described in Chapter 9, in which an impressive rearranging move enabled the KKR/Bain/Vornado consortium to win the deal. The KKR club insisted on substantial "deal protection" as part of the merger agreement. The centerpiece of this deal protection was a $247.5 million "breakup fee" that Toys "R" Us would have to pay to the KKR club if another bidder appeared and stole the company away by paying more for Toys "R" Us. Think of it as a quarter-billion-dollar consolation prize for the KKR club in the event they lost the deal.

Of course, any outside bidder would be crazy to make a bid for Toys "R" Us under these terms. If the outsider won, the company would have to pay the KKR club a quarter billion dollars—about 4 percent of the total value of the company. The breakup fee gave the KKR club a 4 percent leg up against any competing bidder. Making matters worse, if an outsider made a bid, the KKR deal mandated a three-day waiting period, during which the Toys board had to "negotiate in good faith with [the KKR club] to make such adjustments in the terms and conditions of the Agreement such that such [outside] Acquisition Proposal would no longer constitute a Superior Proposal."

What have you learned if you make a bid in this situation, three days pass, and you win? You've learned, three days too late, that some really smart people at KKR, Bain Capital, and Vornado didn't want to match your offer. The combination of the breakup fee and the so-called matching right meant that winner's curse concerns ran rampant for a third party considering whether to enter the deal. The potent combination of deal terms effectively shut down the negotiauction for Toys "R" Us.[11]

The KKR club also negotiated one other deal protection feature that blocked a potential rearranging move by others. Toys "R" Us consisted of two divisions: a very profitable Babies "R" Us division and a lagging Toys division. Because the original search process was quite convoluted, it seemed likely that certain bidders could make a blockbuster bid for Babies and leave Toys with the KKR club—a classic value-creating rearranging move. But the KKR club anticipated this possibility and included an unusual provision in the merger agreement that would require the full breakup fee to be paid if more than half of the Toys "R" Us assets were acquired by somebody else. Babies, not surprisingly, constituted more than half the assets. So the KKR club effectively blocked a potentially value-creating rearranging move through a shut-down move of its own. No other bidders appeared, and the KKR club closed its deal in November 2005.

OPENING-UP MOVES: RESIDENTIAL REAL ESTATE EXAMPLE

Unlike setup and rearranging moves, shut-down moves can also operate in the other direction—as what one might call *opening-up moves*. To see how, consider the typical residential real estate transaction. The traditional deal binds the seller irrevocably between the time of the purchase and sale agreement (P&S) and the closing. The seller can continue receiving "backup offers" in the event that the buyer walks away (say, because a financing condition isn't met), but the seller cannot legally walk away, even if another buyer emerges who can pay more. This is a so-called "tight" deal that shuts down any negotiauction that the seller might have been running. It is obviously useful for the buyer. But sometimes an opening-up move can provide a better deal for both the buyer and the seller.

Consider a situation in which the buyers are close to indifferent in the current deal. They love the house but they are also very happy rent-ing for another year; or they have their eye on another house down the street that they would be equally happy with. In this context, it might be useful to structure a "looser" deal—for example, a deal in which the seller can withdraw between the P&S and the closing by paying the buyers a breakup fee of, for example, $50,000. In the event that a much better deal came along, the seller would be free to take it and pay the initial buyers $50,000. The initial buyers would be ecstatic—having their out-of-pocket costs reimbursed, with plenty left over to contribute to the down payment on the house down the street. The seller is also better off, getting a higher price for the house. By opening up the deal to competition, the buyers and the seller have created the potential for a win-win outcome.

Consider another scenario. The seller is asking $500,000 and the buyer is offering $450,000. The offers reflect the parties' true beliefs about the fair market value of the house. One possible solution is that the parties split the difference, but an alternative deal structure makes use of an opening-up move. Imagine a deal at $450,000 that allows the seller to walk away between signing and closing by paying a very mod-est breakup fee—say, the buyer's out-of-pocket costs.

This deal creates value based on the different beliefs about the value of the house. The buyer, in effect, is saying this: "You think the house is worth $500,000, and I think the house is worth $450,000. We don't know who is right, but I'm so confident in my belief that I'm willing to give you sixty days to shop around to prove me wrong. If you don't find a better deal, we'll close in sixty days at my price." The buyer likes it because he thinks he is likely to close at his price. The seller likes it too, because he thinks he will find a higher offer, but just in case he's wrong he's got the "bird in hand." Again, an opening-up move creates value for the parties by transforming a one-on-one negotiation, which has resulted in impasse, into an implicit or explicit negotiauction.

Although I have not done a systematic survey on this question, experienced real estate brokers tell me that these more sophisticated deal structures are not used. Why not? Residential real estate transactions are typically the most important deals in an individual's life. One would think that buyers and sellers would seize on anything that can create value in this high-stakes world. One explanation is simply inertia. Over the past ten years I have studied the ways in which new deal technologies disseminate, and it's no surprise that dissemination is haphazard and typically slow.[12] "Boilerplate"—the legalese that lawyers pull out of their files as the starting point for any transaction—is a big obstacle to innovation, and boilerplate runs rampant in just about every aspect of a residential real estate transaction.

Another potential explanation—in my view more compelling—involves the incentives of the real estate agents on both sides of the deal. What do residential real estate agents want? Both the buy-side agent and the sell-side agent want a higher sale price, because the brokers' fees are calculated as a percentage of the final sale price. So from the outset, the buy-side agent has financial incentives that are squarely at odds with the incentives of the buyers themselves. But a higher price is not really what real estate agents want. Behind closed doors, real estate agents will tell you that what they really want, above all else, is for the deal to close. Price, on both the buy-side and the sell-side, is secondary to deal certainty. And opening-up moves run exactly counter to deal certainty.

Of course, I can't prove that the reason opening-up moves aren't used in residential real estate transactions is the incentives of the agents at the table. I can, however, point to an academic study showing that real estate agents leave their own houses on the market longer than they leave their clients' houses, on average, and sell their own houses for higher prices.[13] This study is consistent with the view that what real estate agents really want for their clients is a quick and certain sale, and price is secondary. Opening-up moves offer a slower and less certain sale, but in ways that ensure the best possible price for the seller.

To see how a more opened-up residential real estate market might work, consider the United Kingdom, where a homeowner can formally accept an offer from one buyer but remain open to competing offers up to the moment of closing. The British even have a word for this practice—when a third party jumps a deal, it's called *gazumping*. There is also *gazundering*, in which the buyer tries a last-minute reduction in the purchase price, just before the closing. The basic picture in the United Kingdom is a free-for-all up to the moment of closing. As a result, the buyer engages in a mad dash from the moment the offer is accepted until the deal is closed.

Gazumping and gazundering can create chaos for buyers and sellers who crave more certainty than the default legal rules provide. So British solicitors (a.k.a. lawyers) have developed "lock-in" agreements, under which the buyer and seller each put a certain amount of money into escrow—say, 2 percent of the purchase price, or 4 percent total. If either party walks away or tries to change the purchase price other than for one of the enumerated reasons (for example, problems found in the inspection), that party forfeits its deposit. So, as the name suggests, lock-in agreements create a tighter deal than the default UK law provides. According to one website:

> These [lock-in] agreements can cost more money in legal fees but should give invaluable peace of mind at what is a very stressful time. Note that if your solicitor [lawyer] doesn't like the idea then it might be an idea to look elsewhere for legal advice. Their reluctance might only be because these agreements are relatively uncommon and your solicitor may not know how to write one.[14]

And just in case your seller doesn't agree to a lock-in agreement, you can also achieve the benefits unilaterally by buying "gazumping insurance," which pays you a specified amount to cover your out-of-pocket expenses if you are gazumped.

It is certainly true that some buyers and some sellers in the United States want tight deals. Take for example a chain of homeowners who are all buying and selling on the same day, to avoid "bridge" financing or living in temporary housing. All of these buyers and sellers are likely to want tight deals to minimize the chance of wreaking havoc on the entire chain with a single busted deal. But the point is that one size does

not fit all, and the looseness or tightness of the deal should be a heavily negotiated point in residential real estate. In the United States, it is
not. The reason might involve lawyers' reliance on boilerplate contract
language and/or the misaligned incentives of real estate agents. Whatever the explanation, it is clear that creative deployment of opening-up
moves could create enormous value for certain kinds of buyers and sellers in the most important transaction of their lives.

CHAPTER 11

THE SHADOW OF THE DEAL: LEGAL CONSTRAINTS IN NEGOTIAUCTIONS

In this final chapter I turn to the legal "shadow" of the deal.[1] The goal of this chapter is not to arm you with all the tools you need to resolve the legal issues that you will face in negotiauction situations. As the saying goes, the person who tries to be his own lawyer has a fool for a client. Instead, the goal of this chapter is to increase the likelihood that you will identify potential legal issues and consult lawyers as appropriate, before it's too late.

In many deals, the businesspeople negotiate a term sheet or an agreement in principle, and then they "throw it over the fence" to the lawyers to work out the details and write up the contract. This approach assumes that legal issues arise only after the business terms have been resolved. As this chapter demonstrates, legal issues often arise in the deal process itself. This is especially true in negotiauctions.

In the traditional dealmaking paradigm, lawyers are rarely present during the negotiation process. As a result, two kinds of mistakes are made. First, many of my executive education and MBA students don't recognize when they are in legal hot water. "Really?!? I didn't know you can't say that." In most dealmaking situations you won't have a lawyer by your side scripting what you say and do, nor would you want one. But without a general awareness of the law you can be blindsided when the legal challenge comes after the fact.

The second category of mistake is the opposite of the first. Business-people assume that certain moves are off-limits when in fact they are very much available and ought to be part of the dealmaking tool kit. Here's just one example: "You can't talk to competitors on the same side of the table!" Sometimes this assumption is 100 percent correct, but it is not as categorical as the conventional wisdom on collusion would suggest. So this chapter tries to help you flag the legal issues, or non-issues, before it is too late.

I focus on the legal issues that arise uniquely and specifically in negotiauctions, rather than the legal issues that arise in negotiations generally. For example, fraud is a general legal doctrine that governs all negotiations, so I don't cover it here.[2]

I begin my analysis with two categories of moves that process setters often use in negotiauctions: using fictitious bidders to extract a better price, and reneging on process commitments. I then turn to two cat-egories of moves used by process takers that generally raise legal issues: bidding through others, and bidder collusion. To make the legal points salient, I will revisit several of the case studies and other vignettes that I have used in this book. And so in the instances where I have said, "We'll get to the legal issues in Chapter 11," now we're here.

PROCESS SETTER MOVES

Using Fictitious Bidders

Consider again Joe and Alice Townsend's house purchase on Martha's Vineyard, which we discussed in Chapter 8, but let's change the facts a bit. Imagine that Joe and Alice are visiting the house for the first time, along with their broker and the seller's broker. The asking price is $1.39 million, as before. Joe and Alice are asking questions about the house that indicate they are clearly going to make an offer. In the middle of the conversation, the seller's broker gets a call on her cell phone. She looks at the number and excuses herself to another room. A few minutes later, she returns with a grave look on her face: "That was my office on the phone just now. Apparently, an offer has just come in, at the full asking price and with no conditions other than septic compliance and an inspection condition." Joe and Alice retreat to the front yard for a prolonged conversation. They come back inside and make an offer of $1.45 million, with a thirty-minute deadline for acceptance. Fifteen minutes later, the seller accepts the Townsends' offer.

The Townsends quickly sign the paperwork and put down $5,000 in "good faith" money. A small party erupts in the front yard, with hugs and handshakes all around. The seller's broker then leaves the happy couple and their broker to rush to another appointment. She unwittingly leaves her cell phone on the front porch, which Joe and Alice discover only after she is gone. They can't call her number to reach her, so Joe and Alice decide to call her office to alert her to pick up her phone. Alice dials the most recent incoming call, remembering that it was from her office. "Hello?" comes the all-too-young voice on the other end. After some puzzled questioning, Alice discovers that she is talking to the broker's ten-year-old niece. When confronted with the evidence the next day, the seller's broker admits that the other offer never existed. But the Townsends' $5,000 check has already been deposited.

Can the Townsends get out of the deal, or sue the seller's broker for fraud? The answer is likely yes. Historically, courts took the view that lies about competing offers did not give buyers a cause of action.[3] Under this view, competing offers just provided information about the value of the asset—something that the buyer had a responsibility to investigate for himself rather than relying on claims from the seller. But since at least the 1950s, US courts have been more protective of buyers such as the Townsends. The courts' reasoning is that sellers have much better information about competing offers than buyers have, so buyers have no choice but to rely on sellers' claims. In a 1976 Oklahoma case with facts similar to those in the Martha's Vineyard vignette just described (minus the cell phone), the court granted punitive damages to the buyers against the seller's real estate agent, stating:

> A prospective buyer has a right to rely on the veracity of the seller (or his agent) without investigation . . . In the instant case the evidence so far adduced establishes that realtor Taylor, upon becoming aware of plaintiff's desire for the Spanish villa, undertook to bring about a rather rapid resolution of the price problem by using, as it were, a dynamite sales technique to blast an immediate positive response out of plaintiff. The deliberate lie did indeed achieve the intended and expected effect and induced plaintiff to purchase the property for a figure higher than he would have had to pay absent the fraud.[4]

In the scenario described here, then, the Townsends are likely to be able to rescind the contract, or recover damages against the seller's agent.[5] Of course, just because there are legal protections against fictitious buyers doesn't mean you shouldn't try to protect yourself through moves at the table and with contract language. Recall the Townsends' actual written offer, as described in Chapter 8, which was conditioned on the existence of a competing offer. As a legal matter, the condition meant that the offer would not bind the Townsends if no other offer in fact existed. This contractual protection is far better, if you can get it, than having to rely on the court system.

In part the reason is evidentiary: it is very difficult, after the fact, to determine exactly what was said in a tense and high-stakes dealmaking situation. Did the seller's broker actually say that there was another offer on the house, or just that there was another interested buyer? These shades of gray make a difference, because courts have drawn a line between specific claims about competing offers and vague, nonspecific claims about competing offers.[6] In a Massachusetts case from 1996, for example, the court found no liability for a seller who claimed he had "a buyer waiting in the wings" for his property, even though there was no such buyer. The court found that:

There was no evidence that Zais [the seller] represented that he had a bona fide offer at $990,000 from another specific buyer which he would accept if Ravosa did not agree to Zais's asking price. At best, the evidence indicates only that Zais expressed a willingness to deal with other potential buyers, the existence of which might be assumed . . . Conspicuously lacking here are such further deliberate affirmations having a tendency to deceive the purchaser . . . Absent such specific affirmations, the judge was correct in concluding that Zais's general statements fall within the range of acceptable "seller's talk."[7]

To see the contours of this middle ground, let's leave the Martha's Vineyard case study and reconsider the example of the deceptive Chinese food boxes from Chapter 4. Recall that the selling investment banker had informed his one buyer that all other time slots were "taken," and when the unsuspecting buyer arrived to conduct due diligence on Sunday morning, Chinese food boxes were strewn around the data room. Legal? In my opinion this is close to the line, though probably legal. On one hand, the banker was vague (indeed, completely silent) about who left the food boxes. It could have been the sell-side deal team, the janitors who ate dinner the night before, or, indeed, another potential buyer. On the other hand, the banker had said that the other time slots were "taken"—an overt misrepresentation that strongly implied the existence of other bidders. If instead the banker had said the other slots were "unavailable," he would have been on safer ground.[8]

What about the carefully worded sentence from my London investment banker to his sole buyer (also in Chapter 4): "I'm not going to lie to you. But you are the low bidder right now." This is also close to the line but probably okay in the United States under the same reasoning as above. However, Daniel Daeniker, head of the M&A practice group at Homburger, a Swiss law firm, informs me that the line would likely be crossed in many European countries: "A legal analysis in a civil law country would likely lead to the result that this statement would be considered deceitful, and hence, illegal." Interestingly, when Daeniker presented this example to a group of international lawyers, *all* of the US-based lawyers thought that the comment was legal, while a majority of the European-based lawyers believed that the comment crossed the line into illegal behavior. This straw poll suggests an important difference between common law countries such as the United States and civil law countries in continental Europe on what is considered permissible in negotiauction situations.

Daeniker also highlighted some of the practical realities of making this kind of statement:

> I have seen many auctions in which the truth about bidding parties and sometimes even relative prices came out shortly after announcement of the deal. The investment banker in your example has no assurance that his underhanded tactic will remain secret. If it comes to light, he will probably be out of business: even the client who benefited from his tactic will not trust him the next time around, since he knows that this is a banker who does not play with his hands on the table.

The point reminds us that the legal rules provide only a baseline for what is appropriate behavior in negotiauction situations.

Reneging on Process Commitments

Another common tactic among process setters is to renege on process commitments. Imagine a classic setup move, in which a bidder approaches a potential seller with the following: "We are willing to negotiate with you, but we are not interested in having our deal shopped around to others. So if you can commit to that process point, then we are happy to make you a full and fair offer." The seller accepts this process, and the parties negotiate a deal. Then, just before signing on the dotted line, the seller reneges on his process commitment and shops the offer to others. Sure enough, another buyer bites, and the seller abandons the first partner in favor of the better deal. The setup move has failed.

Can the jilted bidder get his deal back? Or at least get damages for having his deal stolen away? The answer is likely yes, under a couple different potential theories. One plausible ground for recovery is a general "duty of good faith" in negotiations. Clearly, the seller who reneges on a process commitment is not negotiating in good faith. The Uniform Commercial Code, which governs the purchase and sale of goods in the United States, imposes a general duty of good faith once the contract has been signed.[9] The problem is that US courts have been generally reluctant to impose a duty of good faith before the contract is signed, during the negotiation process, though it is important to note that civil law countries such as France, Germany, and Japan have been more willing.[10]

A second, and more promising, theory for recovery is the breach of the specific promise that the seller made to the potential buyer regarding deal process. As eminent contracts scholar Allan Farnsworth notes: "Precontractual liability [can arise from] the specific promises that one party makes to another in order to interest the other party in the negotiations . . . A negotiating party may not with impunity break a promise made during negotiations if the other party has relied on it."[11]

In some ways this theory goes back to first principles of contract law, because a contract is just a promise to do something. We can construe the seller's actions as breach of a contract that was formed around a deal process. The buyer offered a process choice, the seller accepted it, and the result is that the seller promised not to shop the offer around. Offer and acceptance are two elements that are needed in order to form a contract, and here we have an offer and an acceptance of a process choice.

To form a legally enforceable contract, both sides must also provide something of value, known as *consideration*. For the seller, finding consideration is no problem: the seller is giving up the right to shop around to other buyers. For the buyer, consideration is murkier. Did the buyer give something up when the seller accepted the process choice?

The buyer's consideration in this scenario has to be something along the lines of giving up the pursuit of other deals. The key, then, is to make this consideration explicit in the setup move itself: "I'm sitting down with you in exclusive negotiations in reliance on the point that you will not shop our offer to others, if we reach a deal." If a line like this appears somewhere in the setup move (ideally in written form, such as an e-mail) then consideration becomes less of a problem on the buyer's side, and a contract is likely formed around the process.

To see how the legal notion of consideration can have bite in a negotiauction situation, consider again the retailer reverse auction from Chapter 4. Recall that, after understanding the incentives that its post-auction round had created, the retailer decided to "show bidders the finish line" by having a single, final-round auction for the construction contract. After the switch to this new system, imagine that an unsuccessful bidder approaches the retailer thirty minutes after the end of the auction: "We had some technical glitches with our hardware, so we weren't able to submit our intended best and final bid by the bid deadline. But we're here now with an offer that is substantially better than the bid you accepted in your auction." Imagine further that the retailer accepts the offer. What recourse would the jilted bidder have?

Unfortunately for the bidder, probably no contract was formed, because there wasn't a "bargained-for exchange" regarding the deal process, and, in particular, no consideration on the bidder side. The retailer held an auction, and contractors showed up to bid. The jilted bidder is likely to be out of luck. The retailer will suffer damage to its reputation, but it won't suffer liability from accepting the after-the-fact bid.

An important exception to forming a contract around a setup move arises when the contract is unenforceable as a matter of law. This can be the case when the process setter is a fiduciary who is negotiating on behalf of others. For example, in Chapter 8 we examined Genesis's deal to buy NCS HealthCare for $42 million. As a condition to the deal, the NCS board agreed to "lock up" a majority of its shares in favor of the deal, in effect preventing NCS from looking at a higher offer from Genesis's rival, Omnicare. A nice setup move by Genesis.

Rolling the tape forward, however, reveals an important limit on forming a contract on process through a setup move. Just as Genesis feared, after the deal was announced Omnicare made an offer to buy NCS for $91 million, and then $144 million—more than three times what Genesis was offering. Genesis didn't increase its bid, comfortable in the fact that NCS had committed irrevocably, through the shareholder lockup agreement, to accept its $42 million offer.

Omnicare sued, seeking a declaration that Genesis's setup move was invalid under Delaware corporate law. Surprisingly, in a controversial three-to-two decision, the Delaware Supreme Court agreed, holding that the NCS board could not contract out of its fiduciary duty to maximize shareholder value in the sale of the company. Omnicare paid Genesis a small breakup fee and walked away with the prize. The decision suggests an important limit on the enforceability of setup moves. When the process setter is acting as a fiduciary, a court may be unwilling to enforce setup or shut-down moves that are too draconian.

In a dramatic illustration of this point, consider the bidding contest between Citigroup and Wells Fargo to acquire Wachovia. Like too many other banks, Wachovia fell victim to the financial crisis in the fall of 2008. With its stock in free fall, Wachovia Chairman and CEO Bob Steel went searching for a savior over the weekend of September 27–28. If Steel did not find a buyer that weekend, he knew that Wachovia would have to follow Lehman Brothers and Washington Mutual into bankruptcy protection on Monday morning.

The most likely buyer was Wells Fargo, the fourth-largest US bank behind Bank of America, JPMorgan Chase, and Citigroup. Unlike Wachovia, Wells Fargo did not have large exposure to subprime mortgages, and Wachovia's south and southeastern geographic focus provided a nice complement to Wells Fargo's west coast focus. Despite these apparent affinities, Wells Fargo Chairman Dick Kovacevich unexpectedly walked away from the negotiations that weekend.

Enter Citigroup. In a late-night/early-morning negotiation that went down to the wire, Citigroup CEO Vikram Pandit, with encouragement from Federal Deposit Insurance Corporation (FDIC) Chairman Sheila Bair, threw Wachovia a lifeline. Late on Sunday, September 28, Citigroup announced that it would buy Wachovia's banking assets, thereby saving Wachovia from a bankruptcy filing on Monday morning. Pandit struck a hard bargain: a price of $1 per share, plus a significant "backstop" in which the FDIC would cover any losses on the Wachovia assets in excess of $42 billion.

On Monday morning, September 29, the deal was announced: Citigroup and Wachovia had a letter of intent around the key terms, with the details and a formal merger agreement to come within a week. Citi would provide Wachovia with a line of credit to keep it afloat until the merger was completed. To make sure that their engagement would lead to a marriage, Citi locked up the deal, just as Genesis had done with NCS HealthCare. The letter of intent stated that for one week, "Wachovia shall not . . . enter into agreement in principle, letter of intent, term sheet, merger agreement, acquisition agreement, option agreement or other similar instrument" with another buyer.[12]

The next day—Tuesday, September 30—Treasury Secretary Paulson changed the IRS regulations to eliminate the annual cap on built-in losses that could offset profits after the acquisition in financial institution deals.[13] (This change was controversial at the time, with some observers questioning the ability of the Treasury Secretary to unilaterally change the tax code, and in February 2009 the American Recovery and Reinvestment Act reversed it.) Paulson's idea was to make the troubled financial institutions more attractive for potential acquirers, by allowing acquirers to use built-in losses immediately to offset profits. Analysts estimated that Wachovia had approximately $70 billion of built-in losses in its loan portfolio,[14] which would yield roughly $25 billion in value for any bank that had sufficient profits to offset those losses. Only a few banks did. Among them was Wells Fargo. After walking away from buying Wachovia just days before, Wells Fargo was suddenly very interested.

Sure enough, Wells Fargo came knocking. Bob Steel, Wachovia's CEO, described Wells Fargo's approach to him on Thursday of that week:

On October 2, 2008 at approximately 7:15 pm, I received an unexpected call from [FDIC] Chairman [Sheila] Bair. She asked me if I had heard from [Wells Fargo Chairman] Kovacevich. I assured her I had not spoken to him since the initiation of the negotiations with Citi. She advised me that it was her understanding that he would be calling me to propose a merger transaction . . . At approximately 9:00 pm, I received a call from Mr. Kovacevich telling me that momentarily he would be sending me a signed, Board-approved merger agreement for the acquisition of all of Wachovia . . . Wachovia's board of directors met by telephone conference at approximately 11:00 pm to review the Wells Fargo proposal . . . After extensive consideration and discussion by the Board, the Board approved accepting the Wells Fargo proposal.[15]

On Friday morning, October 3, Wells Fargo and Wachovia announced their shocking deal: Wells Fargo would buy Wachovia for $7 per share, and with no FDIC backstop. The Wells Fargo board was happy, Bob Steel was called a genius (taking the ailing bank from imminent bankruptcy protection to an offer of $7 per share within a week), and the Wachovia shareholders were ecstatic. The only unhappy party, of course, was Citigroup, which had been left at the altar by Wachovia, the bank that it had saved from disaster and nursed back to health for four days. Citigroup lost 14 percent of its market capitalization, amounting to approximately $17 billion, when the deal between Wells Fargo and Wachovia was announced.

And what about Citi's exclusivity agreement with Wachovia, which barred Wachovia from accepting Wells Fargo's offer? In another breathtaking twist to the story, Section 126(c) of the Emergency Economic Stabilization Act of 2008, signed into law by President Bush on Friday October 2, states the following:

UNENFORCEABILITY OF CERTAIN AGREEMENTS—No provision contained in any existing or future standstill, confidentiality, or other agreement, that directly or indirectly—

(A) affects, restricts, or limits the ability of any person to offer or acquire,

(B) prohibits any person from offering to acquire or acquiring, or

(C) prohibits any person from using any previously disclosed information in connection with any such offer to acquire or acquisition of, all or part of any insured depository institution, including any liabilities, assets, or interest therein, in connection with any transaction in which [the FDIC] exercises its authority under section 11 or 13, shall be enforceable against or impose any liability on such person, as such enforcement or liability shall be contrary to public policy.

Wells Fargo claimed that Section 126(c) rendered the Citi-Wachovia exclusivity agreement unenforceable. As best we can tell, the FDIC inserted the provision into the bailout bill, with virtually no commentary or public debate. (Wells Fargo insisted that it had played "no role in suggesting the language.")[16] The FDIC's logic seemed to be the same as the reasoning used by the Delaware Supreme Court to invalidate Genesis's shareholder lockup agreement with NCS HealthCare: when the process setter is acting as a fiduciary for others, setup and shut-down moves that are too draconian should be unenforceable, as "contrary to public policy." Here, Citi's setup move eliminated the possibility of competition a few days later from Wells Fargo, which would have prevented the Wachovia shareholders from receiving its clearly superior offer. Section 126(c) sweeps clear this barrier to "allocational efficiency" in the marketplace, allowing Wachovia's assets to go to their highest-value use at Wells Fargo. At the time of this writing, Citigroup, Wells Fargo, and Wachovia are embroiled in litigation over this multibillion-dollar negotiauction.

I will close this discussion with a bit of editorializing about the wisdom of the legal principle that we see in the *Omnicare* case and in Section 126(c) of the bailout law. With the benefit of hindsight, it is easy to prefer Omnicare's $144 million offer over Genesis's $42 million offer, or Wells Fargo's $7 per share over Citi's $1 per share. But as we have seen repeatedly throughout this book, setup moves can create value for both parties because, by definition, such moves, when accepted, are better than the perceived BATNAs on both sides. NCS HealthCare and Wachovia were both desperate sellers, and Genesis and Citigroup, respectively, were induced to do deals only through setup moves that prevented further competition.

If the legal rules take such setup moves out of the tool kit, future buyers won't come to the table in the first place, and future sellers such as NCS and Wachovia will be worse off. The *Wall Street Journal* noticed as much, stating in the aftermath of the deal between Wells Fargo and Wachovia, "Government officials are concerned that the way the competing deals unfolded might deter US banks from agreeing to government-assisted transactions."[17] A lawyer who was observing the deal at the time put it more starkly: "A deal is a deal from the agency's perspective. Nobody would believe them [the FDIC] in the future if they did that."[18] But the FDIC brokered the Wells-Wachovia deal anyway.

To use the law and economics terminology, the rule set out in *Omnicare* and endorsed in Section 126(c) has some *ex post* appeal but creates significant *ex ante* costs by limiting the permissible terms of the deal. The better rule would be that, absent self-dealing or conflicts of interest, the setup moves that Genesis and Citigroup made should be enforceable as a matter of law.

Isn't society better off, though, when Wells Fargo owns the assets rather than Citi? Wachovia's troubled assets are no longer backstopped by the FDIC, and there is no doubt that the Wachovia shareholders are happier with the Wells Fargo offer than they would have been with the Citi offer. Wouldn't Citi's setup move have prevented this desirable outcome? Not at all. Enforcing the setup move would still allow Wells Fargo to buy the Wachovia assets—just from Citi rather than from Wachovia. (Economists will recognize this as a straightforward application of the Coase Theorem.) Allocational efficiency would be achieved, but Citi would get some of the profit from the deal. This result seems appropriate, since Citi saved Wachovia from bankruptcy in the first place.

In fact, we may be coming to something resembling this outcome, though in a backhanded way. Citi has renounced its claim on Wachovia's assets, and instead is suing Wells Fargo for "tortious interference" with the Citi-Wachovia exclusivity agreement. In its lawsuit, Citi is seeking $60 billion in damages, more than half of Wells Fargo's market capitalization. In part, the theory of the case is that Section 126(c) did not invalidate the Citi-Wachovia exclusivity agreement until Friday, October 3, when President Bush signed it into law—twelve hours *after* Wachovia had breached its exclusivity agreement with Citi and Wells Fargo's tortious interference had occurred. Section 126(c) of EESA invalidates any "existing or future standstill," so it reaches back to invalidate Citi's contract, but it doesn't reach back to invalidate Wells Fargo's tort against Citi.

So for this and other reasons, Section 126(c) isn't a showstopper, and the case has significant settlement value for Citi. In the end we may have what law and economics scholars would call "efficient breach": Wells Fargo gets the assets, Citigroup makes a profit from the deal through the settlement, and Wachovia shareholders get their $7 per share. My proposed approach to setup moves would get to the same place the parties are likely to end up at, but without the cost and hassle of bitter litigation among the parties.

PROCESS TAKER MOVES

In this final section I shift from process setter moves to process taker moves. I examine two categories of moves used by process takers that frequently raise legal issues: bidding through others, and bidder collusion.

Bidding through Others

In Chapters 4 and 5, I discussed the negotiation that takes place between the seller and buy-side experts or other insiders. In general, the seller wants an open and transparent process, in which uninformed bidders can ride the coattails of expert bidders. In the sale of Revlon, for example, the Revlon directors got a great price for the company because Ron Perelman was able to get a free ride off the bids of Ted Forstmann, who was the favored bidder in the deal. One common tactic that experts or insiders use to short-circuit this dynamic is to bid through agents.

Consider a hypothetical case. A well-known Degas painting is for sale at Sotheby's. Before the auction starts, bidders are nervously eyeing each other to see who will vie for the painting. As the auction gets under way, a mysterious bidder—unknown in the closely knit world of art collectors and curators—is bidding aggressively. Puzzled glances fly around the room among the usual suspects. The mystery bidder wins the auction and only then reveals that he was bidding on behalf of Madame Engelworth, an art collector and well-known Degas expert. Engelworth used an agent to bid on her behalf so that other bidders would not be able to get a free ride off her expertise in valuing Degas paintings.

Has Sotheby's been defrauded? Not at all. Engelworth used the well-established device of an undisclosed principal. Buyers often act as undisclosed principals in situations where sellers would charge higher prices if they knew the buyer's identity. In the late 1990s, for example, Harvard University bought residential real estate around its current campus as an undisclosed principal. It seems likely that Harvard would have paid far more if it had acted directly. Buyers also act as undisclosed principals in negotiauction situations to prevent others from getting a free ride off their expertise. Engelworth would have likely paid a higher price, or not won at all, if others could have observed her bids.

Regardless of the motivation, undisclosed principals are well established in the law and generally legal. Agency law allows an agent to "bind," in contract, a third party to his or her principal. Imagine that Sotheby's feels deceived by Engelworth's tactic and decides not to sell the painting to her. Engelworth can sue Sotheby's to get the painting, even though Sotheby's wasn't aware of her existence and had never agreed to sell the painting to her.

Conversely, if Engelworth has a change of heart and decides not to purchase the painting, Sotheby's can sue her to enforce the contract against her. This is true even if the agent violated Engelworth's explicit instructions. For example, imagine that Engelworth had instructed her agent to bid up to $2.0 million and then drop out, but the agent got caught up in auction fever and won with a $2.2 million bid. Sotheby's can get enforcement of the contract against Engelworth because it had no idea that the agent was bidding on behalf of someone else. Put differently, agency law gives Engelworth the benefit of being an undisclosed principal, but then puts on her the risk of a "loose cannon" agent. (Matters might stand differently if Sotheby's knew that the agent was bidding on behalf of Engelworth, or at least on behalf of someone else.)[19]

There is an important exception when the principal knows that the third party would not do the deal if true identities were known. Imagine, for example, that Madame Engelworth has been blacklisted at Sotheby's because of the strong suspicion (never proven) that she had paid bidders not to participate in auctions for Degas paintings. When Sotheby's discovers that Engelworth has surreptitiously bought the painting through an agent, it has the right to call off the sale. Bidders can't hide behind agents to buy something that they couldn't have bought on their own.[20]

Bidder Collusion

In addition to bidding through others, another common tactic among process takers—one that certainly starts legal warning lights flashing—is bidder collusion. Are bidders *ever* allowed to talk to each other in a bidding situation? And if so, what are they allowed to say? Antitrust law clearly casts an important legal shadow on the kinds of rearranging moves that can be made in negotiauctions.

The starting point in the United States is Section 1 of the Sherman Act, which provides that "every contract, combination in the form of trust or otherwise, or conspiracy, in restraint of trade or commerce among the several States, or with foreign nations, is declared to be illegal." Without knowing what the Sherman Act actually says, many businesspeople assume that US antitrust law prohibits any conversation among bidders in a negotiauction. If that assumption were correct, then many of the rearranging moves that we discussed in Chapter 9 would be categorically illegal.

In some cases, the businessperson rule of thumb is exactly right. Take a classic bidder collusion example from the mid-1970s. The US Forest Service regularly uses auctions to sell tracts of land to lumber and plywood manufacturers. Four of these manufacturers made 90 percent of the timber purchases in a particular region near Detroit. For most of the 1960s, there was ferocious competition among them, which of course led to high prices in the timber auctions. Then, according to the court:

> This "bidding war" came to a sudden end on June 2, 1967, when defendant Vernon Morgan "was surprised" to find no one bidding against him at an auction of a small offering of government timber. Morgan decided, he said, "to experiment," and later that same day he offered no bid against defendant Freres on another sale.[21]

The implicit collusion continued, prices plummeted, the Department of Justice brought suit, and the court had no trouble convicting the lumber manufacturers of violating Section 1 of the Sherman Act. Notice that the bidders did not actually speak with each other, which highlights the point that words are not necessary to find an antitrust violation. As the court had said in a different antitrust case, a "knowing wink can mean more than words."[22]

In other situations, however, even explicit agreement among bidders does not violate the Sherman Act, if the agreement promotes (rather than hinders) competition or efficiency in the marketplace. Throughout this book we have seen several rearranging moves that create value and therefore are likely to meet this condition. Consider again the sale of ABN AMRO (see Chapter 9), in which the consortium of the Royal Bank of Scotland, Banco Santander, and Fortis clearly colluded but their collusion unlocked value that enabled them to deliver a block-buster price to the ABN AMRO shareholders, far in excess of what Barclays could pay. Or consider the Toys "R" Us negotiauction (also discussed in Chapter 9), in which KKR's rearranging move unlocked significant value that enabled the Bain/KKR/Vornado consortium to beat the two other bidders.

"Club deals" in private-equity buyouts provide an interesting application of these points. Beginning in the early 2000s, private-equity buyers began "clubbing" (read: colluding) to make bids for public companies. The Neiman Marcus and Toys "R" Us cases discussed in Chapter 9 are both examples of this trend. By 2006, club deals accounted for approximately half of the $400 billion in private-equity deal volume. The Department of Justice (DOJ) became alarmed about the potential anticompetitive effects of club deals, and in October 2006 the DOJ sent out "inquiries" to several prominent private-equity firms seeking further information.

Private-equity investors defended themselves with the idea that clubbing was a classic rearranging move (to use my terminology) that created value by spreading their risk and increasing their overall firepower. Private-equity investors further pointed out that it would be impossible, in most deals, to bring all conceivable buyers into the club, which means that price pressure from other bidders in the negotiauction would force the club to pay a full and fair price. Perhaps implicitly acknowledging these points, the DOJ has not yet brought any lawsuits against the private-equity firms for antitrust violations, after three years of investigation. The case study illustrates the point that without anticompetitive behavior, there is no antitrust violation. The conventional wisdom among practitioners that you can never talk to competing bidders is too categorical, and it may hinder rearranging moves in negotiauctions that unlock significant value.

CONCLUSION

In this book I have tried to synthesize what I have learned from my research on auctions and negotiations over the past decade. The result is a descriptive claim and a prescriptive claim. The descriptive claim is that most deals in today's competitive marketplace have both negotiation and auction elements. If I have convinced you of this point, or if you knew it already, then you will agree with me that it is somewhat surprising that the academic thinking on auctions and negotiations has developed in separate silos. As I noted in the Introduction, auctions and negotiations are the only two ways in which assets are transferred in any market economy. Yet to my knowledge, this is the first book that brings together these two academic fields, to study auctions and negotiations together.

As I hope readers will agree, however, it is not good enough to simply summarize what auction theory and negotiation theory have to say for dealmaking practice, because sophisticated dealmakers are constantly combining these two mechanisms, intertwining them in ways that bear little resemblance to the pure models of auctions and negotiations that academics have traditionally studied. In fact, "negotiauctions" have become the most common mechanism for buying and selling assets in our increasingly competitive global marketplace. To be clear, not all negotiations are negotiauctions: if you are negotiating with your spouse or settling a legal dispute, for example, it's a negotiation. And not all auctions are negotiauctions either: if you are buying art at Sotheby's or selling flowers in Holland, it's an auction. But these pure cases are the exception rather than the rule.

The point is that most of what we have always called "negotiations" and "auctions" are actually negotiauctions. I hope that this claim itself has value, in that it is a lot easier to play the game well when you understand what game you're playing.

My objective, however, is not solely descriptive; it is also to provide prescriptions for how to play in this complex arena. The traditional academic methodologies that I have used in all my prior work, such as large-sample empirical testing, cannot be deployed to answer the prescriptive question here because negotiauctions are by definition difficult to pin down. For example, standard academic approaches in the field of negotiations require some definition of the negotiation process, but one of the important characteristics of a negotiauction is that the rules of the game are themselves up for grabs.

Thus, I have adopted an inductive approach for this project, examining negotiauction situations to look for common patterns. This case-based methodology has been used at the Harvard Business School for more than a century now, and during this period it has led to some important contributions to business practice. The approach has the benefit of grappling with the messiness that is inherent in real situations rather than just "looking where the light is." Of course, it can easily fail if common themes don't emerge from systematic analysis, and sometimes there just aren't common themes—each situation is idiosyncratic.

Instead, however, what struck me in examining negotiauctions across industries and geographies was the regular appearance of certain kinds of moves. Rather than taking the game as given, sophisticated dealmaking practitioners are constantly assessing the possibility of setup moves, rearranging moves, and shut-down moves. This prescriptive insight for how to play in negotiauction situations is not a single organizing framework, such as what negotiation theory offers. It is also not a set of strong predictions or theorems, such as what auction theory offers. Rather, it is a taxonomy of moves that highlights what you should be looking for in complex dealmaking situations.

In some ways, then, the prescriptions provided in this book are less ambitious than what negotiation theory and auction theory currently offer. It seems possible that a single organizing framework for negotiations, auctions, and negotiauctions will develop over time. But it also seems possible that we have reached the appropriate level of generality for negotiauctions, and that further insights can come only from deep analysis of the specific problem at hand. If the latter, I believe that the taxonomy presented in this book still makes an important contribution by identifying three—and only three—types of moves. Rather than looking broadly for game-changing moves, the categories of setup moves, rearranging moves, and shut-down moves tell you where to look.

To illustrate this last point, I will finish where I began, with the sale of Cable & Wireless America. Recall that seven bidders showed up on Wednesday, January 21, 2004, at 8:30 a.m. The CWA sellers held a multi-round sealed-bid auction for the next thirty-four hours, and then shifted to an open-outcry auction between the two last bidders—Savvis Communications and Gores Technology. Savvis won the auction with a bid of $168.3 million, and then promptly sold five data centers to DuPont Fabros for $52 million and leased them back for fifteen years.

Imagine a different sequence of events, in which the CWA sellers used an auction-then-negotiate negotiauction approach, as suggested by the BASC framework. In the endgame, could the sellers have extracted a higher price through parallel negotiations with Gores and Savvis, in view of the large private value that Savvis perceived from diversifying its customer base? Could the CWA sellers have captured some of the value from the Savvis–DuPont Fabros side deal through these private negotiations, or through a hub-and-spoke rearranging move? Perhaps most importantly, could one of the bidders have won the company at a significantly lower price through a well-timed shut-down move when the auction was stalled in the mid–$60 millions?

The truth is that we will never know the answers to these questions, because they are all counterfactuals. But this book tries to put such questions on the table for dealmakers in the heat of battle. The answers, I hope, will help even experienced and sophisticated practitioners "take their game to the next level" in complex dealmaking situations.

ACKNOWLEDGMENTS

One of the big perks of my job is that I get to learn from an extremely talented group of colleagues, students, and practitioners. Their many contributions are reflected in this book. Bob Mnookin, chair of the Program on Negotiation at the Harvard Law School, has urged me to write a book about auctions and negotiations for several years now, and his encouragement was pivotal in my taking on this project. Max Bazerman of the Harvard Business School has also been a long-standing mentor, and I am grateful for his detailed suggestions on all aspects of this book, even though I know that he does not agree with everything in it. Jim Sebenius at HBS first encouraged me to think about the interplay between auctions and negotiations on a memorable walk over the Weeks Footbridge on a fall evening in 1999. Jim and I also cotaught a course on corporate dealmaking, in which his emphasis on "deal setup" shaped my thinking on deal process design. Richard Zeckhauser of the Kennedy School of Government at Harvard was an early collaborator on the topic of auctions and negotiations, and I have learned immensely from his insights over the years.

At HBS, I am fortunate to be a member of the Negotiations, Organizations, and Markets (NOM) Unit, a unique collection of economists, social psychologists, and lawyers. My interest in the interplay between auctions and negotiations can be traced directly to my conversations with the members of this group over the past decade: Nava Ashraf, George Baker, Greg Barron, Max Bazerman, Peter Coles, Amy Cuddy, Ben Edelman, Jerry Green, Brian Hall, Ian Larkin, Deepak Malhotra, Kathleen McGinn, Al Roth, Jim Sebenius, Andy Wasynczuk, and Mike Wheeler. At HLS, I feel equally lucky to be affiliated with the Program on Negotiation (PON), a consortium of Boston-area schools focused on improving the theory and practice of negotiations. I thank Susan Hackley (the managing director of PON) and the members of the PON executive committee for their encouragement and feedback on this project: Jes Selacuse, Iris Bohnet, and Larry Susskind, in addition to Bob Mnookin, Jim Sebenius, and Max Bazerman noted above.

I also thank my two deans. Elena Kagan of the Harvard Law School enthusiastically supported my request to teach a different kind of course—one that would draw deeply on practitioners' insights in order to better understand corporate deals. It was the school's loss but the country's gain when she left HLS to become the Solicitor General of the United States in March 2009. Dean Jay Light of the Harvard Business School also contributed to this project, providing wise counsel in the early stages and intervening with others within the university as the book began to take shape.

Robert Barnett of Williams & Connolly contributed generously of his time to explain his various book deals to me. Daniel Daeniker of Homburger AG provided helpful guidance on the European approach to several of the legal issues raised in negotiauctions. Mark Gordon of Wachtell, Lipton, Rosen & Katz introduced me to the Cable & Wireless America case study, which is featured prominently throughout this book. David Lax of Lax Sebenius LLC provided detailed comments on earlier drafts and is a coauthor (with Jim Sebenius) of *The Manager as Negotiator* and *3-D Negotiation*, two classic books that have greatly influenced my thinking on corporate dealmaking. Brad Peterson of Mayer Brown LLP constructed a theoretical model of negotiauctions that helped clarify my thinking on certain aspects of the project.

Roger Ritt of WilmerHale walked me through the tax aspects of the Citigroup/Wachovia/Wells Fargo deal that is described in Chapter 11. Hal Movius of the Consensus Building Institute and Tom Kinnaird of the WPP Group also contributed in important ways, particularly in my examination of auctions and negotiations in the procurement context.

I also thank the numerous guests in my Corporate Dealmaking class at Harvard. Among this group, a few deserve particular note for their significant contributions: Doug Braunstein, Managing Director and Head of Investment Banking Coverage, JPMorgan Chase; Donald Gogel, President and CEO, Clayton, Dubilier & Rice; Marc Graboff, President, NBC Universal Television Group; Richard Hall, partner at Cravath, Swaine & Moore; Sam Heyman, Chairman and CEO, International Specialty Products; Phillip Mills, partner at Davis Polk & Wardwell; Jim Morphy, Head of Mergers & Acquisitions, Sullivan & Cromwell; Steve Munger, Chairman of Global Mergers & Acquisitions, Morgan Stanley; Dan Neff, Managing Partner, Wachtell, Lipton, Rosen & Katz; Eileen Nugent, Partner and Co-Chair, Private Equity Group, Skadden, Arps, Slate, Meagher & Flom; Jeff Walker, Senior Vice President, BMG North America; and Bruce Wasserstein, Chairman and CEO, Lazard Inc. I also thank the thousand-plus students and executive education participants at HLS, HBS, and the Kennedy School of Government at Harvard who have listened to my lectures on negotiauctions over the past decade—particularly those students in the early years who tolerated with good nature my preliminary thinking on the subject.

Nithya Sharma provided outstanding research assistance, and Ranjan Ahuja, Barbara Karasinski, and Lisa Carlivati provided excellent administrative help. I thank Professor Jeffrey Teich of New Mexico State University for his permission to use the term *negotiauction*, which he trademarked in 2001. My editor at Norton, Brendan Curry, was an excellent sounding board and supporter throughout this project; and my copy editor, Stephanie Hiebert, did a terrific job translating my academic terms to everyday language. For financial support, I thank the Program on Negotiation at Harvard Law School, the Harvard Law

School Summer Research Fund, the Olin Foundation for research in law and economics, and the Division of Research at the Harvard Business School.

Finally, I thank my wife, Helen, for her support and encouragement. Proposing to her was by far the best shut-down move of my life. This book is dedicated to her, with love.

NOTES

Introduction

1. Unless otherwise specified, all facts from this case come from Guhan Subramanian and Eliot Sherman, "Cable & Wireless America," Harvard Business School Case 908-004 (July 2007).
2. I use the word with Professor Teich's kind permission, to the extent that such permission is needed.
3. Cable & Wireless America auction transcript, January 21–22, 2004, 6.
4. Ibid., 15.
5. Interview with Cable & Wireless America banker, August 17, 2007.
6. "Savvis to Pay $155M for C&W USA," *ComputerWire News*, January 26, 2004.
7. "We Must Have Order!" *Washington Post*, February 2, 2004.

Chapter 1. Preparing to Negotiate

1. Unless otherwise specified, all facts from this case come from Guhan Subramanian and Michelle Kalka, "Frasier (A)," Harvard Business School Case 801-447 (May 2001).
2. Sallie Hofmeister and Greg Braxton, "NBC, Paramount at Impasse over Frasier Renewal," *Los Angeles Times*, December 7, 2000.
3. Gary Levin, "Grammer Gets Wish: 11 Seasons for Frasier," *USA Today*, March 7, 2001.

4. Kerry McCluggage, interview with the author, September 20, 2008.

5. Ibid.

6. Geraldine Fabrikant, "High Hopes at Viacom for Paramount Studio," *International Herald Tribune*, January 6, 2005.

7. Bill Carter, "The Thursday Night Fights; CBS Giving NBC Stiff Competition on a Day It Owns," *New York Times*, January 18, 2001.

8. Robert J. Robinson, "Errors in Social Judgment: Implications for Negotiation and Conflict Resolution, Part 2—Partisan Perceptions," Harvard Business School Case 897-104 (February 1997).

9. Bill Carter, "NBC Faces Prospect of Losing 'Frasier' in Contract Renewal Talks," *New York Times*, December 7, 2000.

10. McCluggage, interview.

Chapter 2. At the Table

1. Unless otherwise specified, all facts from this case come from Guhan Subramanian and Michelle Kalka, "Frasier (A)," Harvard Business School Case 801-447 (May 2001).

2. David A. Lax and James K. Sebenius, *3-D Negotiation: Powerful Tools to Change the Game in Your Most Important Deals* (Boston: Harvard Business School Press, 2006), 191.

3. Richard P. Larrick and George Wu, "Claiming a Large Slice of a Small Pie: Asymmetric Disconfirmation in Negotiation," *Journal of Personality and Social Psychology* 92 (2007): 212–33. Larrick and Wu propose an interesting evolutionary story for their finding. When you estimate that the pie is bigger than it actually is, and therefore make a first offer that is too aggressive, what happens? You find out: the other side tells you that you aren't in the ZOPA, and you either make concessions to get in the ZOPA (if you believe them) or you walk away (if you don't). What happens when you estimate that the pie is smaller than it actually is, and therefore make a first offer that is too cautious? You never find out: the other side plays the game a bit further to make you feel good but quickly closes the deal. So, when you overestimate the size of the pie you get corrected, but when you underestimate the size of the pie you don't get corrected. Over a lifetime of negotiations, the result is a bias toward thinking the pie is smaller than it actually is.

4. Deepak Malhotra and Max Bazerman, *Negotiation Genius: How to Overcome Obstacles and Achieve Brilliant Results at the Bargaining Table and Beyond* (New York: Bantam Dell, 2007), 35.

5. What follows comes from Max H. Bazerman and James J. Gillespie, "Betting on the Future: The Virtues of Contingent Contracts," *Harvard Business Review*, September 1999, 155–60. There are, however, some important limits on the benefits of contingent contracts. See Guhan Subramanian, "A Contingent Contract? Weigh the Costs and Benefits of Making a 'Bet,'" *Negotiation*, August 2006, 9–11.

6. David A. Lax and James K. Sebenius, *The Manager as Negotiator: Bargaining for Cooperation and Competitive Gain* (New York: Free Press, 1986), 38–39.

Chapter 3. When to Auction, When to Negotiate?

1. Mark Gongloff, "Treasury Debt Hasn't Lost Much Luster," *Wall Street Journal*, November 12, 2008.

2. Mark Gongloff, "The World Still Lines Up for Treasurys," *Wall Street Journal*, February 17, 2009.

3. Chantale LaCasse, Marcia Kramer Mayer, Arun Sen, and Elaine Buckberg, "Buying the Bad Stuff: Implementation Considerations for the Paulson Plan" (NERA Economic Consulting white paper, September 27, 2008).

4. Economists Avinash Dixit and Barry Nalebuff make a similar point. See Avinash Dixit and Barry Nalebuff, "$700 Billion Going Once, Going Twice . . . : How to Make Toxic Asset Auctions Work," *Big Money*, September 29, 2008, www.thebigmoney.com/articles/making-bail/2008/09/29/700-billion-going-once-going-twice.

5. Davis Polk & Wardwell, memo to clients, October 4, 2008.

6. Deborah Solomon, "Bailout's New Phase: Consumers," *Wall Street Journal*, November 13, 2008.

7. Deborah Solomon, Jon Hilsenrath, and Damian Paletta, "U.S. Plots New Phase in Banking Bailout," *Wall Street Journal*, January 17, 2009.

8. Stanley Foster Reed and Alexandra Reed Lajoux, *The Art of M&A: A Merger Acquisition Buyout Guide*, 3rd ed. (New York: McGraw-Hill, 1999), 486.

9. Noel Dunn, JPMorgan Chase, e-mail message to the author, July 9, 2008. Used with permission.

10. Jeremy Bulow and Paul Klemperer, "Auctions versus Negotiations," *American Economic Review* 86 (1996): 180. Professors Xiaohua Lu and Preston McAfee similarly find that auctions, but not negotiations, are evolutionarily stable in the marketplace. See Xiaohua Lu and R. Preston McAfee, "The Evolutionary Stability of Auctions over Bargaining," *Games and Economic Behavior* 15 (1996): 228–54.

11. Tom Kinnaird, Head of Commercial & Procurement Services, WPP Group, e-mail message to the author, July 2, 2008. Used with permission.

12. Steve New, Tony Meakin, and Ruth Southworth, *Understanding the E-Marketspace: Making Sense of B2B* (Oxford: Said Business School, 2002), 10.

13. "Most Buyers Shun E-Auctions," *Supply Management*, November 29, 2007, 10.

14. The equation is $(n − 1)/(n + 1)$, where n is the number of bidders.

15. Josh Lerner, Felda Hardymon, and Ann Leamon, "Apax Partners and Xerium S.A.," Harvard Business School Case 804-084 (September 2006).

16. US Bankruptcy Court, District of Delaware, transcript of motions hearing before the Honorable Charles G. Case III, (January 23, 2004), 57.

17. Interview with lead Cable & Wireless America banker, August 14, 2007.

18. Ibid.

19. Alvin E. Roth and Axel Ockenfels, "Last-Minute Bidding and the Rules for Ending Second-Price Auctions: Evidence from eBay and Amazon Auctions on the Internet," *American Economic Review* 92 (September 2002): 1093–1103.

20. US Bankruptcy Court, District of Delaware, transcript of motions hearing, 68.

21. I thank Professor Ian Larkin of the Harvard Business School for this analysis.

22. Savvis Communications Corporation, earnings conference call, February 10, 2004.

23. Rachel Melcer, "Savvis Soars: Things Are Looking Up at Company That Survived Dot-Com Bust," *St. Louis Post-Dispatch*, March 4, 2007 (accessed December 15, 2008, via Factiva, www.factiva.com).

24. See US Code title 11, sec. 363; Local Rules for the US Bankruptcy Court, District of Delaware Rule 6004-1. To the contrary, the local rules explicitly invite the possibility of not auctioning the asset. See Rule 6004-1(b)(iv)(D): "The Sale Motion must disclose whether an auction is contemplated, and highlight any provision in which the debtor has agreed not to solicit competing offers for the property subject to the Sale Motion or to otherwise limit shopping of the property."

25. Tobias Schoenherr and Vincent A. Mabert, "Online Reverse Auctions: Common Myths versus Evolving Reality," *Business Horizons* 50 (2007): 373–84 (quoting interview respondent).

26. The precise wording has been changed slightly for confidentiality reasons. The substance remains unchanged.

27. John Asker and Estelle Cantillon, "Properties of Scoring Auctions," *Rand Journal of Economics*, 39, no. 1 (Spring 2008): 69–86. One implementation of such a scoring system approach is the "Negotiauction" algorithm, devised by Professor Jeffrey Teich of New Mexico State University along with his colleagues. Jefferey E. Teich, Hannele Wallenius, Jyrki Wallenius, and Alexander Zaitsev, "Designing Electronic Auctions: An Internet-Based Hybrid Procedure Combining Aspects of Negotiations and Auctions," *Electronic Commerce Research* 1 (July 2001). The Negotiauction algorithm introduces negotiable bid issues (NBIs), which are issues besides price and quantity that bidders care about (for example, warranty and delivery time). The process setter sets prices for these NBIs, and the software then penalizes or rewards each bid according to the NBIs. This process enables comparison across bids, even though the bids have different features.

28. This point dates to Victor Goldberg, "Competitive Bidding and the Production of Precontract Information," *Bell Journal of Economics* 8, no. 1 (1977): 250–61.

29. Patrick Bajari, Robert McMillan, and Steven Tadelis, "Auctions versus Negotiations in Procurement: An Empirical Analysis," *Journal of Law, Economics & Organization* (2008), http://jleo.oxfordjournals.org.

30. Interview with New York City practitioner, August 11, 1999.

31. See, for example, Guhan Subramanian, "Go-Shops vs. No-Shops in Private Equity Buyouts: Evidence & Implications," *Business Lawyer* 63 (May 2008): 729–60.

32. John R. Wilke, "Pittsburgh's Rooneys Quietly Shop the Steelers," *Wall Street Journal*, July 8, 2008.

33. Kris Maher, "'Hail Mary': Steelers Fans Face Realities of a Sale," *Wall Street Journal*, July 9, 2008.

34. Gerry Dulac and Ed Bouchette, "Rooney Brothers Agree on Price for Steelers; Obama Tax Increase Is a Factor," *Pittsburgh Post-Gazette*, November 15, 2008.

Chapter 4. Choosing the Right Kind of Auction

1. Paul Milgrom and Robert Weber, "A Theory of Auctions and Competitive Bidding," *Econometrica* 50 (September 1982): 1089–1122.

2. Empirical evidence from timber auctions in the US Northwest is consistent with this conclusion. Jonathan D. Levin, Susan Athey, and Enrique Seira, "Comparing Open and Sealed Bid Auctions: Theory and Evidence from Timber Auctions" (FEEM Working Paper no. 142.04, December 2004).

3. "Betting on Blockbusters: Lessons from Book Auctions," *Negotiation*, April 2009, 5–6.

4. Consistent with this point, one academic study finds that sellers receive higher prices on eBay when they start with a lower starting price. See Steven T. Anderson, Daniel Friedman, Garrett H. Milam, and Nirvikar Singh, "Seller Strategies on eBay" (UC Santa Cruz Economics Working Paper no. 564, April 2004).

5. Phil Mindlin, interview with the author, June 9, 2008.

6. Elizabeth Pope, "Wall Street of Flowers," *American Way Magazine*, April 15, 2005, www.americanwaymag.com/dirk-hogervorst-luc-ribberink-new-york-stock-exchange-chicago-board-of-trade.

7. Ibid.

8. Sydney Fish Market, "Sydney Fish Market Fast Facts," www.sydneyfishmarket.com.au (accessed August 4, 2008).

9. Ken Steiglitz, *Snipers Shills, & Sharks: eBay and Human Behavior* (Princeton, NJ: Princeton University Press, 2007), 11–12.

10. See, for example, Paul Milgrom and Lawrence Ausubel, "The Lovely but Lonely Vickrey Auction," in *Combinatorial Auctions*, Peter Crampton, Richard Steinberg, and Yoav Shoham, eds. (Cambridge MA: MIT Press, 2005), 17–40.

11. Michael H. Rothkopf, Thomas J. Teisberg, and Edward P. Kahn, "Why Are Vickrey Auctions Rare?" *Journal of Political Economy* 98, no. 1 (1990): 94–109 (accessed August 5, 2008, via JSTOR, www.jstor.org/pss/2937643).

12. Ibid.

13. eBay, "About Bid Increments," http://pages.ebay.com/help/buy/bid-increments.html#how (accessed November 23, 2008).

14. Cited in Axel Ockenfels and Alvin E. Roth, "Late and Multiple Bidding in Second Price Internet Auctions: Theory and Evidence concerning Different Rules for Ending an Auction," *Games and Economic Behavior* 55 (May 2006): 297–320.

15. Ibid.

16. Peter Tufano and Alberto Moel, "Bidding for Antamina," Harvard Business School Case 297-054 (September 1997).

17. Saul Hudson, "Forty Firms Qualify for Peru Copper Prospect Sale," *Reuters Financial Service*, June 21, 1996.

18. Tufano and Moel, "Bidding for Antamina."

19. "Canadian Group Hopes to Double Antamina Reserves," *Reuters Financial Service*, July 12, 1996, quoted in Peter Tufano and Alberto Moel, "Bidding for Antamina Teaching Note," Harvard Business School Case 298-102 (February 9, 1998).

20. "Antamina Surpasses Rio Algam, Inmet Hopes," *Reuters News*, February 27, 1997 (accessed July 15, 2008, via Factiva, www.factiva.com).
21. Alistair Scrutton, "Canada Group Says Yes to $2.2 Bln Peru Mine," *Reuters News*, September 16, 1998 (accessed July 15, 2008, via Factiva, www.factiva.com).
22. "Antamina Makes US$111.5mn 'Complimentary' Payment," *Business News Americas*, August 5, 2002 (accessed July 15, 2008, via Factiva, www.factiva.com).

Chapter 5. Playing the Game as Process Taker

1. Max Bazerman and William Samuelson, "I Won the Auction but Don't Want the Prize," *Journal of Conflict Resolution* 27 (1983): 618–34.
2. Deepak Malhotra, Gillian Ku, and J. Keith Murnighan, "When Winning Is Everything," *Harvard Business Review*, May 2008, 7.
3. Imagine that Ernie just bought the partnership for $130. There is an interesting and subtle question as to why Ernie might resell the partnership to Bert for less than the amount he just bought it for, as suggested in the text. The reason is that Ernie's BATNA in this renegotiation is to buy the partnership for $130, which represents a $30 loss for him. Therefore he should be willing to sell it at any price that reduces this loss because it is better than his new BATNA. Analytically, the price at which Ernie just bought the partnership is irrelevant to the price at which Ernie will then resell the partnership to Bert.
4. James Surowiecki, *The Wisdom of Crowds: Why the Many Are Smarter Than the Few and How Collective Wisdom Shapes Business, Economies, Societies and Nations* (New York: DoubleDay, 2004).
5. James Surowiecki, "The Agony of Victory and the Thrill of Defeat," *New Yorker*, January 8, 2001, 31.
6. Ibid.
7. Clintons' Earnings Exceed $100m" (April 5, 2005), BBC News Online, http://news.bbc.co.uk/2/hi/americas/7331834.stm.
8. US Department of the Interior, Mineral Management Services, *Federal Offshore Statistics: 1995, Part I—Federal Offshore Lands*, MMS 97-0007 (1995). The Outer Continental Shelf Lands Act of 1954 and subsequent amendments provide for federal jurisdiction over the submerged lands of the OCS (outer continental shelf), and also authorize the Secretary of the Interior to lease those lands for mineral development.
9. E. C. Capen, R. V. Clapp, and W. M. Campbell, "Competitive Bidding in High-Risk Situations," *Journal of Petroleum Technology* 23 (June 1971): 641–53.

10. Unless otherwise specified, the following account comes from Guhan Subramanian and Michelle Kalka, "Auction Vignettes," Harvard Business School Case 902-072 (January 7, 2002).

11. Surowiecki, "Agony of Victory."

12. "252," *60 Minutes* (television broadcast, March 25, 2001).

13. "Selig Gives Blessing to Mega-merger" (February 15, 2004), ESPN.com.

14. "Rangers Would Get Soriano, Financial Flexibility" (February 14, 2004), ESPN.com.

15. Howard Raiffa, *Negotiation Analysis: The Science and Art of Collaborative Decision Making* (Cambridge, MA: Harvard University Press, 2002), 173–77.

16. Roe Stamps, personal communication, May 1, 2008.

17. www.auctionwatch.com/awdaily/tipsandtactics/buy-bid2.html, cited in Alvin E. Roth and Axel Ockenfels, "Last-Minute Bidding and the Rules for Ending Second-Price Auctions: Evidence from eBay and Amazon Auctions on the Internet," *American Economic Review* 92 (September 2002): 1093–1103, fn. 8.

18. Axel Ockenfels and Alvin E. Roth, "Late and Multiple Bidding in Second Price Internet Auctions: Theory and Evidence concerning Different Rules for Ending an Auction," *Games and Economic Behavior* 55 (May 2006): 297–320.

19. Quoted in Guhan Subramanian, "The Drivers of Market Efficiency in Revlon Transactions," *Journal of Corporation Law* 28 (2000): 691, 700.

20. Interview with auctioneer at major international auction house, March 9, 2009.

21. "Revlon Set to Oppose Pantry Pride," *Globe and Mail*, August 21, 1985.

22. Malhotra, Ku, and Murnighan, "When Winning Is Everything."

23. Robert B. Cialdini, *Influence: The Psychology of Persuasion* (New York: Morrow, 1993), 79.

24. Interview with auctioneer, April 21, 2009.

25. This example comes from Malhotra, Ku, and Murnighan, "When Winning Is Everything."

26. "Background of the Paramount Merger," Paramount Communications Inc., Securities and Exchange Commission Form SC13E-3/A (filed May 25, 1994).

27. Johnnie L. Roberts and Randall Smith, "Paramount Opts to Put Itself Up for Auction—Heeding Courts' Orders, Company Opens Bidding and Drops Viacom Pact," *Wall Street Journal*, December 15, 1993.

28. "Background of the Paramount Merger."

29. John Greenwald, "The Deal That Forced Diller to Fold," *Time*, February 28, 1994.

30. Pekka Hietala, Steven Kaplan, and David Robinson, "What Is the Price of Hubris? Using Takeover Battles to Infer Overpayments and Synergies," *Financial Management*, 32, no. 3 (2003): 5–31.

Chapter 6. The Limits of Existing Theory

1. Guhan Subramanian, "Fixing Freezeouts," *Yale Law Journal* 115, no. 1 (October 2005): 43. I thank Professors Victor Goldberg and Richard Zeckhauser for helpful conversations on this point.
2. David Bank, "Browser Breach: How One Sweet Deal Unraveled for Netscape After Microsoft Called," *Wall Street Journal*, November 13, 1997.
3. Ibid.
4. Connie Bendersky and Kathleen L. McGinn, "Phenomenological Assumptions and Knowledge Dissemination within Organizational Studies" (Harvard Business School Working Paper, 2008), table 2. It wasn't always this way: another study reports that in the 1940s and '50s, when social psychologists first began using experimental methods, academic studies used a wide variety of subject populations, including industrial workers in factories, soldiers in training and combat, and the League of Women Voters. David O. Sears, "College Sophomores in the Laboratory: Influences of a Narrow Data Base on Social Psychology's View of Human Nature," *Journal of Personality and Social Psychology* 51 (1986): 515–30. The study reports, with considerable concern, that "by the 1960s, [the] conjunction of college student subject, laboratory site, and experimental method, usually mixed with some deception, had become the dominant method in social psychology."
5. Pablo Guillén and Róbert F. Veszteg, "Subject Pool Bias in Economic Experiments" (Papers from Department of Economic Theory and Economic History of the University of Granada no. 06/03, March 2006).
6. CLER Lab personnel, personal communication, June 6, 2008.
7. Guillén and Veszteg, "Subject Pool Bias."
8. Carl Bialik, "The Numbers Guy: Too Many Studies Use College Students as Their Guinea Pigs," *Wall Street Journal*, August 10, 2007.
9. Ellen Langer, Arthur Blank, and Benzio Chanowitz, "The Mindlessness of Ostensibly Thoughtful Action: The Role of 'Placebic' Information in Interpersonal Interaction," *Journal of Personality and Social Psychology* 36 (1978): 635–42.
10. Ibid. The study was based on fifteen students in each experimental condition. Nine out of fifteen (60 percent) agreed to let the experimenter cut in front without any justification, and fourteen out of fifteen (93 percent) agreed

to let the experimenter cut in front with a meaningless justification. If just one person in either group of fifteen had come out the other way toward the mean, the result would no longer hold at 95 percent confidence, the conventional level of statistical significance that researchers look for. So the difference is fragile, particularly when considered in conjunction with the gender difference that the study also finds. There were two experimenters, a man and a woman; and the study mysteriously reports, without further explanation, that "not surprisingly, the female experimenter had a higher rate of compliance than the male experimenter." Even more bizarrely, the male experimenter knew about the hypothesis being tested while the female experimenter did not—another factor likely to skew the results, and for that reason a clear no-no in experimental methodology. I do not dwell on these problems, because in 2009, more than thirty years after the original study was published, a group of researchers replicated the basic finding using eighty-four undergraduate students at Northern Illinois University. M. Scott Key, John E. Edlund, Brad J. Sagarin, and George Y. Bizer, "Individual Differences in Susceptibility to Mindlessness," *Personality and Individual Differences* 46 (2009): 261–64.

11. Langer, Blank, and Chanowitz, "Mindlessness."

12. Quoted from www.amazines.com/Photocopier_related.html.

13. Quoted from David A. Lax and James K. Sebenius, *3-D Negotiation: Powerful Tools to Change the Game in Your Most Important Deals* (Boston: Harvard Business School Press, 2006), 190.

14. E-mail message from a senior manager, July 18, 2008.

15. Paul Klemperer, *Auctions: Theory and Practice* (Princeton, NJ: Princeton University Press, 2004), 104.

16. Mark Gordon, interview with the author, April 3, 2007.

Chapter 7. An Introduction to Negotiauctions

1. From Guhan Subramanian and Michelle Kalka, "Auction Vignettes," Harvard Business School Case 902-072 (January 7, 2002).

2. Kerry McCluggage, interview with the author, September 26, 2008.

3. Brit Grosskopf and Alvin Roth, "If You Are Offered the Right of First Refusal, Should You Accept? An Investigation of Contract Design," *Games and Economic Behavior*, 65 (2009): 176–204. Grosskopf and Roth explain the intuition for this result as follows: "Because [Last Offer mechanisms such as the one in *Frasier*] require the right holder [NBC] to exercise the right *before* a third party [CBS] for some offers, while retaining the right

to take better offers *after* they have been proposed to the third party, they permit the asset owner [Paramount] to present the third party with an ultimatum, in a way that gives the asset owner an advantage, and the right holder a disadvantage, compared to the case where negotiations are conducted without such a right" (ibid., 196–97, italics in the original).

4. Steve Munger, "Advanced Negotiation: Deal Design & Implementation" (guest lecture, Harvard Business School Dealmaking class, April 7, 2006).

5. Brad Peterson, e-mail message to the author, December 8, 2008. Used with permission.

6. Bruce Wasserstein, visit to Dealmaking class at Harvard Business School, April 23, 2007.

Chapter 8. Setup Moves

1. Unless otherwise specified, facts for this case come from James Sebenius, "Bidding on Martha's Vineyard (A)," Harvard Business School Case 908-044 (January 24, 2008). The names have been changed from the original in order to preserve the pedagogical value of the case.

2. In their excellent book *3-D Negotiation*, David Lax and Jim Sebenius use the similar term *deal setup*, but their usage is more general than mine. *Deal setup*, as defined by Lax and Sebenius, "means acting to ensure that the *right parties* have been involved, in the *right sequence*, to deal with the *right issues* that engage the *right set of interests*, at the *right table or tables*, at the *right time*, under the *right expectations*, and facing the *right consequences of walking away if there is no deal*" (italics in the original). David A. Lax and James K. Sebenius, *3-D Negotiation: Powerful Tools to Change the Game in Your Most Important Deals* (Boston: Harvard Business School Press, 2006), 12.

3. Unless otherwise noted, the facts from this case study come from a presentation by five students in my Dealmaking class on March 23, 2006: Duston Barton, Ryan Gavin, Magnus Karlberg, Thomas Ling, and Raluca Papadima.

4. *Omnicare v. NCS HealthCare, Inc.*, 818 A.2d 914 (Del. 2003).

5. Kerzner International, Securities and Exchange Commission Form SC13E-3 (filed July 19, 2006), 18.

6. In my research, I find that no bidder has ever "jumped" a management buyout (MBO) go-shop deal. (Party A in Kerzner has come the closest.) This (non) finding illustrates the significantly unlevel playing field in go-shop MBOs. Guhan Subramanian, "Go-Shops vs. No-Shops in Private Equity Deals: Evidence & Implications," *Business Lawyer* 63 (May 2008): 729–60.

Chapter 9. Rearranging Moves

1. Unless otherwise noted, the facts from this case study come from a presentation by seven students in my Dealmaking class on March 30, 2008: Erin Archerd, Shlomit Azgad-Tromer, Shilpa Bhandarkar, G. J. Ligelis, Akhil Monappa, Kenneth Moon, and Maria Toneva.
2. "Deals of the Future? Consortiums," *Wall Street Journal*, October 5, 2007.
3. Ibid.
4. "Three Amigos, Only One Conquistador: Mixed Fortunes for the Buyers of ABN AMRO," *Economist*, July 17, 2008.
5. Julia Werdigier, "ABN Amro's Feast of Fees," *New York Times Dealbook*, October 5, 2007, http://dealbook.blogs.nytimes.com/2007/10/05/abn-am ros-feast-of-fees.
6. Ibid. I thank Professor Ian Larkin of the Harvard Business School for this point.
7. Esther B. Fein, "Politics' Tracy and Hepburn Signed by Publishing Rivals," *New York Times*, February 23, 1993.
8. David Streitfeld, "Rivals Join to Publish Political Duo: Random House, S&S Buy Carville-Matalin Campaign Guide," *Washington Post*, February 23, 1993.
9. "An Iconic High-Rise Faces the Auctioneer," *Boston Globe*, March 31, 2009.
10. Stephen Taub, "Will Hancock Tower Be Handed Off?" *CFO Magazine*, February 10, 2009, www.cfo.com.
11. "Hancock Tower Auction: Gone in 60 Seconds," *Boston Globe*, April 1, 2009.
12. Michael Pascoe, "Banks, Property and Mark-to-Market: Eggshells All Round," *BusinessDay*, April 3, 2009, www.businessday.com.au.
13. "Hancock Tower Auction."
14. Kevin O'Shea, Allen & Overy, interview with the author, April 14, 2009.
15. "Deals of the Future?"

Chapter 10. Shut-Down Moves

1. David Carr and Andrew Ross Sorkin, "New York Magazine Sold for $55 Million to Wall St. Figure," *New York Times*, December 17, 2003 (accessed July 10, 2007, via Factiva, www.factiva.com).
2. Keith Kelly and Erica Copulsky, "A Mort-Al Blow: How Cocky Zuckerman Team Flubbed the Deal," *New York Post*, December 18, 2003 (accessed July 10, 2007, via Factiva, www.factiva.com).

3. David Carr, "Post-mortems for a Media Deal Undone," *New York Times*, December 22, 2003.

4. Kelly and Copulsky, "Mort-Al Blow."

5. Bryan Burrough and John Helyar. *Barbarians at the Gate: The Fall of RJR Nabisco* (New York: HarperCollins, 2003), 462.

6. Interview with lead Cable & Wireless America banker, August 14, 2007.

7. HUB International, Securities and Exchange Commission Form DEFM14A (filed May 4, 2007), 10.

8. Unless otherwise noted, the facts from this case study come from a presentation by six students in my Dealmaking class on April 20, 2006: Ching-Yang Lin, Marianna Lopez, Bipul Mainali, Lauren Malan, David McCombie, and Sam Sherry.

9. Paul Robinson and Robert Saunders, "Critical Implications of the Proposed Qwest MCI Merger: A Financial Analysis (Eastern Management Group white paper, 2005).

10. Ibid.

11. It should be noted that I served as an expert witness on this aspect of the Toys "R" Us deal, presenting empirical evidence that the breakup fee was large relative to comparable transactions. See John C. Coates IV and Guhan Subramanian, "A Buy-Side Model of M&A Lockups: Theory & Evidence," *Stanford Law Review* 53, no. 2 (2000), 307–96.

12. Guhan Subramanian, "Post-*Siliconix* Freeze-Outs: Theory and Evidence," *Journal of Legal Studies* 36, no. 5 (January 2007), 1–26.

13. Steven Levitt and Chad Syverson, "Market Distortions When Agents Are Better Informed: A Theoretical and Empirical Exploration of the Value of Information in Real Estate Transactions," *Review of Economics and Statistics* 90 (November 2008), 599–611.

14. Mortgagesorter, "Gazumping," www.mortgagesorter.co.uk/home_buying _guide_gazumping.html.

Chapter 11. The Shadow of the Deal: Legal Constraints in Negotiauctions

1. Robert Mnookin and Lewis Kornhauser, "Bargaining in the Shadow of the Law: The Case of Divorce," *Yale Law Journal* 88, no. 5 (April 1979): 950–97.

2. For those who are interested in a discussion of the legal rules governing fraud, I recommend chapter 11 of Richard Shell, *Bargaining for Advantage: Negotiation Strategies for Reasonable People* (New York: Penguin Group, 2006).

3. See, for example, *Commonwealth v. Quinn*, 222 Mass. 504 (1916).

4. *Beavers v. Lamplighters Realty, Inc.*, 556 P.2d 1328, 1331 (Okla. 1976).

5. As an interesting international comparison, Section 52 of the Australian Trade Practices Act provides the same remedy as a matter of statutory law: "Representations as to fictitious prices or fictitious buyers are the same as any other representation. They must be true in fact and they must give rise to a truthful impression. If they fail either of these tests, then the representor will be liable for damages."

6. Russel Korobkin, *Negotiation Theory and Strategy* (New York: Aspen Law and Business, 2002), 388.

7. *Ravosa v. Zais*, 661 N.E.2d 111, 116 (1996) (internal quotation marks omitted).

8. I thank Dr. Daniel Daeniker of Homburger AG for this point.

9. Uniform Commercial Code Section 1-203: "Every contract or duty within this Act imposes an obligation of good faith in performance and enforcement."

10. Constance Bagley, *Managers and the Legal Environment* (Cincinnati, OH: West/Thomson Learning, 2002), 225.

11. E. Allan Farnsworth, "Precontractual Liability and Preliminary Agreements: Fair Dealing and Failed Negotiations," *Columbia Law Review* 87 (1987): 217, 236.

12. Citigroup/Wachovia letter of intent, September 29, 2008 (on file with the author).

13. Internal Revenue Service Notice 2008-83, 2008-42 I.R.B. 1.

14. Binyamin Appelbaum, "After Change in Tax Law, Wells Fargo Swoops In," *Washington Post*, October 4, 2008.

15. Robert K. Steel, affidavit, October 5, 2008.

16. David Enrich, Dan Fitzpatrick, and Damian Paletta, "Fed Pushes to Resolve Wachovia Deal Dispute," *Wall Street Journal*, October 6, 2008.

17. David Enrich and Dan Fitzpatrick, "Wells Fargo Grabs Wachovia as Citi Walks," *Wall Street Journal*, October 10, 2008.

18. David Marcus and Bill McConnell, "Walking Away Empty-Handed," *Corporate Control Alert* 25, no. 9 (November 2008): 19 (quoting Gilbert Schwartz of Schwartz & Ballen).

19. See, for example, *White v. Thomas*, 1991 Lexis 109 (Ark. App. 1999).

20. Martin Schiff, "The Problem of the Undisclosed Principal and How It Affects Agent and Third Party," *Detroit College of Law Review*, 1984: 47, 70.

21. *U.S. v. Champion Intl. et al.*, 557 F.2d 1270 (1977).

22. *Esco Corp. v. U.S.*, 340 F.2d 1000, 1007 (9th Cir. 1965).

INDEX

Page numbers in *italics* refer to figures.

ABOUT THE AUTHOR

Guhan Subramanian is the Joseph Flom Professor of Law and Business at the Harvard Law School and the H. Douglas Weaver Professor of Business Law at the Harvard Business School. He is the only person in the history of Harvard University to hold tenured appointments at both HLS and HBS. At HLS he teaches courses in negotiations and corporate law. At HBS he teaches in several executive education programs, including Strategic Negotiations, Changing the Game, The Global Negotiator, and Making Corporate Boards More Effective. He is the faculty chair for the week-long HBS executive education program Managing Negotiators and the Deal Process, and the faculty director for the JD/MBA program at Harvard University. Before joining the Harvard faculty he spent three years at McKinsey & Company in their New York, Boston, and Washington, DC offices.

Professor Subramanian's research explores topics in negotiations, corporate dealmaking, and corporate governance. He has published articles in the *Stanford Law Review*, the *Yale Law Journal*, the *Harvard Law Review*, the *Harvard Business Review*, and the *Journal of Legal Studies*, among other places. Over the past ten years he has published more "top ten" articles in corporate and securities law, as selected by academics in the field, than any other scholar in the country. His work has been featured in the *Wall Street Journal*'s "Heard on the Street" column, the *New York Times*, the *American Lawyer*, the *Daily Deal*, and *Corporate Control Alert*, among other places.

Professor Subramanian has served as an expert witness in major public-company deals such as Oracle's $10.3 billion hostile takeover bid for PeopleSoft, Cox Enterprises' $8.9 billion freeze-out of the minority shareholders in Cox Communications, the $6.6 billion leveraged buyout of Toys "R" Us, and Exelon's $8.0 billion hostile bid for NRG Energy. He also advises individuals, boards of directors, and management teams on issues of dealmaking and corporate governance.

Professor Subramanian holds an AB in Economics (*magna cum laude*) from Harvard College, where he was elected to Phi Beta Kappa; an MBA from Harvard Business School; and a JD from Harvard Law School (*magna cum laude*), where he was an editor of the *Harvard Law Review* and a winner of the Ames Moot Court Competition. He is formerly a Fellow of the Harvard Negotiation Research Project and an Olin Fellow for research in law and economics, both at Harvard Law School. He is a member of the New York Bar Association and the American Law and Economics Association.